Squirrelling

Squirrelling

Human–Animal Studies
in the Northern-European Region

Edited by
Amelie Björck, Claudia Lindén & Ann-Sofie Lönngren

Södertörns högskola

Trycksak
3041 0865

Södertörn University
Library
SE-141 89 Huddinge
www.sh.se/publications

Cover layout: Jonathan Robson
Cover image: Ratatoskr in en: Yggdrasill. The text by the animal reads
"Rata / tøskur / ber øf / undar / ord my / llū arnr / og nyd / hoggs".
From the en:17th century en: Icelandic manuscript AM 738 4to,
Árni Magnússon Institute in Iceland.
Graphic form: Per Lindblom & Jonathan Robson
Printed by E-Print, Stockholm 2022

Södertörn Academic Studies 89
ISSN 1650-433X

ISBN 978-91-89109-94-0 (print)
ISBN 978-91-89109-95-7 (digital)

Contents

Introduction

The *Ratatǫskr* Research Group for Literary Animal Studies was founded in 2018 by colleagues working at the Literature department at Södertörn University, Sweden. The name of the group was inspired by Nordic mythology, where *Ratatǫskr* is a squirrel that runs up and down the tree of life, Yggdrasil, carrying messages between the dragon in its roots and the eagle in its crown. Being both a representation of a 'real' animal species and a part of human mythology regarding the organization of the world, the figure of *Ratatǫskr* is situated right in the field of interest for literary and cultural animal studies. While formulated in the tension between metaphorical and linguistic representation on the one hand, and material 'reality' on the other, it is furthermore significant that *Ratatǫskr* is a messenger, a carrier of information and knowledge. However, according to some sources this creature sometimes carries false messages—a circumstance that in the field of literary animal studies points to the challenge posed by non-human perception and cognition and by the agency and agenda of non-human animals. As human beings we approach the non-human worlds in ways available to us, limited as we are by our senses and our language. We approach these worlds as translators of a sort and can only hope that our attention and careful attempts to develop our perspectives and concepts might gradually produce within academic study a greater receptivity towards other beings, and towards our ongoing co-existence inside and outside the literature we analyze and engage with.

The purpose of establishing the *Ratatǫskr* Research Group was to create a platform to discuss questions such as: How is the human-animal relationship depicted in literature and other cultural texts? How can various literary genres and forms and different types of reading contribute in challenging anthropocentric paradigms in the scholarly field of the humanities? How can we understand the relationship between matter, metaphor and agency in literary depictions of non-human animals? What is the relationship between the hierarchically organized animal/ human dichotomy and ideas about categories such as gender, sexuality, 'race' and disability? What ontologies regarding the human-animal relationship can we imagine? And how are these questions linked to ethical issues and dilemmas in the wider humanistic field and in ongoing social interactions between species?

With these questions, it is clear that the scope of the *Ratatoskr* research group for literary animal studies is chiefly in line with the larger transdisciplinary field of human-animal studies that has developed over the past decades within the wider context of posthumanism. Accordingly, the aim with the group is also to develop cooperation with others also active in this field, in both literature and in other subjects, both inside and outside Södertörn University and Sweden. Ultimately, we want to create a space for the group in the international arena for literary and cultural animal studies. However, motivated by both the ecocritical emphasis on place and materiality, and by decolonial thoughts about local knowledges, we also want to direct interest towards Europe's northern-most part, and which the figure of *Ratatoskr* indexes. This is why, when we planned the inaugural symposium for this research group in December 2019, we chose to invite only those human-animal studies scholars who were active in this specific geographic region. This anthology is one concrete outcome of that event, alongside establishing an academic network with representatives from a large number of the Northern-European countries, the *Ratatoskr Network for Literary and Cultural Animal Studies.*

What do we mean, then, with the demarcation 'Europe's northern-most part'? Doubtless this is a rather loose description, understood differently depending on the contexts. Indeed, there are several alternative terms with more exact definitions that might have been employed. 'Scandinavia' often encompasses Sweden, Denmark, and Norway, three countries united by virtue of belonging to the same language family. The problem is that this term (and its associated definition) does not recognize

Sápmi as an equal member of the Northern-European sphere. The term 'Nordic' (with capital N) does not fair better, though it at least has the merit of including Finland and Iceland. It might be argued that the exclusion of Sápmi is because it is not a nation-state. Exclusions of this nature are not without material effects: for instance, Scandinavian literature courses typically do not include works by Sámi authors. In this context, the figure of *Ratatoskr* also serves as a reminder of the still on-going colonialization of Sápmi—since *Ratatoskr* is part of the ancient settler mythology, not the Sámi one.

In the 2016 anthology *The Geopolitics of Nordic and Russian Gender Research 1975–2005* (edited by Ulrika Dahl, Marianne Liljeström & Ulla Manns), the concepts 'Nordic' and 'Scandinavia' are conceptualized as linguistic and political investments based on a politics of demarcation and exclusion. This is of course a relevant understanding from a humanist point of view, but in embracing the lucid concept of 'Europe's northernmost part' we want to establish our rootedness within a more posthumanist understanding of material places as characterized by entanglements of all sorts of human and non-human life. Bears climb, wolves run, fish swim, birds fly, worms crawl, mosquitos swarm and bacteria and other minor organisms spread and multiply, surely under the influence of human actions and desires, but also with the utmost disrespect for it—as was made urgently clear in the outbreak of the COVID 19 pandemic in 2020. What kind of knowledge is produced when beginning with the premise that northern Europe is a material place characterized by multi-species relations, rather than a linguistic and cultural community?

In this anthology, we have contributors situated in Denmark, Norway, Finland, Iceland, Poland, and Sweden. Although a majority of them specialize in the Northern-European area, some researchers work with narratives from other places. Thus, the anthology can be seen as a mapping of the research that is presently being carried out in the field of literary and cultural human-animal studies in this region. Ultimately, however, all the contributions address the same urgent, overarching question: How can we challenge the current paradigm in ways that benefit the production of less violent, more ethically sound and sustainable knowledge regarding the relationship between human and non-human life? This is why we chose the figure of *Ratatǫskr* as a source of inspiration for this collection, since, ultimately, the task is to work up (analogous to the "squirrel") enough good, productive and just knowledge to last us for the future, or in fact to make sure that we even have a future at all.

Since many angles concerning the human-animal relationship elude academic discourse, the anthology proudly includes not only illustrations, but artworks made by the three Swedish artists, Emma Kihl (from the *Ratatǫskr* group), Marta Badenska Hammarberg, and Jacob Broms Engblom, all of whom were invited to present their works at the *Ratatoskr* inaugural conference. Throughout the book, their works appear as traces that nonetheless seek to open up the space for thought; serving as points of transit from section to section, each is followed by short reflections.

The volume could have been arranged in several different ways; many inter-connections can be drawn between individual chapters. We have chosen to group the texts with respect to common interests, and ended up subdividing the contributions into three sections: 1) ontology and culture, 2) norms and hierarchies, 3) our mode of perception when approaching non-human creatures and phenomena.

In the first part of the book, "More-than-human world-making, culture and knowledge," contributors explore what possibilities are afforded for knowledge when mining ontologies and concepts for ideas that go beyond the scope of the human. In order to better understand the complexities of "cultures of animality" a new conceptuality needs to be developed that might more easily cross species boundaries and be explored in various cultural contexts, both human and animal. In his chapter "Idiorrhythmy and Its Discontents: Cultures of Animality in Roland Barthes and Ursula K. Le Guin", Michael Lundblad digs precisely into this conceptual field. The term "idiorrhythmy" was coined by Roland Barthes in a 1977 lecture series, with the aim of capturing how one might "regulate interindividual distance" for the benefit of both individuals and communities. By investigating how this, and other concepts from Barthes, work in relation to different cultures—for instance among Ursula Le Guin's literary ants—fine differences between cultures can be articulated, and where the hunt for keywords and concepts becomes in itself a process of knowledge making.

Questions of knowledge and different world views are also dealt with in Ann-Sofie Lönngren's contribution to this anthology, "Reclaiming a Repressed World. Decolonizing the Human-animal Relationship in three Stories by Contemporary Sámi author Kirste Paltto". Here, Lönngren investigates the human-animal relationship in a small selection of texts from Northern-European indigenous literature. In a comparative close reading of three short stories published in the collection "Stolen" (Norwegian original *Stjålet*) by renowned Sámi author Kirste Paltto in 2003, Lönngren finds that they depict a modern world that gradually reveals elements from a precolonial ontology. Ultimately, she concludes that Paltto's depictions of the relationship between the human and the nonhuman world as a horizontal continuum relies on the traditional Sámi view, rather than the colonizer's hierarchical and static conception, inspired by Christianity.

In Małgorzata Poks' contribution to the anthology, "Between the Tigers of Anger and the Horses of Instruction in Olga Tokarczuk's *Drive Your Plow Over the Bones of the Dead*", attention is largely set on pre-modern ontologies. Poks investigates the relationship between non-human animals and the Polish Nobel Prize-winner of 2018, who, since the beginning of her publishing career has spoken from a position that can be called 'ontological animism', foundational to all pre-modern cultures. In her analysis, Poks foregrounds the author's involved, activist agenda and highlights her sense of responsibility for the animal(ized) Other. In this process, Poks traces the contours of an alternative world based on more just, and less oppressive, human-animal relations.

In the texts placed in the second part of the book, "Making Live and Letting Die: Biopolitics, Literature, and the Human/Animal Divide," the high stakes that are invested in the process of categorization are scrutinized from a variety of angles and starting points. Processes of inclusion or exclusion are addressed as a recurring literary topic with connections to religion, law, sexual norms and the act of naming. What beings are safeguarded, what beings are outcasts—and how are these negotiations played out? The section starts with Claudia Lindéns chapter "The Bear as Ursus Sacer in 19th-century Swedish Literature". In her text, Lindén examines relations between humans and bears in the junction between folklore mythology, the Christian tradition, Darwinism and discourses surrounding animal rights. In the late 1800s, at a moment when the bear was threatened by extinction in Sweden, Pelle Molin's and Selma Lagerlöf's short stories posit the bear as comparable with the human out-law, (den fredlöse). With reference to Giorgio Agamben, this non-human animal appears as a political and precarious creature, caught in limbo before both human and divine law.

In "Tracing the Wolf in Hermann Hesse's Der Steppenwolf", Oscar von Seth's focus on the dividing line between human/animal sheds new light on this famous German novel. By analyzing how the wolf appears in the text, von Seth notes that not only does the animality it brings to the narrative iterate the homo sacer, it also accentuates a connection to queerness. He further claims that the wolf part of the main character's identity functions as a contrast to—and critique of—the anthropocentric paradigm that regards humans as superior to all other animals. However, in reproducing racist stereotypes and promoting racial inequality, so as to foster "wolf-agency," the anthropocentric critique in Der Steppenwolf is, von Seth concludes, undermined and comes across as rather arbitrary.

The question of being recognized as a life worth saving is dealt with in Karin Dirke's contribution to this collection, "Killing Animals to Spare them". Here, the view of the suffering and death of animals and how it was tackled by animal protectionists in Sweden at the end of the 19ᵗʰ century is scrutinized. The empirical focus of the chapter is the writings of poet, newspaper maker and horse slaughterer Karl Johan Ekeblad (1817–1895), who, in bodily as well as social ways, was himself a potential outcast. Yet, his message was completely in line with conserving power, maintaining the biopolitical rule of making live and letting die.

In the process of being conceptualized as a 'subject', naming plays a crucial part. In Sune Borkfelt's chapter, "Names and Namelessness in Animal Narratives", the complications of naming animals in fiction are dealt with. Borkfelt claims that naming places and beings (human and non-human) may work in both their favor and disservice, making them either easier to love or easier to kill. Moreover, he provides an outline for a theoretical basis for discussing what he calls 'literary animal onomastics'. Through the (re)application of theory on names and naming, and a number of exemplifications from different works of fiction, Borkfelt shows how the politics, ethics, and power dynamics of naming are central to depictions of nonhuman animals in literary narratives, while also fulfilling different narrative functions.

Under the third and final section, "Feeling and Thinking Across Species and Scales," we have gathered texts that look into different ways of imagining and learning about the more-than-human world through a different optics—with the help of poetry or video games expanding human perception or by a reading intervention that deliberately pushes its focus beyond the mammal scale. In "Lungs and Leaves. Ecosystemic Imaginaries and the Thematics of Breathing in Finnish Environmental Poetry", Karoliina Lummaa notes that breathing and photosynthesis can be identified as specific and consistent motifs in contemporary Finnish environmental poetry, and that these moreover connect to nonhuman otherness, multispecies relations and ecology. Lummaa ultimately concludes that the motifs of breathing and photosynthesis forms a multimorphic network of meanings emerging between diverse types of animals, plant bodies and machines. She also claims that these networks are part of a quest for new ways of relating to the nonhuman, fueled by a human longing for belonging, coexistence and sharing.

Connections between the human and her surrounding non-human world is placed at the center of the analysis also in "Life as a Lynx: A Digital Animal Story". Here, Gunnar Theodór Eggertsson examines the video game Shelter 2 (2015) and its potential to open up an intermediary space between the human player and the animal avatar. By way of adopting an animal viewpoint, the human player is invited to a "ludo-narrative" practice unhindered by a conventional linear storyline. In Eggertsson's analysis the game's weaving of a multilayered animal experience marks an advancement of traditional literary animal storytelling—while he also critically notes that Shelter 2 engages deeper with promoting identification with the individual animal than with the factual threat that humans pose to the Lynx species.

In "Humans, Cows, and Bacteria: Three Modes of Reading the Film *Bullhead*", Amelie Björck demonstrates how reading a text on different scales will bring out different dramas from one and the same work of art. Generally, the humanities have been preoccupied by an anthropocentric mode of reading that focuses on the human drama. Animal studies have contributed with an alternative way of reading that shifts focus to other animals; in *Bullhead* to the biopolitical drama of cattle. However, Björck suggests that a third mode of reading is possible—and indeed essential, if we want to understand the complex entanglements of life: the micro perspective. By following the traces of hormones and antibiotics through mammal bodies, gutters and ecologies a drama beyond the mammal scale gains the required attention.

The anthology ends with an "Afterword" written by Elsi Hyttinen: "Humans and Seagulls, Paused: Pipsa Lonka's *Sky Every day* (2020) and Theater During the Pandemic". Between our symposium in December 2019, and the publication of this book in September 2021, something crucial happened that may have irreversibly affected both human and non-human life all over Earth: the corona-virus pandemic. In this essay, Hyttinen writes while in the lockdown that the virus caused in Finland, as well as in many other places. Longing for theatre, for bodies, for connectedness, she observes that the pandemic is doing something to 'the animal that therefore she is'. This is surely true also for the rest of us, but exactly what that *something* is, is yet for us all to think about.

Amelie Björck, Claudia Lindén and Ann-Sofie Lönngren (eds.)
Södertörn, November 1st, 2021

MORE-THAN-HUMAN WORLD-MAKING,
CULTURE AND KNOWLEDGE

Idiorrhythmy and Its Discontents:
Cultures of Animality in Roland Barthes
and Ursula K. Le Guin

Michael Lundblad

In a fascinating short story entitled "'The Author of the Acacia Seeds' and Other Extracts from the *Journal of the Association of Therolinguistics*" (1974), Ursula K. Le Guin imitates—if not parodies—an academic discipline of the future called "therolinguistics." The extracts in the story come from a time in which various animal languages have been deciphered and translated into human languages, although sometimes that translation makes more sense as a dance or a kind of kinetic performance. Penguin, for example, is better translated as a ballet. In an editorial to the journal, the president of this fictional organization tells us to "Remember that so late as the mid-twentieth century, most scientists, and many artists, did not believe that even Dolphin would ever be comprehensible to the human brain—or worth comprehending!"[1] Another extract from the journal utilizes linguistic knowledge of Ant dialects to argue for a particular interpretation of specific messages authored by an ant, "written in touch-gland exudation on degerminated acacia seeds laid in rows."[2] Gender plays an important role in a debate over whether the Ant author is a "neuter-female worker" who envies male privilege, or one who wants to resist presumably patriarchal norms by expressing "ultimate blasphemy."[3] Does this suggest that we could be studying gender as an element of

---

[1] Ursula K. Le Guin, "'The Author of the Acacia Seeds' and Other Extracts from the *Journal of the Association of Therolinguistics*," in *Buffalo Gals and Other Animal Presences* (1974; repr., Santa Barbara, CA: Capra, 1987), 175. Editors' note: Concerning Ursula Le Guin see also Sune Borkfelt's and Amelie Björck's chapters in this volume.

[2] Le Guin, 167.

[3] Le Guin, 168–169.

nonhuman animal cultures in literary and cultural studies today? How seriously should we take that kind of question?

At least two apparently different understandings of culture emerge from these extracts, beginning with the assumption that humans are not the only animals that have language or dialects, and that progress can be made in terms of humans trying to understand different modes of animal communication, including aesthetic or even artistic elements. Recent and ongoing forays in multispecies ethnography, philosophical ethology, and theoretical biology can be seen as pursuing this kind of work in important and fascinating ways, within a broader understanding of animal communication; different dialects have indeed been found among animal groups within the same species.[4] According to ethologists, patterns of communication that can be learned and passed on to subsequent generations constitute a form of animal culture. But this is a very limited understanding of culture from the perspective of literary and cultural studies. Their typical examples of cultural difference include adapted behaviors that seem to provide some sort of survival benefit, although aesthetic considerations are not always overlooked.[5] Another form of culture in Le Guin's story, however, might seem less realistic, if not egregiously anthropomorphized: the suggestion that an ant, for example, could be understood to have composed texts that express frustration with communal restrictions based upon gender. Is it possible to imagine that ants can have discrimination or othering within their own ant cultures, without sounding like a parody of academia gone wild, or

[4] According to biological research summarized by Joe Roman, for example, "groups of killer whales maintain their own vocal dialects despite interaction with other groups"; while humpback whales "show evidence of cultural transmission" such as, for example, "In 1996, two male humpbacks from the Indian Ocean arrived in the Pacific with a new song. Within two years, all the Pacific males had changed their tune, picking up the migrants' songs." See Joe Roman, *Whale* (London: Reaktion Books, 2006), 202–205.
[5] See, for example, Thom van Dooren, Eben Kirksey & Ursula Münster, "Multi-species Studies: Cultivating Arts of Attentiveness," *Environmental Humanities* 8, no. 1 (2016), 1–23; and Eben Kirksey & Stefan Helmreich, "The Emergence of Multispecies Ethnography," *Cultural Anthropology* 25, no. 4 (2010), 545–576.

anthropomorphic projection worthy of Disney? If we want to expand our understanding of what can constitute animal cultures, which is part of my aim here, what should we pay attention to in Le Guin's story?

In Donna Haraway's discussion of the story in *Staying with the Trouble* (2016), we are told that "[i]t matters what stories we tell to tell other stories with; it matters what concepts we think to think other concepts with."[6] Taking up Le Guin's "carrier bag" theory of fiction in relation to SF writers such as Octavia Butler as well, Haraway focuses primarily on animal cultures in relation to communication and intra-actions, turning to multispecies becomings and specific histories of symbiosis between various species of ants and acacia trees in different geographical locations.[7] But Haraway does not address the question of whether ants might face discrimination, or feel isolated or alone while being pressured to fulfill their roles in relation to the survival of the colony. In literary and cultural studies today, we do not seem to have the most productive concepts for thinking about animal cultures suggested by this story. We might have a long way to go, or actually be quite unwilling, to develop the idea that ants or other species could have language in a poststructuralist sense, with discursive constructions of culture that could find homologies with human gender, sexuality, race, class, and so on. We can be wary of biopolitical hierarchies that position human consciousness at the top, as well as the sins of anthropocentrism and anthropomorphism that could be associated with looking for human cultural categories among animal groups.[8] But there might be better ways of conceptualizing difference and oppression *within* animal cultures, or what I would like to call *cultures of animality*. We need to develop keywords in animality and

---

[6] Donna J. Haraway, *Staying With the Trouble: Making Kin in the Chthulucene* (Durham, NC: Duke University Press, 2016), 118.

[7] On the idea of "becoming with" in multispecies intra-actions, see Donna J. Haraway, *When Species Meet* (Minneapolis, MN: University of Minnesota Press, 2008).

[8] On biopolitical hierarchies, see Cary Wolfe, *Before the Law: Humans and Other Animals in a Biopolitical Frame* (Chicago: University of Chicago Press, 2013).

human-animal studies that might more easily cross species boundaries, with concepts that can be explored in both human and animal cultural contexts.

To that end, I am interested in a lesser-known lecture series by Roland Barthes at the *Collège de France* in 1977, published posthumously as *How to Live Together: Novelistic Simulations of Some Everyday Spaces* (2013). Barthes' concept of what he calls "idiorrhythmy" seems productive to me for identifying what can go wrong between individuals in a community, when individual autonomy is disrupted in relation to what Barthes calls "traits." Barthes' project is what he calls a utopian fantasy, exploring literary texts in dialog with other fields such as ethnography, history, and sociology, in order to imagine better ways of living together. Literary texts can suggest ideal forms of living together, in other words, or else illustrate the forces that can tear them apart.[9] I want to sketch out, then, some of Barthes' concepts and gesture toward ways they might help us to explore cultures of animality in different ways. My focus here will be upon Barthes' concept of idiorrhythmy and other keywords that could be inspired by it. Le Guin's story will serve as a touchstone literary example for exploring these ideas.

One of Barthes' "traits" is "Banc" in French or "School" in English, referring primarily to a school of fish. The key question in relation to developing the idea of idiorrhythmy, according to Barthes, is how to "regulate interindividual distance" when "what's most precious, our ultimate possession, is space."[10] But there is also a desire for "a distance that won't destroy affect," where there is a "relation that's in no way oppressive but at the same time where there's a real warmth of feeling."[11] *How to Live Together* is a collection of Barthes' lecture notes, supplemented by transcriptions from recordings of the lectures themselves, along with the seminars he ran in conjunction with the lectures. As a result, they are often only fragments of thoughts, with

---

[9] Roland Barthes, *How to Live Together: Novelistic Simulations of Some Everyday Spaces*, trans. Kate Briggs (New York: Columbia University Press, 2013).
[10] Barthes, 131–132.
[11] Barthes, 132.

references and allusions to various other texts, rather than a finished book adapted and published by Barthes himself. He was unfortunately killed shortly afterward. But the introductory lecture lays out a path that Barthes will follow in relation to idiorrhythmy: "something like solitude with regular interruptions: the paradox, the contradiction, the aporia of bringing distances together..."[12] The concept comes from Barthes' reading about the history of monks on Mount Athos, "both isolated from and in contact with one another within a particular type of structure [...] Where each subject lives according to his own rhythm."[13] From the Greek, "idios" means "personal, particular, one's own,"[14] which makes it possible to fantasize about "idiorrhythmic clusters" of people living together outside of monasteries as well.

According to Barthes, a school of fish "appears to be the perfect image of Living-together, one that would appear to effect the perfectly smooth symbiosis of what are nevertheless separate individual beings."[15] But before we start thinking that Barthes is closer to Derrida than we might have thought, seriously considering the question of the animal, he stops short: "Clearly: one should never seriously compare traits of animal ethology with traits of human sociology, never infer one order from the other (because between the two there's always at least this separating them: *language*)."[16] Clearly Barthes is not on the same page as those who have deconstructed language as the supposedly definitive dividing line between humans and all other animals on the planet, from Le Guin to Haraway to Derrida.[17] Barthes also draws a problematic line when it comes to culture as limited to humans. When comparing animals with human societies, and

[12] Barthes, 6.
[13] Barthes, 6.
[14] Barthes, 178n31.
[15] Barthes, 37.
[16] Barthes, 37, my emphasis.
[17] See Donna J. Haraway, *Simians, Cyborgs, and Women: The Reinvention of Nature* (New York: Routledge, 1991) and Jacques Derrida, *The Animal That Therefore I Am (Following)* (New York: Fordham University Press, 2008).

in one case specifically insect societies, Barthes admits that "there are parallels…"[18] But, "[e]ven so, they're still not comparable: human society ≠ insect society. Insect society: has its basis in a series of innate behaviors. ≠ Men: [have] intelligence that's individual rather than specific; connections are often learned: *it's what we call 'culture.'*"[19] This definition of culture matches what ethologists and multispecies ethnographers have already found in nonhuman animals: connections and behaviors that are learned rather than innate, and that can be taught to others.

For Barthes, however, a distinction can be made between a school of fish and what he sees as the "extremely banal myth of an anthill-society. Which is: generalized, universalized bureaucratized training…"[20] The anthill becomes "the equalization of individuals, the mechanization of social functions," while the school of fish is "the canceling of subjects, the training of affects, which are wholly equalized."[21] The school of fish can be seen as modeling "collective, synchronized, abrupt shifts in tastes, pleasures, fashions, fears."[22] It can even reproduce itself without sexual intimacy: "a school of male fish will swim above a school of females. As the mass of eggs floats up to the surface it passes through the school of males, which then release their sperm— reproduction without contact, pure species with no subjects. Erotic paradox: bodies are pressed against each other and yet they don't make love."[23] Barthes is careful throughout his work to note that idiorrhythmy is not about the intimacy of lovers, which makes this example more appealing to him: "Idiorrhythmy: protects the body in that it keeps it at a distance in order to safeguard its value: its desire."[24]

The biggest problem with Barthes' concept of idiorrhythmy in terms of cultures of animality is that he never seriously

---

[18] Barthes, 37.
[19] Barthes, 37, my emphasis.
[20] Barthes, 37.
[21] Barthes, 37–38.
[22] Barthes, 37.
[23] Barthes, 38.
[24] Barthes, 38.

considers nonhuman animals as subjects or agents or actors; they are essentially metaphorical models for how humans can interact with each other.[25] But idiorrhythmy is nonetheless a concept that can be considered in relation to nonhuman animals, despite Barthes' own limitations, as well as inter-species relations, particularly as they are constructed in literary and cultural texts. What disrupts the idiorrhythmy of the ant colony, for example, in Le Guin's story? One of the messages from the "Author" of the acacia seeds is this: "As the ant among foreign-enemy ants is killed, so the ant without ants dies, but being without ants is as sweet as honeydew."[26] The commentary then explains, "An ant intruding in a colony not its own is usually killed. Isolated from other ants it invariably dies within a day or so. The difficulty in this passage is the word/mark 'without ants,' which we take to mean 'alone'—a concept for which no word/mark exists in Ant."[27] Clearly in this literary example the individual ant relishes solitude—it can be "as sweet as honeydew"—but the ant lives in a community in which isolation leads to death. The therolinguists here are surprised to find an apparently new concept: the idea of *feeling* alone.

Another way to respond to the story might be to see it as highlighting a potentially idiorrhythmic cluster gone bad, where an individual's desire for solitude leads to death. But how and why does that happen? The most obvious threats to idiorrhythmy in general would be violence, oppression, and death, but the concept allows for subtler forms of disruption to be explored. Barthes' trait of "school" is once again interesting to consider here. What makes an anthill colony more oppressive than a school of fish? What about this particular ant community? Fish schools can inspire us to think about "Schooling" more generally, referring to both a group clustering together and

[25] I develop this point further in relation to Barthes' discussion of *Robinson Crusoe* in my "Opening Up a Dossier: Animals, Animalities, and Living Together with Roland Barthes," in *Animals, Animality, and Literature* (Cambridge: Cambridge University Press, 2018), 217–230.
[26] Le Guin, 168.
[27] Le Guin, 168.

some form of teaching, a means for showing individuals how to avoid swimming into each other, disrupting each other's own rhythm, if not the group as a whole. How does that happen for particular ants in specific conjunctures of time and place? How might various forms of schooling be more or less disruptive to human or inter-species idiorrhythmic clusters as well? What if the "school" does not adapt to individuals needing more space or time alone? What are the mechanisms through which discipline is enforced, to avoid the cluster being disbanded?

These are different kinds of questions compared to Haraway's "closer look" at the story, which moves quickly to a discussion of "symbiosis, symbiogenesis, and ecological evolutionary developmental biology," specifically in relation to ants and acacia seeds, in order to reflect upon these multispecies relations: "The therolinguists were worried about the message they tried to decipher in the writing, but I am riveted by what drew ant and acacia seed together in the first place. How did they know each other? How did they communicate? Why did the ant paint her message on that shiny surface?"[28] She goes on to discuss acacias in Australia, Southern California, and Central America, revealing how, "in evolutionary-ecological terms, these ants and acacias are necessary to each other's reproductive business."[29] There are examples that could even be seen as forms of domestication by the ants, making sure the trees that shelter them are not squeezed out by other kinds of vegetation. According to Haraway, "[t]he more one looks, the more the name of the game of living and dying on earth is a convoluted multispecies affair that goes by the name of symbiosis, the yoking together of companion species, at table together."[30]

From Haraway's discussion, we can think about forms of communication and intra-action between species that are organized primarily in "evolutionary-ecological terms." But what about communication that looks more like literary or cul-

[28] Haraway, *Staying*, 122, 123–124.
[29] Haraway, *Staying*, 124.
[30] Haraway, *Staying*, 124.

tural production in Le Guin's story? Here we might gesture toward different definitions of culture, looking back to those tracked by Raymond Williams in *Keywords* (orig. 1976), around the same time that both Le Guin and Barthes were writing these texts. If culture can be "the works and practices of intellectual and especially artistic activity,"[31] we might argue that the definition could or should apply to animal communication. So, too, might we extend Williams' decidedly humanist bias in more posthumanist directions in relation to another definition of culture he identifies as "a particular way of life, whether of a people, a period, a group, or humanity in general."[32] That understanding can resonate with unique learned behaviors taught and maintained in specific animal groups, ethologically speaking. The third category of usage, which is "a general process of intellectual, spiritual and aesthetic development,"[33] however, might seem less promising in terms of multispecies discussions, whether we highlight individuals or groups of animals somehow acquiring "culture" in this sense. Culture is of course an incredibly complex signifier, with diverse meanings and histories in relation to various academic fields, historical and cultural contexts, and popular usage.[34]

But the concepts of individuality and autonomy might seem problematic when it comes to nonhuman animals, even if they do not necessarily suggest other forms of anthropomorphism. We have other theoretical fields and terms to draw upon, as well as different genealogies that are beyond the scope of this chapter.[35] Rather than showing that animal autonomy can be

---

[31] Raymond Williams, *Keywords: A Vocabulary of Culture and Society* (1976; repr., New York: Oxford University Press, 1983), 90.

[32] Williams, 90.

[33] Williams, 90.

[34] George Yudice tracks many of these complexities, for example, in his entry on "Culture" for the 2nd edition of *Keywords for American Cultural Studies* (New York: New York University Press, 2014), 68–72. The volume as a whole suggests ongoing keywords for the study of U.S. human culture, which can also be related to human interactions with other species.

[35] I have in mind here, for example, actor-network theory's development of the idea of distributed agency; the philosophical and biological concept of *umwelt*;

"just like humans," posthumanism, for example, can reveal that *humans* are not "just like humans," in the sense of a stable humanist conception of Self and free will.[36] As a result, we do not need to be fixated upon concepts such as intent in relation to either human or animal autonomy. Le Guin's story of an ant author does seem to suggest a decipherable intent, however. What should we do with that? What about the question of cultural production, in which ants in the story are seen as having created literary texts?

Vinciane Despret, among others, argues that these kinds of questions could be seen as the least promising or interesting, when it comes to animals themselves in ethological studies. Why insist upon the idea of an author, for example, of the ant-kind in Le Guin's case, and privilege the messages whose meanings seem to be derived in some form in relation to intent? We might also be reminded here of Barthes' own rejection of authorial intent in "The Death of the Author" (1967). In *What Would Animals Say If We Asked the Right Questions?* (2016), Despret argues that we should reject the question of whether animals can "be granted the status of artist," precisely because it privileges the question of intent.[37] Despret focuses instead on the "agencements" that lead to "achievement" when "beasts and humans accomplish a work together."[38] Despret wants to "welcome new ways of speaking, describing, and narrating that allow us to respond, in a sensitive way, to these events,"[39] and her work suggests multiple ways of doing that.

How might we respond, in a sensitive way, to the event of writing in Le Guin's text? Is it realistic enough to be taken seriously? How do we decide? How does it relate to idior-

Haraway's and others' thinking about *becoming-with*; autopoietic organisms in systems theory; and various poststructuralist deconstructions of the "I."

[36] See Cary Wolfe, *What Is Posthumanism?* (Minneapolis: Unniversity of Minnesota Press, 2010).

[37] Vinciane Despret, *What Would Animals Say If We Asked the Right Questions?* trans. Brett Buchanan (Minneapolis: University of Minnesota Press, 2016), 1.

[38] Despret, 6.

[39] Despret, 6.

rhythmy? The final message "written" (by exuding from a touch-gland, that is) on the acacia seeds seems emphatic, but we might not know how to interpret it or respond to it: "Eat the eggs! Up with the Queen!"[40] The fictional commentary in the story tells us that in one interpretation, "the author, a wingless neuter-female worker, yearns hopelessly to be a winged male, and to found a new colony, flying upward in the nuptial flight with a new Queen."[41] But the assumption that "up" connotes "good" is dismissed as "ethnocentric" by the authors of the commentary, who argue instead that "this strange author, in the solitude of her lonely tunnel, sought with what means she had to express the ultimate blasphemy conceivable to an ant."[42] These are all loaded words, of course, from blasphemy to Queen to nuptial flights. They might seem far too anthropomorphic, including the projection of gendered frustrations and desires. It is worth noting that Le Guin's text could be seen as *parodying* academic discourse, on the one hand, or, on the other hand, suggesting a provocative way of drawing attention to parallel problems of rigid gender roles policed within human cultures, particularly in the 1970s. Le Guin could be writing more about disruptions to human idiorrhythmy on the basis of gender, in other words, than ant cultures. But these projects can be far more intertwined than we might think.

Le Guin's story also evokes the language of class, from the Queen down to worker and soldier "castes." We are told, for example, that an ant of the "soldier caste" would have been "illiterate" and therefore "presumably not interested in the collection of useless seeds from which the edible germs had been removed."[43] Here we might pause to consider whether or how the language of class could or should be applied to cultures of animality in better ways, while looking back to Barthes for alternatives. Through his dossier on "Domestiques/ Servants,"

[40] Le Guin, 168.
[41] Le Guin, 168.
[42] Le Guin, 169.
[43] Le Guin, 169.

Barthes raises questions such as, "[h]ow do needs get satisfied? Who takes care of the domestic tasks? Thorny issue for modern 'communes': Who does the washing up? → The problem of servants."[44] Problems can come when distinctions are made between members of a community who work and those who do not work to meet the basic needs of the community. According to Barthes, "this communitary problem repeats the major structural problems of all societies: the division of labor, exchange, class divisions, the reconstruction of a social microcosm at the margins of society, the circumscription of an idle, privileged group."[45] This problem can begin even with a voluntary master/servant relationship in the case of apprentice monks, but can also be seen in literary examples such as Robinson Crusoe and the character Friday, which Barthes describes more accurately as a master/slave relationship: "Living-Together with Friday is a matter of living with a slave. [...] Friday places Robinson's foot on his head himself (as if it were the essential nature of a black man to be instantly enslaved..."[46] My question here becomes: what would it mean to think about "servants" in an anthill society? Could they be aware of their comparative positions? Who works for the common good in various ways, and who does not? Are there any opportunities for changing roles? How might the consideration of who works in different ways lead to better comparisons between human and animal cultures? The word "servants"—as well as "work"—is of course loaded with human history as well, along with racism and oppression, but perhaps it allows us to see something different from imposing the specificities of class onto other species.

Which other "traits" or keywords from Barthes might have more or less potential for exploring cultures of animality? My claim is not that all of his terms have equal promise, nor that they are necessarily even the best "traits" for exploring idiorrhythmy. Rather, I want to highlight the process of considering

---

[44] Barthes, 75.
[45] Barthes, 77.
[46] Barthes, 76.

and developing keywords that might more productively cross species lines. If the terms and discourses we analyze in relation to human cultures seem less productive in relation to cultures of animality, how might we take a step back, or even upwards, to a level of generalization that feels not only less anthropomorphic but also more sensitive and imaginative? As Barthes suggests, literary texts, particularly fiction, can provide the means for opening up these imaginative dossiers, which are not only informed by, but also inform, the work of researchers intra-acting with "actual" animals.[47]

I would like to mention a few more "traits" from Barthes that could be developed further, or, contrarily, could lead to even better, perhaps different, keywords identifying particular factors that disrupt idiorrhythmy in various human and animal cultures. According to Barthes, under the "trait" of "Chef / Chief," for example, the idiorrhythmic space can be disrupted as soon as there is a chief, rather than a community of equals, or even a group with an informal guru: "the introduction of a hierarchy: the invention of the chief."[48] Perhaps hierarchy would be a better keyword, as it could relate to "servants" as well. But is it the existence of hierarchy itself, or is it more precisely when hierarchy impinges upon individual choice, when the individual does not agree that the decisions being made are best for the community as a whole? Can SF help us to imagine something like choice for ants, without requiring a humanist subject? What if hierarchy is based not upon work but upon something like othering that can lead to discrimination, or prejudice, or favoring within a group? Barthes' reflections on "Idyllique / Idyll," suggest that there must be "an absence of conflict," where the idyllic "refers to a literary representation (or fantasmatization) of its relational space."[49] Certainly conflict can lead to obvious disruptions of idiorrhythmy, such as aggression and

---

[47] On "intra-action," see Karen Barad, *Meeting the Universe Halfway: Quantum Physics and the Entanglement of Matter and Meaning* (Durham, NC: Duke University Press, 2007); and Haraway, *When Species Meet*.

[48] Barthes, 54.

[49] Barthes, 88.

violence. But what if the enforcement of rules deemed important for survival, if not also the common good, is perceived as violent by some but not all? Under "Règle / Rule," Barthes concludes that idiorrhythmy can be threatened when the development of habits or customs leads to more rigid rules: "Perhaps, after a certain period of time (historical, personal), every rule, even an inner one, becomes abuse?"[50] All of these threats to idiorrhythmy—servants, chiefs, hierarchies, conflicts, rules—might be imaginatively considered in relation to historically and culturally situated cultures, not only within human or non-human groups, but also between groups, between species.

Barthes is quite explicit in the end about not making any social prescriptions. He ends his lectures intentionally with a dossier on "Utopie / Utopia," indicating that he had initially planned to "dedicate the thirteenth [and final lecture] to constructing, in front of you, a utopia of idiorrhythmic Living-Together—since the lecture course started out from that particular fantasy."[51] Instead, he admits that he "didn't have time to collect your contributions"; that he "lacked the necessary enthusiasm"; and that he had realized over the course of the lectures that "a utopia of idiorrhythmic Living-Together is not a social utopia."[52] Although it's not in his written notes, orally he says, simply: "I don't have a philosophy of Living Together."[53] While he suggests vaguely that the lectures of the following year will "involve an *Ethics*," Barthes also resists committing to any particular method for dealing with the dossiers he has opened up thus far: "the preparation for method is an infinite, infinitely open process. It's a form of preparation whose final achievement is forever postponed."[54] Despite the fact that he begins the lecture series by talking about a "non-method," he now concludes that "[a]s always, the 'non-' is too simple. It would be

---

[50] Barthes, 120.
[51] Barthes, 130.
[52] Barthes, 130.
[53] Barthes, 196n12.
[54] Barthes, 136.

better to say: pre-method. As if I were preparing my materials with a view to dealing with them methodically at some later stage; as if I actually weren't too bothered what method would take them up. Anything is possible: psychoanalysis, semiology, ideological criticism could make use of them..."[55] But Barthes is content to leave those kinds of possibilities undeveloped.

I will end with one of the key traits to which Barthes ultimately pays less attention: "Cause / Cause." When considering "small, flexible groups of several individuals who are attempting to live together (within a certain proximity to one another), while each preserving his or her *rhuthmos*," Barthes acknowledges the importance of the question: "What brings them together?"[56] Whether it is a monastery or the sanatorium of *The Magic Mountain*, "[f]or there to be idiorrhythmy—or a dream of idiorrhythmy—there has to be: a diffuse, vague, uncertain Cause, a floating *Telos*, more a fantasy than a belief."[57] For those of us in the humanities and social sciences working on animalities broadly conceived, the fantasy might be not just a small community but larger societal structures and ecological relations that allow for different species to live together in better ways, toward Lestel's hybrid communities or Haraway's "becoming with."[58]

But we might also think about animalities scholarship itself as uniting behind "a diffuse, vague, uncertain Cause" in which opening up dossiers on animalities in literary and cultural texts is more than just a "pre-method." Finally, then, how might we aspire toward idiorrhythmy ourselves, as scholars committed to a vague common cause as well as our own solitary pursuits, without impinging upon each other? Perhaps we can re-open a

[55] Barthes, 136.
[56] Barthes, 43.
[57] Barthes, 46.
[58] On Lestel, see, for example, Matthew Chrulew, "The Philosophical Ethology of Dominique Lestel," *Angelaki: Journal of the Theoretical Humanities* 19, no. 3 (2014), 17–44; on animalities, see my "Introduction. The End of the Animal: Literary and Cultural Animalities," in *Animalities: Literary and Cultural Studies Beyond the Human*, (Edinburgh: Edinburgh University Press, 2017), 1–22.

dossier on "response" following Derrida: how might we do more than just react to each other? What forms of indifference or non-responsiveness are intolerable or even fatal?[59] As Haraway declares, and I'm with her: "With Le Guin, I am committed to the finicky, disruptive details of good stories that don't know how to finish. Good stories reach into rich pasts to sustain thick presents to keep the story going for those who come after."[60] In order to develop new keywords for cultures of animality, we can learn from writers and theorists, from ethologists and anthropologists, as well as from indigenous and non-eurocentric epistemologies and ways of being in the world. We can explore a wide range of texts related to specific animal species, particularly if we want to understand relationships between ants, for example, in Le Guin's story and beyond. We need to keep our eyes and other senses open for forces and factors that not only limit and shut things down, but also those that point toward productive or fulfilling possibilities for better ways of living together.

References

Barad, Karen. *Meeting the Universe Halfway: Quantum Physics and the Entanglement of Matter and Meaning.* Durham, NC: Duke University Press, 2007.

Barthes, Roland. *How to Live Together: Novelistic Simulations of Some Everyday Spaces.* Translated by Kate Briggs. New York: Columbia University Press, 2013.

Chrulew, Matthew. "The Philosophical Ethology of Dominique Lestel." *Angelaki: Journal of the Theoretical Humanities* 19, no. 3 (2014): 17–44.

Derrida, Jacques. *The Animal That Therefore I Am (Following).* Edited by Marie-Louise Mallet, translated by David Wills. 2006. Reprint, New York: Fordham University Press, 2008.

Despret, Vinciane. *What Would Animals Say If We Asked the Right Questions?* Translated by Brett Buchanan. Minneapolis: University of Minnesota Press, 2016.

---

[59] On response vs. reaction, see Derrida.
[60] Haraway, *Staying*, 125.

Dooren, Thom van, Eben Kirksey & Ursula Münster. "Multispecies Studies: Cultivating Arts of Attentiveness." *Environmental Humanities* 8, no. 1 (2016): 1–23.

Haraway, Donna. *Simians, Cyborgs, and Women: The Reinvention of Nature.* New York: Routledge, 1991.

Haraway, Donna, *Staying With the Trouble: Making Kin in the Chthulucene.* Durham, New York: Duke University Press, 2016.

Haraway, Donna. *When Species Meet.* Minneapolis, MN: University of Minnesota Press, 2008.

Kirksey, Eben & Stefan Helmreich. "The Emergence of Multispecies Ethnography." *Cultural Anthropology* 25, no. 4 (2010): 545–576.

Le Guin, Ursula K. "'The Author of the Acacia Seeds' and Other Extracts from the *Journal of the Association of Therolinguistics.*" In *Buffalo Gals and Other Animal Presences.*1974. Reprint, Santa Barbara, CA: Capra, 1987.

Lundblad, Michael. "Introduction. The End of the Animal: Literary and Cultural Animalities." In *Animalities: Literary and Cultural Studies Beyond the Human,* 1–22. Edited by Michael Lundblad. Edinburgh: Edinburgh University Press, 2017.

Lundblad, Michael. "Opening Up a Dossier: Animals, Animalities, and Living Together with Barthes, Roland." In *Animals, Animality, and Literature,* 217–230. Edited by Bruce Boehrer, Molly Hand, and Brian Massumi. Cambridge: Cambridge University Press, 2018.

Roman, Joe, *Whale.* London: Reaktion Books, 2006.

Williams, Raymond. *Keywords: A Vocabulary of Culture and Society.* 1976. Reprint, New York: Oxford University Press, 1983.

Wolfe, Cary. *Before the Law: Humans and Other Animals in a Biopolitical Frame.* Chicago: University of Chicago Press, 2013.

Wolfe, Cary. *What Is Posthumanism?* Minneapolis: University of Minnesota Press, 2010.

Yudice, George. "Culture." In *Keywords for American Cultural Studies,* 68–72. Edited by Bruce Burgett and Glenn Hendler. New York: New York University Press, 2014.

Reclaiming a Repressed World: Decolonizing the Human-Animal Relationship in Three Stories by Contemporary Sámi Author Kirsti Paltto

Ann-Sofie Lönngren

When the field of literary animal studies started to take shape, one of the first methodological issues addressed regarding literary interpretation was to question the general practice of viewing fictive animals primarily as metaphors for something else, for example, human emotions or desires. Instead, it was argued that literary depictions of animals should be understood according to the logic of metonymy, that is, as 'real animals,' leaving traces in the text for the reader to follow and interpret. This redirection of attention ultimately led to the conclusion that literary animals can be agents in the text, thus capable of affecting or even defining the course of events in a fictive story. Theoretically, these discussions were typically grounded in the works of Gilles Deleuze and Félix Guattari, as well as Donna Haraway.[1] But these ideas are also remarkably similar to lines of thought to be found in the field of indigenous studies. Indeed, one of the fundamental pillars of indigenous ontologies is the presumption that the non-human world has agency,[2] an assumption that of course includes non-human animals, meaning that the human exceptionalism of Western colonial know-

---

[1] For an overview, see Ann-Sofie Lönngren, "Metaphor, Metonymy, More-than-anthropocentric. The Animal that therefore I Read (and Follow)," in *The Palgrave Handbook of Animals and Literature* (Basingstoke: Palgrave MacMillan, 2021), 23–50. Throughout this article, I mostly employ the terms "human" and "animal" as shorthand for the more accurate but longer phrase "human and non-human animals." In this praxis I am inspired by Laura Brown's *Homeless Dogs and Melancholy Apes. Humans and Other Animals in the Modern Literary Imagination* (Ithaca, London: Cornell University Press, 2010), 2.

[2] Jerry Lee Rosiek, Jimmy Snyder & Scott L. Pratt, "The New Materialisms and Indigenous Theories of Non-Human Agency: Making the Case for Respectful Anti-Colonial Engagement," *Qualitative Inquiry* 26, no. 3–4 (2020), 331–346.

ledge production and philosophy is undermined.[3] From the point of view of human-animal studies, these circumstances call for a mapping of the characteristics of these ontologies and of the role and accounts of animal agency within them. In order to discuss these questions, I turn to literature, which has been described as "storage for knowledge" in indigenous contexts.[4] More precisely, I will analyze three stories written by acknowledged Sámi author Kirsti Paltto (b. 1947).

Background

Sámi is the name of the indigenous people that traditionally inhabit Sápmi, stretching over approximately 400,000 km^2 of the northern-most parts of Norway, Sweden, Finland and Russia. Depending on how 'Sáminess' is defined, one can speak of 70,000–101,000 people belonging to this minority, living in Sápmi and other places.[5] Contacts between people living in this area and the rest of Europe have been continuous since the settlement of Northern Europe at the end of the last Ice Age.[6]

---

[3] Jacques Derrida, *The Animal That Therefore I Am (Following)*, trans. David Wills (New York: Fordham University Press, 2008), 1–11; Donna J. Haraway, *Primate Visions. Gender, Race, and Nature in the World of Modern Science* (New York, London: Routledge, 1989); Donna J. Haraway, *When Species Meet* (Minneapolis, London: University of Minnesota Press, 2008), 9–15; Elina Helander-Renvall, "Animism, Personhood and the Nature of Reality: Sami Perspectives," *Polar Record* 46, no. 236 (2010): passim; Barbara Noske, *Humans and Other Animals. Beyond the Boundaries of Anthropology* (Winchester: Pluto Press, 1989), xi.

[4] Rauna Kuokkanen, "Border Crossings, Pathfinders and New Visions: the Role of Sámi Literature in Contemporary Society," *Nordlit* 15 (2004): 93.

[5] Johanna Domokos, *A Writing Hand Reaches Further—Čálli giehta olla guhkás'. Recommendations for the Improvement of the Sámi Literary Field* (Finland: Nordic Council, 2018), 8. In English, the name of the Sámi people is variously spelled as Sámi, Saami and Sami. I follow Domokos' praxis and use the ethnonym Sámi, and the term Sápmi for their historical and present primary area (Domokos, *Writing Hand*, 8). The older word 'Lapp' is nowadays considered derogatory. See Ildikó Tamás, "The Colors of the Polar Lights (Symbols in the Construction of Sami Identity)," in *The Concept of Freedom in the Literatures of Eastern Europe* (Võro: Publications of Võro institute, 2017), 12.

[6] Stéphane Aubinet, *The Craft of Yoiking. Philosophical Variations on Sámi Chants* (University of Oslo: Department of Musicology, 2020), 4.

During the Middle Ages, Sámi and other people co-existed in this area, but as the process of forming nation-states intensified, measures were taken to increase control over Sápmi. Thus, churches were built from around the 16th century, and from around the beginning of the 17th century, the Swedish state started to interfere more regularly with the lives of the Sámi. The most effective period of missionary work was the second half of the 19th century, when shamanism and joiking[7] were punished by religious and secular authorities alike. Up until the last third of the 20th century, these repressive tendencies would increase, particularly in Norway and Sweden, who employed never-before-seen tactics to try to assimilate the Sámi. Apart from having to deal with the loss of societal prestige and discrimination, people struggling to maintain their Sámi identity could no longer use their native language publicly, and everything connected with Sámi culture was stigmatized. In Sweden, the State Institute for Racial Biology (established in 1922 and operative until the 1970s) was used to demonstrate their inferiority. From around the 1960s, however, the claims for Sámi rights and recognition, which had started to form at the beginning of the 20th century, became more insistent and successful. Today, the Sámi people have largely regained their rights to language and culture, and, in some cases, also managed to get legal rights to the land they traditionally inhabit. However, the extent to which their demands are met varies across the four nation-states over which Sápmi stretches. Currently, Norway is the country in which Sámi rights are most extensively acknowledged.[8]

---

[7] The joik is a singing tradition that touches the whole life of the Sámi. The joiks function as entertainment, as a communication tool, and as an expression of identity. It is also a system for the classification and identification of the Sami's surroundings, and a summary of their experiences and knowledge of the world (Tamás, 11n1).

[8] John Trygve Solbakk, *The Sámi People—A Handbook* (Karasjok: Davvi Girji, 2006), 18–78; Tamás, 17–28.

The Sámi flag.

The reconstruction of a Sámi cultural past that had been shattered by colonial interventions intensified in the 1970s. In this process, fiction came to play an important role. There was now a rise of Sámi authors writing in Sámi about the traditional way of living in this community, but also about conflicts with modern society and between generations, as well as the effects of a history of repression.[9] One of these authors is Kirsti Paltto from Ohcejohka, Utsjoki in Finland, who is sometimes called the first Sámi female writer. The transition from a traditional to a modern society is a recurring theme in Paltto's work, and she is heavily influenced by the indigenous peoples' movement and anti-colonial currents. Since the 1970s, Paltto has published

---

[9] Domokos, *Writing Hand*, 8–9; Johanna Domokos & Michal Kovář, "Terveisiä Lapista as an Example of Intercultural Dialogism," *Kirjallisuudentutkimuksen aikakauslehti A VAIN* 3 (2015), 51–67. For a thorough review of the history of Sámi literature, see Rauna Kuokkanen & Kirsti Paltto, "Publishing Sámi Literature—from Christian Translations to Sámi Publishing Houses," *Studies in American Indian Literatures* 22, no. 2 (2010), 42–58 and Vuokko Hirvonen, *Voices from Sápmi: Sámi Women's Path to Authorship*, trans. Kaija Anttonen (1988; repr., Kautokeino: DAT, 2008).

texts in a range of different genres, encompassing poetry, short stories, children's books, novels and plays, as well as essays, tracts, and scholarly works. Many of her texts have been translated into other languages such as Swedish, Norwegian, English and Hungarian. Paltto has also received several awards for her authorship.[10] Paltto is a writer who is often mentioned in overviews of the development of Sámi literature.[11] Scholars have primarily been interested in her significance for reconstructing (in particular women's) Sámi identity and culture, the postcolonial context of her authorship, the ways in which she refers to Sámi folklore and mythology in narratives that are situated in the Sámi community today, and the political significance of the fact that she has written most of her works in the northern Sámi language rather than in Finnish.[12] Although I certainly see the relevance of these perspectives, I claim that there is one aspect of her works with which has not been thoroughly dealt. Many scholars acknowledge the fact that Paltto (and other Sámi and indigenous authors) depict the non-human world as 'animist', a concept that includes the spiritualization of the object world,[13] and a view of nature as alive. Moreover, it includes the existence of a social

[10] Enikő Molnár Bodrogi, "Dissenting Narratives of Identity in Saami, Meänkieli and Kven Literatures," *Revista Română de Studii Baltice și Nordice / The Romanian Journal for Baltic and Nordic Studies* 11, no. 1 (2019), 27; Anne Heith, "Putting an End to the Shame Associated with Minority Culture and its Concomitant Negative Self-Images—On Gender and Ethnicity in Sami and Tornedalian Literature," in *The History of Nordic Women's Literature Online* (Odense: Syddansk Universitet, 2016), 2.

[11] See, for example, Kaisa Ahvenjärvi, "Reindeer Revisited. Traditional Sámi features in contemporary Sámi poetry," in *Rethinking National Literatures and the Literary Canon in Scandinavia* (Newcastle upon Tyne: Cambridge Scholars Publishing, 2015), 104–129 and Kathleen Osgood Dana, "Sami Literature in the Twentieth Century," *World Literature Today* 71 (Winter 1997), 22–28.

[12] Due to the dispersion of relatively small groups over large areas, there are several different Sámi languages with varying numbers of speakers (Domokos, *Writing Hand*, 8–9; see also Tamás, 13–15).

[13] Harry Garuba, "Explorations in Animist Materialism: Notes on Reading/ Writing African Literature, Culture, and Society," *Public Culture* 15, no. 2 (2003), 267.

space for humans and non-humans to interrelate to each other.[14] But there is still a lack of studies regarding the details of this ontology in relation to the agency of non-human animals as well as the precise ways in which non-human agency and their narrative effects are accounted for in the works of Paltto.[15]

These questions gain relevance against the background of the traditional Sámi way of living in close kinship with natural elements. This is not unusual in native contexts,[16] and there are rich references to the non-human world in Sámi cultural expressions such as joik.[17] As for non-human animals, the reindeer has always been a cornerstone of Sámi society, even if there are also Sámi villages that have lived off fishing and hunting.[18] Moreover, there are frequent occurrences of bears, cats, dogs and also hybrid creatures in Sámi folklore, joik, literature and mythology.[19] In the following, I will conduct a comparative close reading of the ontology and agency of non-human animals in three short stories from Paltto's collection of stories *Stjålet* (*Stolen*) from 2003.[20]

<hr />

[14] Helander-Renvall, 44.

[15] There has, however, been studies conducted regarding the human-animal relationship in other indigenous literature. Within this wider field, my analysis adds a Sámi perspective to previous publications such as *Indigenous Creatures, Native Knowledges, and the Arts: Animal Studies in Modern Worlds* (London: Palgrave MacMillan 2017); Susan McHugh, *Love in a Time of Slaughters. Human-animal Stories against Genocide and Extinction* (Pennsylvania: The Pennsylvania University Press, 2019) and Daniel Heath Justice (Cherokee), *Why Indigenous Literature Matter* (Waterloo & Ontario: Wilfrid Laurier University Press, 2018).

[16] Kathleen Osgood Dana, "Áillohaš and his Image Drum. The Native Poet as Shaman," *Nordlit* 15 (2004), 27.

[17] Stéphane Aubinet, "Chanter les territoires Sámi dans un monde plus-qu'humain," *Information géographique* 81, no. 1 (2017), 20–37.

[18] Tamás, 12–13. Although a large part of the Sámi population lives in cities today, reindeer keeping remains a central element to the internal and external expressions of 'Sámi identity', and Swedish and Norwegian law guarantee the Sámi monopoly in this area. In Finland, however, only 20% of the Sámi population is employed in reindeer keeping, and the percentage is even lower in Russia (Tamás, 15).

[19] Helander-Renvall, passim.

[20] This collection was originally published in 2001 in the northern Sámi language, but I have read it in its Norwegian translation. There are altogether 15 separate stories in the book.

Three stories

In "The bedbug," we learn about Egá, an older solitary man who, due to his fear of ghosts and other supernatural beings, is the laughing stock of the little Sámi community in which he lives. The course of events begins when Egá sets out for a hike to a headland, where there is an old timber cottage for all to use. Having safely reached the hut, Egá stretches out on the reindeer skin on the floor to sleep. At that point, it strikes him as odd that while there are swarms of mosquitos outdoors, there are none inside the hut. This riddle is solved as Egá becomes aware of what is described as a huge bedbug crawling out of one of the cracks in the wall. Egá hastily collects his few belongings and runs screaming into the night, throws himself in a river and swims across it before he dares to stop. Inside the cabin, the bedbug scuttles across the floor to watch Egá's escape through the window while sadly contemplating why humans hate bedbugs so much even though they never mean to do anything wrong—just get themselves a meal, and not even by killing, as humans do, but simply by sucking some blood. It then watches Egá sitting on the other side of the river, soaking wet, and shakes its head at the stupidity of man. Next time, the bedbug ponders, it will be smarter not to reveal itself, but climb onto the ceiling and let itself drop down silently onto the nose of the next human who spends the night in the hut. Then the bedbug goes to sleep, and the focalization goes back to Egá, who does not dare to return to the hut. Instead, he walks until he reaches his friend Olle's house, where he is given warm coffee and new clothes while his own are drying. There, however, he is also laughed at—what ghost is he scared of now? But Egá says nothing, ever, to anyone about the bedbug. The only thing that has changed is that he is no longer afraid of ghosts.[21]

---

[21] Kirsti Paltto, *Stjålet*, trans. Ellen Anna Gaup, Mikkel A. Gaup and Laila Stein (2001. Repr., Karasjok: Davvi Girji, 2003), 7–13. This is the first story in the collection. It has not been translated into English and the translation of the title is my own. Norwegian original: "Vegglusa."

"The bear-girl" depicts its main character Rásttôs as an elderly man who is reasonable yet somehow different. At the story's beginning, we learn that he has a family; however, they live elsewhere than in the small Sámi community in which he himself resides. In his remembrance of his youth, we get to follow how this came about. When Rásttôs was a young man, he was sent into the mountains to collect a few runaway reindeer cows. Exhausted after the non-successful chase, he sits down to smoke, and that is when, to his horror, he discovers a big bear close to him. Rásttôs pulls out his knife to protect himself, but as he watches the bear it becomes transparent and reveals a beautiful naked girl inside. He follows the bear-girl to its lair where they spend the night together. The day after, when Rásttôs goes back to the village, he is surprised to learn that the reindeer herd he thought he had lost is safely back in the enclosure. After that event, Rásttôs will spend the rest of his life visiting his bear-girl. Returning to the present time in the story, Rásttôs is old, but he still looks forward to going into the mountains to spend time with his bear family. The story ends with him imagining that maybe one day, one of his now grown-up bear-daughters will run into a young Sámi man and enchant him like their mother once did to Rásttôs.[22]

"Tracks," finally, features Sámmol as its main character, an elderly man living with his dog Guksi in a modern Sámi community. Sámmol is known to be hot-tempered, and at the beginning of the story, he is angry at a young Sámi journalist, Ole, who interviewed him for a Sámi newspaper some days previously. That man had got it all wrong! Sámmol had told the journalist about the footprints he has often seen in the mountains, half reindeer, half woman, and now Ole has written that these tracks go down the mountain and disappear into a lake, which is not true. Sámmol is so angry that he calls the journalist

---

[22] Paltto, 31–41. This is the third story in the collection, but for the sake of clarity in relation to my argument, I have placed it second in my analysis. It has not been translated into English and the translation of the title is my own. Norwegian original: "Bjørnejente." Editors' note: Concerning bear-stories see also Claudia Lindén's chapter in this volume.

and tells him to get in his car and come to see him immediately. When he arrives, Sámmol takes him on a skiing tour into the mountains so that he can see the tracks firsthand. The journalist is amazed and takes photos of them, but then continues to follow them once he has parted ways with Sámmol. Together with Guksi, Ole follows the tracks until all of a sudden the hybrid creature stands before him—half reindeer, half naked woman. While he watches it, the creature splits in two, and then he himself unites with the girl instead of the reindeer. They run in the northern lights together, an event which, for Ole, is characterized by an otherworldly bliss. Then the reindeer comes back and pushes him from the girl's side so that he falls out of the sky and lands on the mountain, just beside his skis. After that, the journalist does not remember anything until he wakes up, together with Guksi, in the basement of his workplace and finds out that 24 hours have passed since he journeyed into the mountains. When Ole's boss calls Sámmol in an attempt to solicit some answers about what happened, the old man simply asks to speak to his dog Guksi, who listens carefully to what Sámmol says before hanging up.[23]

Discussion: Re-enchanting the world

In order to understand the significance of non-human agency in these stories, we need to start with a conceptualization of their general ontology. This is, however, easier said than done, since they seem to depict at least two different ontologies that are partly at odds with one another. Firstly, there is the modern world we all know where people drive cars, speak over the phone, use cameras for documentation and read newspapers. Secondly, there is a world that contains unrealistic and magical elements that are not possible to account for with modern, scientific concepts. This duality can be understood with help

[23] Paltto, 15–29. This is the second story in the collection, but for the sake of clarity in relation to my argument, I have placed it third in my analysis. It has not been translated into English and the translation of the title is my own. Norwegian original: "Spor."

from some lines of thought advanced by Harry Garuba, who claims that there is a joint "animist unconscious" in all societies that has been subjected to a colonial takeover by monotheistic religions. Thus, this term should not be seen as a doctrine or a specific set of beliefs, but rather as a presupposition for "the re-enchantment of the world," an umbrella term that Garuba has coined for the recurrence of pre-colonial beliefs and images in the modern world.[24]

While Garuba speaks of the recurrence of such symbols in, for example, commercial contexts of the majority population, I think that his idea can equally be applied to Paltto's stories as well, since she depicts a modern world that gradually reveals elements from a pre-colonial ontology. Also, on a meta-level, the very medium of 'literature' can be seen as colonial, since the Sámi story-telling tradition has always been oral. Thus, the realistic outset of each of the three stories that I study here can be seen as being gradually 're-enchanted' by the oral tradition that is working in them in this specific Sámi context. This discussion is in line with Osgood Dana's reading of Nils-Aslak Valkeapää (1943–2001), a renowned Sámi poet who was a con-temporary of Paltto. Osgood Dana claims that today, the realm of the Sámi shaman (the *noaidi*) in many instances has shifted from the private domain of the family and family group to the public domain of literature and art. She contends that "both poet/artist and shaman are equipped in remarkable ways to negotiate between worlds, and in the hands of shaman-poets, text becomes the tool of prophecy and mediation."[25] In Paltto's stories, the occurrence of competing worldviews makes visible the difference between indigenous literature and other kinds, namely the former's strong reliance on oral story-telling.[26] Since it is the ontology constructed in this tradition that has non-human agency as the norm, then this is the one we need to map.

---

[24] Garuba, 265.
[25] Osgood Dana, "Áillohaš," 7.
[26] Kuokkannen, "Border," 93.

To this end, focusing on the stories' main characters seems like a constructive start. As Garuba notes, the spiritualization of the physical world that characterizes the animist worldview involves literary representational strategies that give "the abstract or metaphorical a material realization" and thus add a "concrete dimension to abstract ideas."[27] In Paltto's stories, the three main characters appear as such literary materializations because of the striking similarities between them. They are all elderly and all are known for being somewhat temperamental, due to some specific character trait: Egá is laughed at for being superstitious, Rásttôs is both respected and questioned for his unusual choice of family, and Sámmol seems to be close to feared due to his hot temper. If these characters are understood according to what Garuba refers as animist literature's habit of "'locking' spirit within matter,"[28] and if we presume that this 'spirit' is the alternative ontology in these stories, then we can conclude that this worldview is old and that it is both ridiculed, respected, questioned and feared.

Further information regarding this issue is gained if we consider the relationship between these characters and the place in which they reside, a small Sámi community. Indeed, these men are all part of the communities in which they live and from which they are marginalized. This marginalization is partly due to their unusual personality traits and partly to the fact that none of them live with a family in a traditional sense. The latter circumstance can be understood with an argument made by Kim Tallbear in a North American and Canadian context, namely, that the ideal of the nuclear family was brought with the colonizers. Before that, the extended family was the norm,[29] something that surely seems to have been the case in Sámi contexts as well.[30] Thus, by living outside of the norm of the

---

[27] Garuba, 273, 284.
[28] Garuba, 267.
[29] Kim Tallbear, "Making Love and Relations Beyond Settler Sex and Family," in *Making Kin Not Population* (Chicago: Prickly Paradigm Press, 2018), 145–164.
[30] Rauni Magga Lukkari, "Where did the Laughter Go?" in *No Beginning, No End: The Sami Speak Up* (Edmonton: Canadian Circumpolar Institute, 1998), 109.

nuclear family, the three main characters in Paltto's stories make visible a long since established part of the Sámi community that has now been pushed aside to its fringes. Indeed, they may have actively taken that place as a point of resistance; we do not learn much about Egá, but both Rásttôs and Sámmol seem to be openly at odds with certain normative expectations of the society in which they live.

The significance of place recurs in the fact that all three of these men, in either the story's past or present time, have gone into their surroundings on a quest for something. These recurring movements from the small village into the mountains can be seen as part of a "social imaginary," which, according to Garuba, is close to the "animist unconscious" in colonized cultures.[31] But even if the images are very similar, there are significant differences regarding what the three men are searching for and find. Egá is aiming for the hut on the headland, and only accidentally stumbles upon a non-human animal so unexpectedly large his fears for ghosts and gnomes—which are part of the colonial folklore—disappear forevermore. Indeed, the fact that he is not looking to find something else but rather is fully oriented in the postcolonial ontology is shown in the fact that he, while he wanders to the headlands, thinks that the mosquitos are "as large as angels"—"angels" of course being part of the Christian mythology of the colonizers.[32]

Rásttôs, on the other hand, is searching for an essential part of Sámi culture and ways of living—i.e. reindeers—when he is surprised to encounter a creature from Sámi mythology. Sámmol, finally, is consciously looking for a supernatural being that he is firmly convinced exists—and he is proven right. If we, again, regard these men as materializations of the worldview in these stories, we can draw the conclusion that the characteristics of this ontology are made clear and visible only in the surroundings, not in the community itself. We can also make the assumption that regardless of what someone is searching for, they may

---

[31] Garuba, 283.
[32] Paltto, "Vegglusa," 8. Translation by me. Norwegian original: "store som engler."

instead find proofs of this alternative worldview which, once they have seen it, they can always return to if they want. These latter circumstances can be understood by way of Garuba's argument about the forming of a "collective subjectivity that structures being and consciousness in predominantly animist societies and cultures."[33] If one is Sámi, then the animist ontology is always accessible by definition.

For all three men, the encounter in the mountains gives them knowledge of the world that changes their lives forever, but the way in which this occurs depends on their reactions. For Egá, the encounter with the bedbug is terrifying, and so he flees. Also Rásttôs is frightened when he first encounters the bear, reaching for the knife in his pocket. But as he lingers, he learns that the creature before him is not what it appears to be at first sight, but rather something beautiful and desirable which ultimately, as he abandons his fear and follows it, gives him pleasure and a sense of community that will last for life. Regarding Sámmol, we do not learn anything about how he gained the knowledge he has, only that it is now, when he is old, rooted in him to such a degree that he appears to regard it as 'common sense.' In sum, the alternative ontology in these three stories might at first appear scary and overwhelming, but if one dares to linger, they provide a certain dimension of the world that lasts a lifetime.

The images of both the bear-girl and the reindeer-girl hybrid connects this dimension to a pre-Christian worldview which, according to Tamás, plays a determining role in Sámi discourses.[34] In particular, with the case of the bear it is difficult, however, to distinguish between the imaginary reality and the 'real animal' since according to traditional Sámi belief, as Helander-Renvall claims, there are at least three kinds of bears: an ordinary bear, a transformed human in a bear shape, and a bewitched bear. In addition, spirits may take a bear look, and bears may assume the role of helpers to humans.[35] In Paltto's

[33] Garuba, 269.
[34] Tamás, 23.
[35] Helander-Renvall, 51.

story, the bear-girl seems to be a variant of "a transformed human in bear shape," and this depiction is clearly part of the indigenous ontology made visible in the text.

Together, these three stories reveal in what ways the implications of this alternative ontology are so challenging to modern-day discourse that they cannot be spoken about, only passed on by experience. If and how that knowledge—which indeed forms a lesson to be learned—is passed on differs fundamentally between the three stories, however. In the first, Egá learns something for himself, though he never attempts to share his knowledge with anyone else. However, since the focalization shifts to the bedbug the moment Egá flees from it, the reader is given the chance to follow its inner monologue and learns that it possesses agency, an agenda and a sense of perspective, and also that it means no harm. Indeed, the bedbug's perspective takes up a good 1½ pages of a story that is only 6 in length. This can be seen as an example of what Garuba defines as a recurring aspect of de- and postcolonial literature, namely "representational strategies and narrative techniques, which are demonstrably superstructural effects of an animist conception of reality and the world," based in an oral tradition.[36] In the story about Egá, this narrative strategy presents an alternative ontology to the reader, even though the main character has fled the scene.

Contrary to the first, the question of how knowledge about the world should be passed on is openly discussed in the second and third stories. Rásttôs, who was sent into the mountains to look for the reindeer cows by an older Sámi man, imagines that the knowledge he possesses about the world—including the destabilization of the binary categories 'human' and 'animal'— will be passed on by the next generation of bear-girls, his daughters, who will encounter and enchant a young Sámi man in the same way as their mother had. In the third story, the narrative strategy of shifting the focalization to a non-human animal, present in the first story, is partly repeated; we occasionally get the perspective of Sámmol's dog. This technique relates

[36] Garuba, 270.

to the fact that Sámmol has such confidence in his non-human companion's abilities that he even speaks to him over the phone. Thus, Sámmol clearly shows that he knows that non-human animals have both agency, perspective, and abilities that go unacknowledged. But Sámmol is also knowingly and consciously striving to make visible the alternative ontology in which he lives to a younger Sámi man.

When taken together, the circumstances within which these three stories play themselves out point to the fact that while the ontology they depict can be experienced by any Sámi person, it is transferred to just a few, and can only be gained when human and non-human elements interfere with one another. While those who make visible this alternative ontology are all men, in the stories of Rásttôs and Sámmol the non-human element is depicted as an active and desirable female. This is interesting given that historically, there are indications of relatively strong matrilineal and matrilocal traditions and of Sámi women being regarded as equal to man.[37] Also, Sámi women have traditionally been responsible for passing down cultural knowledge to future generations.[38] These circumstances have further connotations for the part of the third story in which the reindeer-girl takes the male journalist on a journey in the northern lights: this natural phenomenon has been identified by Tamás as a universal image for the Sámi people.[39]

Moreover, it is apparent that in both the agency of non-human animals and in the stories' depictions of human-animal hybrids, the scientific categories of species are overthrown. Indeed, the very fact that such creatures exist in these stories, as well as the ways in which they engage with humans, point to the fact that the stories' alternative ontology entails a questioning of the modern notion that there is a clear-cut distinction between

[37] Rauna Kuokkanen, "Indigenous Women in Traditional Economies: The Case of Sámi Reindeer Herding," *Signs: Journal of Women in Culture and Society* 34, no. 3 (2009), 500.
[38] A task that recurs in the 'memory work' carried out by Sámi women writers in the 20th century. See Hirvonen, *Voices from Sápmi*, 81–90.
[39] Tamás, 16–17, 29–30.

human and animal. These subversions can be understood with an argument from Garuba, who claims that animist logic "subverts the authority of Western science by reinscribing the authority of magic within the interstices of the rational/secular/modern." In undermining Western binarism, Garuba claims animist culture "opens up a whole new world of poaching possibilities." Indeed, this process takes place in Paltto's stories by destabilizing "the hierarchy of science over magic and the secularist narrative of modernity [and] by reabsorbing historical time into the matrices of myth and magic."[40]

By extension, the undermining of the Western scientific discourse entails a subversion of normative (human) notions of time and place. In the first story, the reader will notice that when the narrative voice shifts to the bedbug, it appears as if no human time passes, since Egá does not move at all. Again, then, the reader of this story learns more about the animist ontology than about the human protagonist; the presence of a non-human animal has the potential to upset the human timeline. In the other two stories, the rupturing of linear time is connected to a destabilization of the notion of 'place.' In the second story, Rásttôs notices the passing of an unexpectedly long duration of time while he has been with the bear-girl in the mountains. He is also surprised to find the lost reindeer cows mysteriously back in their enclosure when he returns to the village. Here, the stories are in line with Garuba's definition of 'animism,' which "opens up a different time outside the usual linear, positivist time encoded with notions of progress and increasing secularization."[41] Indeed, the fact that the subversion of time is also connected to the undermining of normative conceptualizations of place has been discussed by Kumkum Sangari, who claims that de- and postcolonial literature conceptualize time as "poised in a liminal space, which, having broken out of the binary opposition between circular and linear, gives a third

[40] Garuba, 270–271.
[41] Garuba, 271.

space and a different time the chance to emerge."[42] As Osgood Dana notes, this subversion of time and place is a common trait in indigenous ontologies all over the world.[43] In Paltto's stories, it is a fundamental part of the ontology that human conceptualizations of time and place can, at least temporarily, be overruled by non-human ones.

I would like to end this analysis with a closer look at the subversion of time and space in the third story, paying particular attention to the depiction of the journalist, Ole. When he wakes up in the basement of his workplace, he has no idea of how he got there. He finds that, because he had been away for so long, people have been worried about him. I claim that the fact that he is a journalist gives this story's disruptions of normative time and space specific connotations. As a journalist, his job is to report and spread knowledge about the 'truth.' But since he is originally only capable of thinking and seeing within the modern ontology of the colonizers, he ends up reporting according to their history and timeline. What Sámmol does, however, is to let him experience another history, which was present before the takeover and which has a 'truth' that abides.

In line with the thought of Sangari, what is happening here can be understood as the "absence of a single linear time need not be read as the absence of a historical consciousness but rather as the operation of a different kind of historical consciousness."[44] Although Sangari discusses the works of Gabriel García Márquez and Salman Rushdie, the emphasis on alternative histories goes together well with indigenous literature's reliance on the oral tradition and anti-colonial writings of history. Against this background, it certainly seems relevant that it is in the *basement*, specifically, of Ole's workplace that he wakes up after his experience in the mountains. This is a place where the marginalized and old are typically stored away, but without disappearing fully. A point that goes together

---

[42] Kumkum Sangari, "The Politics of the Possible," *Cultural Critique* 7 (1987), 176.
[43] Osgood Dana, "Áillohaš," 13–17.
[44] Sangari, 172.

remarkably well with Garuba's concept of the 'animist unconscious.'[45]

Summary

The alternative ontology presented in these stories consists in the old, which is ridiculed, respected, questioned, feared; the articulation of a specific form of experience universal for all Sámi communities; a defiance against normative colonial discourses, which have become a long-established part of the Sámi community, now marginalized and/or resilient; a mode of being that is visible only outside the village, in its surroundings, that is displayed in an encounter which can be both consciously searched for and randomly found. It opens up for an insight that one does not risk losing once it has been received, an insight that can at first be frightening, yet (erotically) blissful if one lingers there. An alternative ontology that is made visible in both form and content, providing a lifelong community/worldview/knowledge/dimension. It makes itself felt by certain characters, only possible to transfer by experience. Though possible to gain by anyone, it is only acquired by a few. This alternative ontology is a gendered affair, it encompasses the possibility of non-human animals having agency, an agenda and their own perspective. This alternative ontology thus subverts the modern scientific discourse of species. The transmissibility of this ontology relies on an oral tradition, and is grounded on alternative notions of 'history' and 'truth', ones that make possible the overruling of human conceptualizations of time and place by non-human understandings. All of these points take the form of literary human- and non-human materializations of ideas.

In light of the above, I would like to finish this article with a few more general remarks.

Firstly, the modern setting for the stories, the marginalized position of the three characters in the societies in which they live, the all-Sámi world within which they move, and the over-

---

[45] Considering the Freudian concept of 'the unconscious' as a kind of undercurrent, haunting the stability of the 'normal.'

whelming assurance for which this alternative ontology provides, in terms of experiencing the overall process as a 'decolonization of the mind.' This concept has been defined in an indigenous studies context and describes the conscious return to images, beliefs, thoughts, concepts, cultural practices and worldviews that were used before colonization.[46] In Paltto's stories, this process is partly carried out through non-human agency, but humans who have had their minds decolonized can also pass these insights on to younger generations. This circumstance is made particularly visible in the third story, in which Sámmol goes through much trouble to show Ole what he knows to exist and be true. Sámmol, then, joins sides with the non-human forces in decolonizing the Sámi mind, and in relation to this circumstance, it is interesting to note that he is the character who is depicted as living closest and equally with a non-human animal in his daily life, his dog. Indeed, this aspect points to something that is relevant on a general level for all of these stories, namely that Paltto's depictions of the relationship between the human and the non-human world relies on the traditional Sámi view of a horizontal continuum, rather than the colonizer's hierarchical and static Christian view.

Secondly, it is clearly the case that the alternative ontology in Paltto's stories does not make up a firm system of concepts and beliefs. This is perfectly in line with an argument made by Garuba, who claims that the process of "re-enchanting the world" is not about believing in any specific gods or even about embracing the animist worldview. What it does instead is to provide broad "avenues for knowing our way around our world and society."[47] Moreover, although the traditional ontology is surely at odds with the stories' hegemonic one, no attempt is made to replace or overthrow it. This can be understood by way of another argument by Garuba, namely that to "question the

---

[46] See Ngũgĩ wa Thiong'o, *Decolonising the Mind. The Politics of Language in African Literature* (London: Currey, 1986) and Linda Tuhiwai Smith, *Decolonizing Methodologies. Research and Indigenous Peoples* (1999, repr., London: Zed Books, 2012), 24, 111–126.

[47] Garuba, 283.

homogenizing narrative of Western modernity and then replace it with another homogenizing narrative of an animist modernity would be to undermine the various other subaltern modernities struggling for voices." Indeed, he then makes the politically important claim that in de- and postcolonial contexts, "an animistic understanding of the world applied to the practice of everyday life has often provided avenues of agency for the dispossessed."[48]

However, in the field of indigenous studies, the 'avenue of agency' that is opened up not only concerns the human, but also the non-human world in general, and in particular the non-human animal. Billy-Ray Belcourt has made the case that the colonization of indigenous people and the natural world, including non-human animals, are closely connected processes and that decolonization thus does not happen for only one or the other.[49] It is hoped that my discussion of how humans and non-human animals are related horizontally, making a joint case against the colonization of the mind in Paltto's stories, has made this clearly visible.

Finally, I would like to briefly return to the beginning of this article, which spoke of a development in literary studies about whether fictional animals should be read metonymically or metaphorically. As we have seen, the specificities in de- and postcolonial literature encourage us to choose a third option: to read depictions of humans and non-humans alike as literary materializations of the stories' abstract ideas. According to Garuba, such narrative techniques should not be understood as extended metaphors, but, rather, as accounts of the significance of the concrete in the text's worldview.[50] Interestingly, these depictions not only float somewhere between metonymy and metaphor but also add their own unique element to an understanding of literary representations. As such, they are certainly

---

[48] Garuba, 284–285.
[49] Billy-Ray Belcourt, "Animal Bodies, Colonial Subjects: (Re)Locating Animality in Decolonial Thought." *Societies* 5, no. 1 (2015): 1–11.
[50] Garuba, 274.

of interest far beyond the scope of the fields of both indigenous studies and literary human-animal studies.

References

Ahvenjärvi, Kaisa. "Reindeer Revisited. Traditional Sámi features in Contemporary Sámi Poetry." In *Rethinking National Literatures and the Literary Canon in Scandinavia*, 104–129. Edited by Ann-Sofie Lönngren, Dag Heede, Anne Heith and Heidi Grönstrand. Newcastle upon Tyne: Cambridge Scholars Publishing, 2015.

Aubinet, Stéphane. *The Craft of Yoiking. Philosophical Variations on Sámi Chants.* University of Oslo: Department of Musicology, 2020.

Aubinet, Stéphane. "Chanter les territoires Sámi dans un monde plus-qu'humain." *Information géographique* 81, no. 1 (2017): 20–37.

Belcourt, Billy-Ray. "Animal Bodies, Colonial Subjects: (Re)Locating Animality in Decolonial Thought." *Societies* 5, no. 1 (2015): 1–11.

Bodrogi, Enikő Molnár. "Dissenting Narratives of Identity in Saami, Meänkieli and Kven Literatures." *Revista Română de Studii Baltice și Nordice / The Romanian Journal for Baltic and Nordic Studies* 11, no. 1 (2019): 19–55.

Brown, Laura. *Homeless Dogs and Melancholy Apes. Humans and Other Animals in the Modern Literary Imagination.* Ithaca, London: Cornell University Press, 2010.

Derrida, Jacques. *The Animal That Therefore I Am (Following).* Edited by Marie-Louise Mallet, translated by David Wills. 2006. Reprint, New York: Fordham University Press, 2008.

Domokos, Johanna. *A Writing Hand Reaches Further—'Čálli giehta olla guhkás'. Recommendations for the Improvement of the Sámi Literary Field.* Finland: Nordic Council, 2018.

Domokos, Johanna & Michal Kovář. "Terveisiä Lapista as an Example of Intercultural Dialogism." *Kirjallisuudentutkimuksen aikakauslehti AVAIN* 3 (2015): 51–67.

Garuba, Harry. "Explorations in Animist Materialism: Notes on Reading/ Writing African Literature, Culture, and Society." *Public Culture* 15, no. 2 (2003): 261–285.

Haraway, Donna J. *When Species Meet.* Minneapolis, London: University of Minnesota Press, 2008.

Haraway, Donna J. *Primate Visions. Gender, Race, and Nature in the World of Modern Science.* New York, London: Routledge, 1989.

Heith, Anne. "Putting an End to the Shame Associated with Minority Culture and its Concomitant Negative Self-Images—On Gender and Ethnicity in Sami and Tornedalian Literature." In *The History of*

Nordic Women's Literature Online, 1–10. Edited by Anne-Marie Mai and Anita Frank Goth. Odense: Syddansk Universitet, 2016.

Helander-Renvall, Elina. "Animism, Personhood and the Nature of Reality: Sami Perspectives." *Polar Record* 46, no. 236 (2010): 44–56.

Hirvonen, Vuokko. *Voices from Sápmi: Sámi Women's Path to Authorship.* Translated by Kaija Anttonen. 1988. Reprint, Kautokeino: DAT, 2008.

Indigenous Creatures, Native Knowledges, and the Arts: Animal Studies in Modern Worlds. Edited by Susan McHugh & Wendy Woodward. London: Palgrave MacMillan 2017.

Justice, Daniel Heath (Cherokee). *Why Indigenous Literature Matter.* Waterloo & Ontario: Wilfrid Laurier University Press, 2018.

Kuokkanen, Rauna. "Indigenous Women in Traditional Economies: The Case of Sámi Reindeer Herding." *Signs: Journal of Women in Culture and Society* 34, no. 3 (2009): 499–504.

Kuokkanen, Rauna. "Border Crossings, Pathfinders and New Visions: the Role of Sámi Literature in Contemporary Society." *Nordlit* 15 (2004): 91–103.

Kuokkanen, Rauna & Kirsti Paltto. "Publishing Sámi Literature—from Christian Translations to Sámi Publishing Houses." *Studies in American Indian Literatures* 22, no. 2 (2010): 42–58.

Lukkari, Rauni Magga. "Where did the Laughter go?" In *No Beginning, No End: The Sami Speak Up,* 103–110. Edited by Elina Helander-Renvall & Kaarina Kailo. Edmonton: Canadian Circumpolar Institute, 1998.

Lönngren, Ann-Sofie. "Metaphor, Metonymy, More-Than-Anthropocentric. The Animal That Therefore I Read (and Follow)." In *The Palgrave Handbook of Animals and Literature,* 37–50. Edited by Susan McHugh, Robert McKay & John Miller. Basingstoke: Palgrave Macmillan, 2021.

McHugh, Susan. *Love in a Time of Slaughters. Human-Animal Stories against Genocide and Extinction.* Pennsylvania: The Pennsylvania University Press, 2019.

Noske, Barbara. *Humans and Other Animals. Beyond the Boundaries of Anthropology.* Winchester: Pluto Press, 1989.

Osgood Dana, Kathleen. "Áillohaš and His Image Drum. The Native Poet as Shaman." *Nordlit* 15 (2004): 7–33.

Osgood Dana, Kathleen. "Sami Literature in the Twentieth Century." *World Literature Today* 71 (Winter 1997): 22–28.

Paltto, Kirste. *Stjålet.* Translated by Ellen Anna Gaup, Mikkel A. Gaup & Laila Stein. 2001. Reprint, Karasjok: Davvi Girji, 2003.

Rosiek, Jerry Lee, Jimmy Snyder and Scott L. Pratt. "The New Materialisms and Indigenous Theories of Non-Human Agency: Making the

Case for Respectful Anti-Colonial Engagement." *Qualitative Inquiry* 26, no. 3–4 (2020): 331–346.

Sangari, Kumkum. "The Politics of the Possible." *Cultural Critique* 7 (1987): 157–186.

Smith, Linda Tuhiwai. *Decolonizing Methodologies. Research and Indigenous Peoples.* 1999. Reprint, London: Zed Books, 2012.

Solbakk, John Trygve. *The Sámi People—A Handbook.* Karasjok: Davvi Girji, 2006.

Tallbear, Kim. "Making Love and Relations Beyond Settler Sex and Family." In *Making Kin Not Population,* 145–164. Edited by Adele E. Clarke & Donna Haraway. Chicago: Prickly Paradigm Press, 2018.

Tamás, Ildikó. "The Colors of the Polar Lights (Symbols in the Construction of Sami Identity)." In *The Concept of Freedom in the Literatures of Eastern Europe,* 1–52. Edited by Toimõndanuq Szilárd, Tibor Tóth, Roza Kirillova & Jüvä Sullõv. Võro: Publications of Võro Institute, 2017.

Thiong'o, Ngũgĩ wa. *Decolonising the Mind. The Politics of Language in African Literature.* London: Currey, 1986.

Between the Tigers of Anger and the Horses of Instruction in Olga Tokarczuk's *Drive Your Plow Over the Bones of the Dead*

Małgorzata Poks

Honored with the Nobel Prize for her "narrative imagination that with encyclopedic passion represents the crossing of boundaries as a form of life,"[1] Olga Tokarczuk exposes—at no small personal risk[2]—the fiction of stable identities and fixed ideological positions. Consistently dismantling binaries alleged to be natural, her works are a hymn to impurity, mongrelization, hybridity. Her early fascination with aberrations and contestation of socially constructed norms led her to study psychology. It was then that she understood the power of the unconscious, which prevents us from seeing the world as it really is. Her studies also taught her to distrust the norm even further, to discredit statistics and neat methodologies in dealing with the teeming profusion of undisciplined difference. The assumption "that we are constant, and that our reactions can be predicted" seemed "terribly dangerous" to her.[3] Then there was an internship in a geropsychiatric ward, extensive travels, and daily contacts with people from all walks of life, including mentally disturbed and neurodivergent patients, as well as involvement in animal anti-cruelty campaigns. A person with this kind of formation is well-equipped to see similarities where others see differences; to realize that the only certainty is change and transformation.

---

[1] "Press release," *NobelPrize.org* (accessed 07-09-2020)

[2] Most notably, in 2015, after the publication of *The Books of Jacob* and Tokarczuk's criticism of the invented history of Poland as a tolerant and open country, the writer became the object of a hate campaign.

[3] Olga Tokarczuk, *Flights*, trans. Jennifer Croft (New York: Riverhead Books, 2018), 15.

In the essay "The Masks of Animals" Tokarczuk argues for the centrality of empathy[4] in anti-cruelty activism. The ability to enter the pain and share the emotions of vulnerable creatures subjected to human dominance—caged, killed for sport, experimented on, and harvested for meat—is a harrowing experience, one that necessitates action, however doomed it may be. The Nobel Prize laureate has seen the "face" behind the mask of her essay's title and has known it to be the face of our equal.[5]

Since the beginning of her publishing career, Tokarczuk has been speaking from a position that can be called "ontological animism." Foundational to all pre-modern cultures, ontological animism inheres in the belief that consciousness, or sentience, is not the sole property of humans but belongs to all animate life and, possibly, inanimate objects as well. In the words of Graham Harvey, professor of Religious Studies at the Open University in London, new animism is "the understanding that the world is a community of persons, most of whom are not human, but all of whom are related, and all of whom deserve respect."[6] This understanding would be close to what Tokarczuk herself calls "tenderness." In her Nobel Lecture she claims that tenderness "is a way of looking that shows the world as being alive, living, interconnected, cooperating with, and codependent on itself."[7] Although such tenderness is rare in the world of modernist binaries, the writer often speaks from the margins of modernity, from "magical" or premodern epistemologies, "look[ing] at things ex-centrically, away from the center."[8] In my analysis of

---

[4] While Tokarczuk uses empathy in its positive sense, Petra Mayr observes that those who draw satisfaction from killing and torturing others must also be able to exercise empathy—sometimes called negative empathy. This is, for instance, the case with recreational hunters. Quoted in Andrzej Elżanowski, "Motywacja i moralność łowiecka," *Zoophilologica. Polish Journal of Animal Studies*, no. 4 (2018), 128.

[5] Olga Tokarczuk, *Moment niedźwiedzia* [The Bear's Moment] (Warszawa: Wydawnictwo Krytyki Politycznej, 2012), 53.

[6] Graham Harvey, "Animism and Ecology: Participating in the World Community," *The Ecological Citizen* 3, no. 1 (2019), 80.

[7] Olga Tokarczuk, "Nobel Lecture by Olga Tokarczuk: Nobel Laureate in Literature 2018," *NobelPrize.org* (accessed 07–09–2020), 24.

[8] Tokarczuk, "Nobel Lecture," 20.

the image of non-human animals in Olga Tokarczuk's novel *Drive Your Plow Over the Bones of the Dead* I will foreground the author's involved, activist agenda, highlight a sense of responsibility for the animal(ized) Other, and trace the contours of an alternative world based on more just, less oppressive human-animal relations.

The Fall

Drive Your Plow Over the Bones of the Dead (2009) is Tokarczuk's most extensive treatment of the issue of animal suffering. Popularized by its screen adaptation under the title *Spoor*,[9] it is also her most politically engaged novel. It features Janina Duszejko, an elderly woman who lives alone in a small village in the South-West of Poland, close to the Czech border. She talks to animals, destroys snares set up by poachers, attempts to obstruct hunts, and monitors animal abuse. When the nearby town is rocked by a series of mysterious deaths, rumor has it that the victims—hunters and members of the local elite—have been murdered by insurgent animals in an act of vengeance. Duszejko is the first to spread this rumor.

Dubbed an ecological thriller, structurally the novel is built around quotations from William Blake; indeed, it is Blake's mysticism that sets its metaphysical roots deepest in the text. The title comes from *Proverbs of Hell*, a collection of aphorisms included in *The Marriage of Heaven and Hell*, Blake's most influential book, which attempts to depolarize modern opposites. In the Romantic visionary's personal mythology hell embodies energy, heaven—the authoritarian regulations of reason. The marriage of the title points to Blake's belief in the contradictory nature of reality: "Without contraries is no progression,"[10] proclaims the poet. But in Blake's meditation, Reason has banished the unprincipled energy and has usurped

---

[9] *Spoor*, directed by Agnieszka Holland & Kasia Adamik (Warszawa: Studio Filmowe, 2017).
[10] William Blake, "The Marriage of Heaven and Hell," in *The Poetical Works of William Blake* (1908; repr., London, New York: Oxford University Press, 2011).

the whole of reality, making us all prisoners in a decadent, de-energized universe ruled by abstract rationalizations. In the fallen world, scientific knowing is the only legitimate form of knowledge; emotions are discredited, and empathy is seen an obstacle on the way to cognition. The Blakean Fall is the metaphysical condition of the novel's world and Duszejko is its conscience.

The men supposedly murdered by vengeful animals provide the full measure of fallen humanity. The first victim, an uncouth, malicious poacher called Big Foot, chokes to death on a bone of a recently snared deer. Helping to dress him for the funeral, Duszejko discovers a photograph, which reveals the mystery of her two missing dogs. They were shot by a hunting party, with Big Foot being one of the beaters. As it turns out, four of the most prominent hunters from the photo will die within weeks of one another. A corrupt chief of police known as Commandant is apparently murdered by deer; a ruthless land speculator and owner of a fur farm, whom Duszejko names Innerd, is found decomposing in snares, nibbled by foxes; the President, so called because he presided over every company and society in the area, is discovered suffocated by swarms of a rare kind of beetle; and the local Catholic priest, Father Rustle, chaplain of the hunting society and an avid defender of man's mandate to "subdue the earth," dies in a fire apparently started by magpies.

The photograph found by Duszejko is to her proof that a crime had been committed by the town's "decent citizens." It shows uniform-clad men proudly posing for a picture at the end of the annual hunt on the feast day for St. Hubertus.[11] They stand around displaying their game—animal carcasses laid side by side in neat rows, the arrangement of each row regulated by strict rules of hunting etiquette. The men boast of a duty well-accomplished, but the dead boars, deer, hares, and numerous pheasants, teals and mallards look to Duszejko like "dots, as if those

---

[11] Hubertus, the German version of St. Hubert of Liège's name, has become specifically associated with the hunting ritual. In this text both versions of the name will be used.

Animal bodies were a sentence written to me, and the Birds formed a long ellipsis to say 'this will go on and on.'"[12] The woman deciphers the message. She hears the cry of the dead, their plea to put an end to the carnage, to stop the ongoing animal Holocaust.

Throughout the novel hunting towers are strongly associated with the watchtowers of concentration camps, in what seems like an echo of Charles Patterson's book *Eternal Treblinka: Our Treatment of Animals and the Holocaust*.[13] Walking her daily rounds on the plateau, Duszejko knows the exact position of the eight wooden constructions arrogantly but somehow fittingly called pulpits—for it is a gospel of death that is preached from them.[14] The hay stacks next to the pulpits, which are to attract animals for the hunters to have a perfect mark, Duszejko calls "cunning, treacherous, sophisticated evil."[15] Given this frame of reference and following the logic of intersectional oppressions brought to Critical Animal Studies by feminist critics, it would not be off the mark to detect in the crime-documenting photograph an echo of another genocidal practice, recorded in revolting souvenirs called lynching postcards. Popular in 19th century USA, they depicted a happy crowd—partying, smoking cigarettes, and smiling with the sense of a mission well accomplished—pointing their fingers at mutilated black bodies, the atrocity of the crime lost on the decent fathers and sons, the so-called pillars of morality.

As is well known, prior to president Lincoln's Emancipation Proclamation, blacks in the American South had the status of chattel. Animals still do in most parts of the world. Historically, animalized humans (e.g. people of color) shared the socially constructed space assigned to non-human animals; similarly exploited and denied rights, their inclusion in the ranks of

---

[12] Olga Tokarczuk, *Drive Your Plow Over the Bones of the Dead*, trans. Antonia Lloyd-Jones (New York: Riverhead Books, 2019), 253.

[13] Charles Patterson, *Eternal Treblinka: Our Treatment of Animals and the Holocaust* (New York: Lantern Books, 2002).

[14] Tokarczuk, *Drive Your Plow*, 54.

[15] Tokarczuk, *Drive Your Plow*, 104.

humanity has been a relatively recent development. Since they were property, killing a human slave was not punishable by law, the suffering inflicted on her or him of no account. The only reprisal was the financial loss to the slave's owner. This is precisely the non-human animals' situation today, speciesism being one more link in the chain of interlocked oppressions.

Abandoning nuance to make her point clear, Tokarczuk, well-known for her embrace of the intersectional perspective in all her works, reveals the violence behind the hunters' everyday lives, their misogyny, arrogance, contempt for the weak and for those deviating from the norm. In order to hold on to power they endlessly replicate binaries that disadvantage all Others (non-male, disabled, poor, non-human, etc.) and guarantee the maintenance of the status quo—at the apex of this order is the normative, carnophallogocentric[16] subject. Meat-eating, violence, and aggressive masculinity belong together, as demonstrated by the novel's repugnant characters. In the background of the photograph discovered by Duszejko a feast is being prepared: bottles of vodka are soaking in buckets of ice-cold water, "pots of hunter's stew, sausages and kebabs skewered on sticks"[17] are waiting to be roasted in the bonfire. This is the normative male's idea of fun, the celebration of raw masculinity: while eating flesh, they will likely go over the bloody details of the day's hunt, perhaps throwing in a few sexist jokes before returning home drunk. To sum up, in Tokarczuk's handling, hunting becomes the essence of aggressive masculinity, a gateway to privilege, and a confirmation of one's "normative" status. This is the human "norm" Tokarczuk constantly dismantles—embodied in a caste of powermongers who declare themselves

---

[16] Jacques Derrida introduced the idea of carnophallogocentrism in his interview with Jean Luc Nancy, entitled "Eating Well." According to the philosopher, Western subjectivity is quintessentially virile and masculine (phallo), speaking and self-present (logo), and animal-flesh eating. See Carol Adams & Matthew Calarco, "Derrida and the Sexual Politics of Meat," in *Meat Culture* (Leiden and Boston: Brill, 2017), 31–52.

[17] Tokarczuk, *Drive Your Plow*, 254.

lords of creation and misread the Bible to validate their mandate to "subdue."

In the world's fallen state, the political system and organized religion work in tandem, protecting the oppressor and condemning the victim. In the novel, Father Rustle represents the mentality of the institutional Catholic Church in Poland. He is a composite of real-life clergymen who act as spiritual guardians to hunting associations, and also hunt themselves. Duszejko comes into contact with him at the annual pastoral visit. There the priest instructs her about the sin of mourning animals; mourning is reserved for the human dead only. Rather than console or perform the ministry of listening expected of a man of God, Father Rustle pontificates about the animal difference and advises the grieving woman to pray. His crowning argument—that dogs are only animals—reverses history. Remembering Theodor Adorno's famous warning: "Auschwitz begins whenever someone looks at a slaughterhouse and thinks: they're only animals."[18] Father Rustle's ontological credo launches humanity back on a road to another Final Solution. But it is his sermon on St. Hubert's feast that outrages Duszejko. Based on authentic materials accessed on the Internet,[19] the sermon is a combination of militant speciesism and blatant glorification of hunters as true ecologists. Duszejko walks up to the pulpit and calls Father Rustle a murderer, charging him with inciting people to crime.

On crime and sin

From the few extant studies and the hunters' own declarations, we know that most recreational hunters kill for pleasure, though they rarely admit it.[20] A prominent German hunter, Florian Asche, confesses that the often invoked need to shoot game to preserve ecological balance is merely a smokescreen for what

---

[18] Quoted in Patterson, *Eternal Treblinka*, 53.
[19] Tokarczuk, "Author's Note," in *Drive Your Plow*, 257.
[20] Elżanowski, 124.

really drives hunters but cannot be admitted in public: hunters kill, he claims, because they derive pleasure from it.[21] Apart from boosting their adrenaline, shooting game induces a state bordering on ecstasy and arouses sensual desire. With its combination of cruelty and excitement, the violence of the hunt is not unlike the violence of rape, admits Paul Parin.[22] The hunter and the rapist draw satisfaction from the suffering of the powerless victim and delight in their own superiority. But while rape is a crime, the recreational killing of an animal is regarded as "sport," with rules and etiquette of its own. This is the measure of our modern schizophrenia: we justify the crimes we enjoy committing by an appeal to tradition. Yet, traditions evolve, they change along with human consciousness. Today nobody in their right mind would defend slavery by calling it tradition, although it was a "traditional" way of life for many countries. And so was sexual violence against women—in some places it still is. Understood as ritualized social practices which "seek to inculcate certain values and norms of behavior by repetition," tradition is an ideological invention, argues Eric Hobsbawm.[23] The values and norms that the hunting tradition seeks to instill are decidedly atavistic, a throwback to our species' evolutionary violence. Little wonder that it cannot be comfortably disentangled from other kinds of violence; indeed, more often than not, it directly leads to them. Paleontologist, zoologist, and animal rights activist, Andrzej Elżanowski, does not hesitate to call such a tradition "evil," an activity which brutalizes society and socializes children into structures of oppression.[24]

The counterintuitive partnership of the Polish hunting associations and the Catholic Church in Poland has been the subject of many investigative articles in this country. Agnieszka

---

[21] Florian Asche: *Jagen, Sex und Tiere essen: Die Lust am Archaischen* (Neumann-Neudamm Melsungen, 2014), 34–35.

[22] Paul Parin, *Die Leidenschaft des Jägers* (Hamburg: Europäische Va, 2003), 8–9.

[23] Eric Hobsbawm, "Introduction: Inventing Traditions," in *The Invention of Tradition* (Cambridge: Cambridge University Press, 2003), 1–14.

[24] Elżanowski, 122–123.

Sowa and Arkadiusz Panasiuk of the *Polityka* weekly, for instance, worry that the Church gives a moral sanction to hunting by celebrating St. Hubertus masses, appointing chaplains to hunting associations, blessing the animals killed at the annual St. Hubertus hunt, or broadcasting TV programs and publishing books about hunting.[25] Other critics of the alliance between state and church point to the sect-like character of the bloody hunting ritual blessed by priests. Mainstream propaganda, however, reverses this criticism, by referring to ecological organizations as sects while turning a blind eye to the hunting clergymen's gross transgressions of the law—both state and ecclesiastical—let alone hunting etiquette. In a well-publicized case, a hunting chaplain was discovered transporting an illegally killed specimen of an endangered species. The same man has long been suspected of poaching.[26] Duszejko's charges of murder and incitement have a solid base in reality.

The curious disregard for animal suffering in the ranks of Polish clergy, who should be in the forefront of struggles against cruelty and violence, can be partly explained by the influence of the *Catechism of the Catholic Church*, believes Elżanowski, who accuses the Church of misothery, or hatred of animals.[27] Rooted in the Thomist doctrine and enshrined in the *Catechism*, misothery is passed down to children in the course of their state-sponsored religious education. Thus, it not only defines the intel-

---

[25] Agnieszka Sowa & Arkadiusz Panasiuk, "Ksiądz myśliwych," *Polityka*, no. 30, July 21, 2020.

[26] "Ksiądz morderca zwierząt," [Priest—Murderer of Animals], Leśny Patrol—Ludzie Przeciw Myśliwym, *Facebook* 29-01-2018 (accessed 29-08-2020).

[27] See especially paragraphs 2417–2418: "God entrusted animals to the stewardship of those whom he created in his own image. Hence it is legitimate to use animals for food and clothing. They may be domesticated to help man in his work and leisure. Medical and scientific experimentation on animals is a morally acceptable practice if it remains within reasonable limits and contributes to caring for or saving human lives," and "it is contrary to human dignity to cause animals to suffer or die needlessly. It is likewise unworthy to spend money on them that should as a priority go to the relief of human misery. One can love animals; one should not direct to them the affection due only to persons." *Catechism of the Catholic Church* (United States Catholic Conference of Bishops, 1997).

lectual and spiritual horizon of Polish clergy, but becomes naturalized as an effective consciousness of the entire nation. Children, who lack the ability to make moral distinctions for themselves, accept the teachings of their spiritual fathers and carry those teachings into adulthood. In church and in religious education classes, they internalize speciesism as part of "tradition."

The appropriation of Hubert of Liège[28] as the patron saint of hunters is another scandal, a manipulation of tradition which underpins the most celebrated hunting event of the year: St. Hubert's feast day. Already the story of Hubert's conversion is highly questionable,[29] but it is the ideological subversion of its original meaning that is most surprising. According to legend, one Good Friday, when young Hubert skipped prayer and was chasing a stag, he had a vision of a crucifix between the animal's antlers. As a consequence of this encounter, he renounced hunting and became a priest. Deborah Jones, the author of *The School of Compassion*, claims that in the Middle Ages clergy "were forbidden to hunt and, if they did, they would have to take penance."[30] The story of the transformation of the early Church's condemnation of the hunt into its co-partnership in "wildlife management," under the unlikely auspices of the medieval anti-hunt convert, remains instructive for staunch defendants of "tradition," and downright outrageous for everyone else. The Hubert of the legend would more likely expect God to appear to the faithful as a lamb than a self-assured huntsman. In Tokarczuk's novel it is Duszejko that receives a similar insight at the time of the Agnus Dei prayer, thinking God should now appear in his true, animal shape—"as a Sheep, Cow or Stag, and thunder in a mighty tone [...] to put an end to this terrible hypocrisy."[31] Yet, if he did, he would be outraged to discover the

---

[28] St. Hubert was born about 656 and died in 727 or 728. He was the first bishop of Liège, and Apostle of the Ardennes.

[29] The miraculous conversion was in all probability appropriated from St Eustace and attributed to Hubert in the 15th century.

[30] Deborah Jones, *The School of Compassion a Roman Catholic Theology of Animals* (Loeminster: Gracewing Publishers, 2001).

[31] Tokarczuk, *Drive Your Plow*, 239.

undigested contents of his flock's stomachs: "the ham ... the Chickens, Rabbits and Calves."[32] Tokarczuk's writings celebrate heterotopias, or places of radical difference. In a thought experiment she calls a parlor game ("How to Invent Heterotopia") she invites her readers to overcome mental passivity by imagining the world otherwise. The rules of the game—which bears uncanny similarity to deconstruction—are both simple and profound: the player chooses a set of truths which seem absolute and examines them for cracks and inconsistencies. This exercise helps to dismantle some of the protective mechanisms of the psyche; it demonstrates how much the world we live in is determined by the social contract and sealed by our mental inertia. Inventing a Heterotopia, or imagining alternative realities, has moral significance.[33] It reveals fabulous possibilities, which could come true if we trusted imagination more and pseudo-universal truths less.

One such pseudo-truth is the idea of human exceptionalism. Self-elevated above other forms of life, our species gives itself the moral mandate to exploit the world, regardless of the destruction to lives and habitats this entails. Again, mental inertia prevents us from understanding the disastrous consequences of our self-appointed human privilege. Tokarczuk's Heterotopians treat others, however problematic they might be, as partners and neighbors. In a world overflowing with suffering, they refuse to exploit other lives for their own interest.

How can Christians adore the Lamb and raise sheep for slaughter?—Tokarczuk seems to be asking. How can priests preach the God of love and compassion while actively seeking to kill God's creatures? Is this the effect of naturalized speciesism, a failure of imagination, the lack of moral compass, or all of the above? Whatever the reason, ultimately it is imaginative inertia that "allows evil to take root."[34] Tokarczuk challenges her readers

---

[32] Tokarczuk, *Drive Your Plow*, 238.
[33] Tokarczuk, *Moment niedźwiedzia*, 43. For the purpose of this article, fragments quoted from Polish language sources unavailable in English have been translated by the author.
[34] Tokarczuk, *Moment niedźwiedzia*, 43.

to shake it off, to look around and take notice of the cracks and faultlines in the world's seemingly natural arrangement. *Drive Your Plow Over the Bones of the Dead* reveals a panorama of human duplicity, intentional or subconscious. It is a plea to wake up from our collective slumber and live decently.

Above all, it asks uncomfortable questions about the meaning of sin and the nature of crime. Crime is a culture-bound concept. As such, it evolves over time to reflect a society's changing moral consciousness. So does sin. Although the most fundamental moral obligation is to respect and protect life, crime (and sin as its religious counterpart) regulates relations within an organized community, while the lives of those excluded from its boundaries are exempt from moral or legal consideration. Historically, the killing and torture of slaves or people considered racially inferior (like Jews in Nazi Germany), was not regarded as a crime. Even today, far from being criminalized, killing an "enemy" is seen as patriotic duty and blessed by clergy, whose vocation is to follow the meek, non-violent Christ—he one who has left his followers the commandment to *love* thy enemy. If we find it difficult to extend love and compassion to those who are most like us—as members of national, ethnic, religious, etc. communities—how much less likely are we to recognize the sanctity of non-human life. As long as the Catholic Church follows the scientifically compromised neo-Thomist line of argument, it will continue to bless the killing of intelligent, sentient creatures, which is a true sin. A character in Tokarczuk's most recent publication, *Tales of the Bizarre*, explains: "In the evolutionary sense, we are still chimpanzees, hedgehogs and larches."[35] It is a crime and a sin to refuse to recognize this.

Janina Duszejko defends the inherent worth of every single creature. She and not Father Rustle is the true servant of the Mystical Lamb. She administers to the most vulnerable, buries

---

[35] Olga Tokarczuk, *Opowieści bizarne* (Kraków: Wydawnictwo Literackie, 2019), 132.

their remains in a self-arranged cemetery, defends their interests, liberates them from slavery, and takes punishment in her hands when established law remains passive in the face of crime. Likewise, it is her "sermon"[36] at the police station that expresses a truly prophetic wrath, not unlike that of Old Testament prophets. Duszejko is faithful to the most sacred, most fundamental law: Thou shalt not kill. And knows that it applies to all life, that divinity knows no borders. Arranging a cemetery for animals and mourning her dogs, she tacitly assumes that all of us—humans as well as non-humans—share the same ultimate destiny, whatever that may be. If there is a heaven, both humans and non-humans will go there, she seems to be saying.

Tigers of wrath

"The tigers of wrath are wiser than the horses of instruction," reads the motto to the climactic 16th chapter of Tokarczuk's novel *Drive Your Plow Over the Bones of the Dead*. When rational arguments fall on deaf ears, written denunciations of crimes on animals are left unanswered, and the criminals are given the green light to continue with their violence, Duszejko's choices are limited. In a nutshell, the situation is like this: the small-town elite dominated by hunters treats animals as though they are objects created for human benefit; they regard killing as entertainment and sacred tradition, never thinking about the cruelty behind it; animals are not real for them. Little wonder they think Duszejko pathetic. Grieving for a young boar mindlessly killed outside of a hunting season or a doe poached by Big Foot, she feels, as she says, "an endless sense of mourning for every Animal dead. One period of grief is followed by another, so I am in constant mourning. This is my natural state."[37] In a murderous world mourning never ends.

Her respect for animals entails responsibility for the living as well as the dead. As a witness to a crime, she believes that—by

---

[36] In the novel's Polish version, the title of chapter VII, "A Speech to a Poodle," reads, literally, "A Sermon to a Poodle."
[37] Tokarczuk, *Drive Your Plow*, 101.

virtue of a justice higher than established law—she has been called to become the agent of retribution. The nature of the crime she witnesses—cruel, ritual, repetitive—seems to demand extreme action. By extending agency to animals, the narrative plays with the possibility that Duszejko has been chosen to be the animals' avenger. The woman does not seem to be in full control of what happens, as if acting on the dictates of a higher power, or possibly, given Tokarczuk's insistence on the fluid nature of reality, even becoming an animal in the act of meting out justice. The woman first starts to feel uneasy when, upon arriving with Oddball at the cottage of Big Foot, who has just choked on a bone, she sees deer standing calmly close to their lethal enemy's place, unafraid, looking at her insistently. The woman has the uncanny impression that "we caught them in the middle of performing a ritual whose meaning we couldn't fathom."[38] Later, she realizes that the moment of decision had come, similar to St. Hubert's conversion. She confesses to Oddball:

> At dawn, by the time we went home after the dreadful night of dressing Big Foot, I knew what I had to do. Those Deer we saw outside the house had told me. They chose me from among others—maybe because I don't eat meat and they can sense it—to continue to act in their Name. They appeared before me, like the Stag to Saint Hubert, to have me become the punitive hand of justice, in secret. Not just for the Deer, but for other Animals too. For they have no voice in parliament.[39]

In meting out justice to the murderers, Duszejko dismantles the myth of human supremacy over the world of nature. The bodies of animal executioners return to the endless circulation of matter, repositioned in the food chain to which they have always belonged, becoming "part of the feast in the chain of recipro-

---

[38] Tokarczuk, *Drive Your Plow*, 4.
[39] Tokarczuk, *Drive Your Plow*, 255–256.

city."[40] The mouldy remains of Innerd or the corpse of President colonized by *cucujus haematodes* dispel the illusion of human-animal difference. We are all eaten as well as eaters.

As far as Duszejko is concerned, there is no essential difference between human and non-human animals: both have agency, make conscious decisions, and experience grief. If deer come up to the carcass of a boar and mourn his death,[41] why should they not be able to take revenge? A fox she calls Consul leads her to the scene of a crime, where she finds the body of a young boar.[42] Two majestic white foxes who "look like diplomatic service of the Animal Kingdom" show up "to reconnoiter,"[43] while a stag attacking a hunter on an internet film seems to confirm Duszejko's hopes that animals have finally launched an offensive against their tormentors, that they are no longer passive in the war humans have waged against them.

The war against animals is the subject of an interesting study by Australian scholar and activist Dinesh Wadiwel.[44] Drawing on Michel Foucault and Giorgio Agamben, he argues that animals have become the spoils of war—objects and disposable property dependent on the arbitrary whims of their masters. Inhabiting a permanent war zone, they live in a state of ethical suspension and are subject to genocidal practices. Heteronormative man—embodied in Tokarczuk's novel in the President, Innerd, Commandant, or Father Rustle—administers an animal death camp. The non-human other, exiled from the sphere of ethical consideration, can be hunted in and out of season, exploited, and murdered with impunity, because the conquered have no rights.

"Killing has become exempt from punishment," complains Duszejko. "And as it goes unpunished," she continues, "nobody

[40] Val Plumwood, *The Eye of the Crocodile* (Canberra: Australian National University, 2012), 19.
[41] Tokarczuk, *Drive Your Plow*, 100.
[42] Tokarczuk, *Drive Your Plow*, 99.
[43] Tokarczuk, *Drive Your Plow*, 137.
[44] Dinesh Wadiwel, *The War Against Animals* (Leiden: Brill, 2015).

notices it anymore. And as nobody notices it, it doesn't exist."[45] With her mystical experience not unlike St. Hubert's and an empathy which could put most Christian saints to shame, she starts to preach a sermon, which is an alternative to Father Rustle's. Addressed not to the town's comfortably saved, but to the unconverted, the unwilling, and the hopeless—and appropriately disregarded by them—she preaches a jeremiad, demonstrating the depth of human depravity, making one more futile attempt to bring the evildoers to their senses. As the woman entwines the human and the animal Holocaust into a single vision, she preaches the apocalypse: "You'll say it's just one Boar [...]. But what about the deluge of butchered meat that falls on our cities day by day like never-ending apocalyptic rain? The rain heralds slaughter, disease, collective madness, the obfuscation and contamination of the Mind."[46] Referring to "someone's body [...] made into shoes, into meatballs, sausages, a bedside rug, someone's bones [...] boiled to make broth," as well as the "shoes, sofas, a shoulder bag made of someone's belly, cutting it into bits and frying it in oil,"[47] she is depicting a bleak panorama of the Blakean Land of Ulro. Her question: "What sort of world is it, where killing and pain is the norm,"[48] a world which is "a prison full of suffering so constructed that in order to survive one must inflict pain on others,"[49] sounds like a blasphemy and an accusation. Although Duszejko's speech has many similarities with the lectures of Elizabeth Costello,[50] a literary character invented by John M. Coetzee,[51] the concluding questions sound

---

[45] Tokarczuk, *Drive Your Plow*, 105.

[46] Tokarczuk, *Drive Your Plow*, 106.

[47] Tokarczuk, *Drive Your Plow*, 106.

[48] Tokarczuk, *Drive Your Plow*, 107.

[49] Tokarczuk, *Drive Your Plow*, 106.

[50] In her essay "Maski zwierząt" [Masks of Animals] Tokarczuk devotes much space to Elizabeth Costello. It is clear the Polish novelist admires Costello's uncompromising veganism and the depth of her academic arguments against human cruelty to animals. Unlike Duszejko, however, Costello embraces non-violence and uses reason in her antisystemic endeavors. Tokarczuk, *Moment niedźwiedzia*, 31–54.

[51] John M. Coetzee, *Elizabeth Costello* (Secker & Warburg, 2003).

more like Milton's Satan[52]—a rebel against the tyranny of heaven, much admired by William Blake. Seized by prophetic anger, Duszejko, not unlike Milton's fallen angel, rejects the unjust arrangement of the world and fights her own war against the powers that be. Her intelligence and empathy lead her to undermine the time-honored, "traditional" truths, which secure the privileges of the world's powerful at the cost of the excluded.

Conclusion

The situation of non-human animals in Poland is far from acceptable. The meat and dairy industries are thriving, fur farms operate legally, slaughterhouses are becoming increasingly more efficient, the number of abandoned pets increases every holiday season, and efforts of anti-cruelty advocates tend to be dismissed as ecoterrorism and attacks on tradition. Against this background, Olga Tokarczuk's 2009 novel *Drive Your Plow Over the Bones of the Dead* cannot *not* be read as political, a manifesto of an involved, interventionist stance. Extending the notion of crime, as well as the religious concept of sin, to misothery and the resulting cruelty towards "inferior" beings, Tokarczuk demonstrates the evil of hunting for pleasure, examines the roots of violence against animals in the context of interlocked oppressions, and dwells on the notion of responsibility for inflicting suffering on sentient beings. It is a philosophical treatise presented in the form of a detective fiction. It is also a manifesto signed with Tokarczuk's "art of tenderness," and an admission of the existential, perhaps even ontological darkness, which can be traced in most of her other novels. Suffering is omnipresent, those novels say. But while humans, equipped with their rights and privileges, can cut out niches of relatively good living out of that sea of suffering, non-human animals depend entirely on human mercy—which is difficult to come by.

---

[52] John Milton, *Paradise Lost* (1667). Being a romantic poet, William Blake believed Satan from Milton's canonical epic poem stole the show from Christ and became the real hero. Rebellious and proud, Satan was a prototype of the dark Romantic (or Byronic) protagonist.

Hence the importance of ethics, of cultivating an attitude informed by a sense of response-ability: the ability to respond to the epiphany of the animal face, most radically embodied in Duszejko. In the overcoming of the illusory human-animal division lies humanity's, and the entire planet's, future.

References

Adams, Carol & Matthew Calarco. "Derrida and the Sexual Politics of Meat." In *Meat Culture*, 31–52. Edited by Annie Potts. Leiden and Boston: Brill, 2017.

Asche, Florian. *Jagen, Sex und Tiere essen: Die Lust am Archaischen.* Melsungen: Neumann-Neudamm, 2014.

Blake, William. "The Marriage of Heaven and Hell." In *The Poetical Works of William Blake*. 1908. Reprint, London, New York: Oxford University Press, 2011.

Catechism of the Catholic Church. United States Catholic Conference of Bishops, 1997.

Elżanowski, Andrzej. "Motywacja i moralność łowiecka" [Hunting Motivation and Morality]. *Zoophilologica. Polish Journal of Animal Studies*, no. 4 (2018): 121–134.

Harvey, Graham. "Animism and Ecology: Participating in the World Community." *The Ecological Citizen* 3, no. 1 (2019): 79–84.

Hobsbawm, Eric. "Introduction: Inventing Traditions." In *The Invention of Tradition*. Edited by Eric Hobsbawm & Terence Ranger, 1–14. Cambridge: Cambridge University Press, 2003.

Holland, Agnieszka & Kasia Adamik, *Spoor*. Warszawa: Studio Filmowe, 2017.

Jones, Deborah. *The School of Compassion a Roman Catholic Theology of Animals*. Loeminster: Gracewing Publishers, 2001.

"Ksiadz mordeca zwierząt." [Priest—Murderer of Animals"]. *Leśny Patrol—Ludzie Przeciw Myśliwym. Facebook* Facebook 29-01-2018 (accessed 29-08-2020).

Tokarczuk, Olga. *Drive Your Plow Over the Bones of the Dead*. Translated by Antonia Lloyd-Jones. New York: Riverhead Books, 2019.

Tokarczuk, Olga. *Flights*. Translated by Jennifer Croft. New York: Riverhead Books, 2018.

Tokarczuk, Olga. *Moment niedźwiedzia*. Warszawa: Wydawnictwo Krytyki Politycznej, 2012.

Tokarczuk, Olga. *Nobel Lecture by Olga Tokarczuk: Nobel Laureate in Literature 2018*. Stockholm: Svenska Akademien, 2019 (accessed 30-08-2020).

Tokarczuk, Olga. *Opowieści bizarne.* Kraków: Wydawnictwo Literackie, 2019.

Patterson, Charles. *Eternal Treblinka: Our Treatment of Animals and the Holocaust.* New York: Lantern Books, 2002.

Parin, Paul. *Die Leidenschaft des Jägers.* Hamburg: Europäische Va, 2003.

Plumwood, Val. *The Eye of the Crocodile.* Edited by Lorraine Shannon. Canberra: Australian National University, 2012.

"Press release." NobelPrize.org. Nobel Media AB 2020 (accessed 07–08–2020)

Sowa, Agnieszka & Arkadiusz Panasiuk. "Ksiądz myśliwych" [Priest of Hunters]. *Polityka* 30, July 21, 2020 (accessed 30–08–2020)

"St. Francis and St. Hubert Awards." *Catholic Concern for Animals.* (accessed 29–08–2020).

Wadiwel, Dinesh. *The War Against Animals.* Leiden: Brill, 2015.

Artistic Intervention I

Marta Badenska Hammarberg: Still from *Condition*, 3:25 min continuous colour video and sound, 2018.

Reflection

During 2019, Marta Badenska Hammarberg was my student at the Royal Art Institute in Stockholm, where I teach writing classes. I had seen Marta's film *Condition* installed at that institution, in a room below the open art space by the school entrance. As I remember, the room was dark but offered light through a wide video projection. There was a backless bench carefully placed at the center of the space, providing the seated viewer a perfect distance to the projector screen. While I was struggling not to project my human self onto what I was watching, I looked at the geese trying to sleep in surroundings that at times created a high-pitched background noise. My aim was to attune to a mode of seeing that might enable me to confront the limits of the very notion of the human. Even though the still does not capture the spirit of the entire film, it nonetheless gives a sense of the living conditions of these birds in the urban setting of Stockholm.

Emma Kihl

MAKING LIVE AND LETTING DIE. BIOPOLITICS,
LITERATURE, AND THE HUMAN/ANIMAL DIVIDE

The Bear as *Ursus Sacer* in 19th Century Swedish Literature

Claudia Lindén

When the new Swedish national hunting statute was passed in 1864 it was decided to intensify the extermination of all the large predators such as bear, wolf, wolverine and lynx. The bounty was increased tenfold, and the policy was a success: by the end of the 19th century the bear was on the verge of extinction, and the price of a bearskin had skyrocketed. In the winter of 1904, the nobleman and hunter Eric von Rosen proudly let himself be photographed outside his home at a fashionable address in central Stockholm, with eight dead bears he had killed. (Finnish bears since the Swedish ones were scarce.)

Photo: Axel Malmström Dagens Nyheter March 13, 1904.[1]

---

[1] The picture was taken by *Dagens Nyheter*'s (DN:s) young photographer Axel Malmström, but it seems as if it was not published at the time, but DN writes about von Rosen's hunt and the bears outside his house on March 13, 1904. The picture was published in DN in an article on Malmström, May 14, 1928.

What seemed like an achievement in the nineteenth century would by the dawn of the new century take on different connotations. When the possibility of the bear's extinction became a reality, public critique emerged against the state's bounty on bears and its devastating effects. Already in 1905, the Swedish Royal Academy of Science argued that the bear had to be protected, since so few bears were left that reproduction was no longer taking place.[2] In a law on national parks from 1909, it was forbidden to hunt bears, and in 1916 the king Gustaf V issued a ban on the cruel tradition of bear-dancing.[3] When the Nordic outdoor museum Skansen, created by Arthur Hazelius in 1891, decided to house animals, bears were among the first animals to be introduced at Skansen. This took place already in 1893.[4] In a couple of years, the bear went from monster, with a bounty on its head, to a literary artefact and protected museum piece.

In the Nordic countries, the bear can, like no other wild animal, be traced in ancient folklore, folk tales, mythic imaginations of shapeshifting, place names and linguistic expressions. Bears are found in a variety of heraldic weapons for both nobility and cities and regions. On the verge of extinction, the bear seems to have spurred the cultural imagination in new ways. In *fin de siècle* Swedish literature, the bear appears in several stories that also criticize or ridicule bear hunting.[5] This literary intervention on the bear's behalf could be seen as yet another answer to Georg Brandes' famous aesthetic and ethical call for literature that

---

[2] Sune Björklöf, *Björnen: i markerna & kulturen* (Möklinta: Gidlund, 2010), 198.

[3] Pelin Tünaydin, "Pawing through the history of bear dancing," *Frühneuzeit-Info* 24 (oct. 2013), 53.

[4] The idea behind Skansen, once created by Artur Hazelius as a microcosm of Sweden, is an open-air museum that collects and preserves the material memory of a nation in one place, not only buildings but also its animals and traditions. See also Claudia Lindén & Hans Ruin, "A Home to Die in: Hazelius, Skansen and the Aesthetics of Historical Disappearance," in *History Unfolds: samtidskonst möter historia: Contemporary Art Meets History* (Stockholm: Historiska, 2017).

[5] Helena Nyblom and Alfhild Agrell also wrote short stories in which the bear plays a central role, but there the bear is still more alien than in Lagerlöf's and Molin's stories. Editors' note: Concerning bear-stories see also Ann-Sofie Lönngren's chapter in this volume.

debates contemporary problems. In *What Animals Mean in the Fiction of Modernity* Philip Armstrong has pointed out that how animals are understood and treated by humans should be considered in relation to the ways we feel about them: "Literary texts testify to the shared emotions, moods and thoughts of people in specific historical moments and places, as they are influenced by—and as they influence—the surrounding sociocultural forces and systems."[6] In this article, I will show, in two short stories from the 1890s by the Swedish authors Selma Lagerlöf and Pelle Molin, how the ethical and emotional similarities between man and bear are accentuated. Thereby a cultural, religious, and political space opens up, where bear and human beings co-exist. In line with Agamben's concept of *homo sacer*, I will also argue that the bear can be understood as *Ursus sacer*, as bare life, pointing towards the always-already crossed line between humans and non-human animals, nature and culture, that according to Agamben is the *urphänomen* of politics.

Bears—between the human and the divine

Its precarious position makes the bear an *Ursus sacer*, to paraphrase the Italian philosopher Agamben's concept *homo sacer*: an ancient roman law specifying a person that may be killed but not sacrificed, someone outside both human and divine law. Agamben interprets the "sacer" category not as a taboo—as it has often been interpreted—but as an "originary political structure that is located in a zone prior to the distinction between sacred and profane, religious and juridical."[7] The person who can be killed but not sacrificed constitutes a kind of double exception, excluded both from human law and at the same time from the divine law, but also—through this double ban—the

---

[6] Philip Armstrong, *What Animals Mean in the Fiction of Modernity* (London: Routledge, 2008), 4.

[7] Giorgio Agamben, *Homo Sacer: Sovereign Power and Bare Life* (1995; repr., Stanford: Stanford University Press, 1998), 48. Editors' note: Concerning Agamben's concept *homo sacer*, see also Oscar von Seth's chapter in this volume.

homo sacer is included in both categories, the human and the divine. This zone in between is what Agamben calls "bare life," that which comes prior to the juridical law. Bare life not only comes *before* the law, but is consubstantial *with* the law, and with this double ban from the profane and the religious. Agamben regards bare life as the originary activity of sovereignty. The sacredness of life, which today is invoked as a fundamental right in opposition to sovereign power, originally expresses both "life's subjection to a power over death and life's irreparable exposure in the relation of abandonment," Agamben writes.[8]

The bear's close resemblance to man, in real life (being omnivorious and a pedimeter, an animal putting its heel first when walking on two legs) as well as the bear's central position in folklore, culture, literature, in pre- or rather non-Christian belief, as well as in the Christian tradition, turns it into a creature that could be viewed as another example of "bare life" in Agamben's sense of a double exception/inclusion in the profane and the religious. As an actual animal the bear is affected by human actions and politics but, concomitantly, it also affects the cultural imagination and, by extension, humans. Agamben connects *homo sacer* with the Germanic and Scandinavian notion of "*den fredlöse*," the outlaw, what in German is called *friedlos* or *Friedlosigkeit*: "founded on the concept of peace (*Friede*) and the corresponding exclusion from the community of the wrongdoer, who therefore became *friedlos*, without peace, and whom anyone was permitted to kill without committing homicide."[9] For Agamben this also connects to the old islandic expression *vargr y veum* for someone who had committed a crime, especially in a church, or a murder: "In the bandit and the outlaw (*wargus*, *vargr*, the wolf and, in the religious sense, the sacred

---

[8] Agamben, 53.
[9] Agamben, 63.

wolf, *vargr y veum*), Germanic and Scandinavian antiquity give us a brother of *homo sacer* beyond the shadow of any doubt."[10] This connection between *homo sacer* and the old Nordic concept of *fredlöshet*, which also has a connotation of animality, of a mix between the human and the animal, opens up for us to see how the bear can be understood as an *Ursus sacer*. When the bear has been made *fredlös*, an outlaw, the old resemblance between the human and bear becomes like a weird, distorted, Dorian Grey-like, mirror of the human.

The Christian tradition has a long complex history with animals, especially bears, and is connected to both older bear cults and the close resemblance between bear and human. In his book *The Bear, History of a Fallen King* from 2011, the French historian Michel Pastoureau traces the millennium-long process of the Church's struggle against the bear: "Almost everywhere, from the Alps to the Baltic, the bear stood as a rival to Christ. The Church thought it appropriate to declare war on the bear, to fight him by all means possible, and to bring him down from his throne and his altars."[11] According to Pastoreau, the Church's struggle against the bear took several forms: demonization as well as the replacement of sacred rituals with Saint days or other Church festivities. Around the year 1000 the bear was replaced with the lion, a more Christological symbol in the eastern tradition.[12] But the definite dethroning of the bear comes with the

---

[10] Agamben, 63. I am grateful to Olof Sundqvist for pointing out that this expression is attested in Óláfs saga Tryggvasonar by Oddr: gerir Hakon j. utlagþan oc scylldi hann heita vargr i veum. er hann hafði brotit hit özta hof i Gautlandi. A person who killed someone on a sanctified ground could be described as a "wolf" in ancient Scandinavia: "In *Egils saga* 49, Queen Gunnhildr's brother, Eyvindr, was considered a 'wolf' after killing at a vé sanctuary: 'Because Eyvindr had committed murder at a sacred place he was declared a defiler [actually a wolf (*vargr*)] and had to go into outlawry at once'", Olof Sundqvist, *An Arena for Higher Powers: Ceremonial Buildings and Religious Strategies for Rulership in Late Iron Age Scandinavia*, (Leiden: Brill, 2016), 294.

[11] Pastoureau, Michel, *The Bear. History of a Fallen King* (Cambridge: The Belknap Press of Harvard University Press, 2011), 3.

[12] Pastoureau, 167.

bestiary *Roman de Renart* in the mid-13th century, where the bear is ridiculed when portrayed as a coward and a glutton, who only thinks of honey.

At the same time, in the Middle Ages, the humiliating tradition of bear-dancing commences. Bear-dancing, with bears in chains and muzzle, were common in the whole of Europe up until the early twentieth century and can be seen as a tradition and late example of humiliating the bear. Being the only four-legged animal that, like humans, also is a plantigrade, the dancing bear becomes uncannily like a human in chains when moving on two legs.[13] Pastoureau points out that the church, which condemned spectacles, tolerated this practice with bears, but looked down on the bear handlers, something that in turn made the bear an even more despised animal: "Associating the bear with them therefore effectively helped to devalue the animal and, therefore through a kind of osmosis, to project onto him all the vices imputed to his masters and companions in misfortunes."[14]

Quakers and animal rights

The same Christian tradition that once subdued the worship of the sacred bear is also behind the emerging animal rights movement, which began in Victorian England. The Quakers were active in the anti-vivisection movement and Quaker Joseph Pease persuaded parliament to insert two clauses in the act to protect animals.[15] These clauses primarily concerned domestic animals, and perhaps, therefore, could run parallel to the long tradition within the Church, from St Augustine, of placing animals both domestic and wild, beneath humans.[16] The Christian tradition is complex however, and, as Rod Preece and David Fraser have pointed out, there are plenty of examples in

---

[13] Tünaydin, 52.

[14] Pastoureau, 172–175.

[15] Peter Hollindale, "Plain Speaking: Black Beauty as a Quaker text," *Children's Literature* 28 (2000), 97.

[16] St. Augustine has a special disregard for the bear, which he calls the devil: *"ursus est* diabolical." Quoted from Pastoureau, 120.

the Bible and in philosophy of how a different position is adopted, to wit all creatures are regarded as God's creatures. How these beliefs can be interpreted and translated into action has of course been the subject of recurring debates, which in turn have been "influenced by economic forces, ecclesiastical institutions, sheer individual and collective self-interest, as well as by honest, legitimate, and well-considered differences of interpretation", as Preece and Fraser write.[17]

When the discussion of stopping cruelty against animals starts in Victorian England it is firmly grounded in Quaker and Christian beliefs about man's relation to his neighbor and kin. When the first 'Society for the Prevention of Cruelty to Animals' was founded in England in 1824, it was initiated as a response to the bad treatment of urban workhorses and stray dogs. Anna Sewell, who came from a British quaker family, wrote *Black Beauty* (1877) as a critique of the treatment of workhorses.[18] It became one of the world's all-time best-selling novels, and a famous argument for the welfare of horses. The novel is written from the perspective of Black Beauty, a horse that starts his life under good circumstances and then by unfortunate events goes through several owners, both poor and cruel, but in a happy ending finds his way back to a good life with kind humans. Sewell connects her animal rights argument to human rights. When a local boy gets into trouble for abusing a horse, Black Beauty overhears one stable hand telling another that it "served him right…he used to swagger about and bully the little boys."[19] Caroline Hagood points out that in this way "Sewell bridges the human-animal rights gap by implying that cruelty to animals often extends to humans."[20]

---

[17] Rod Preece and David Fraser, "The Status of Animals in Biblical and Christian Thought: A Study in Colliding Values," *Society & Animals* 8, no. 3 (2000), 258.

[18] Editors' note: Concerning Black Beauty see also Karin Dirke's and Sune Borkfelt's chapter in this volume.

[19] Anna Sewall, "The Devil's Trade Mark," in *Black Beauty, The Autobiography of a Horse* (London: Jerrold, 1877).

[20] Caroline Hagood, "Animal Rights Versus Human Rights: Anna Sewell's *Black Beauty*, Paula Casal's 'Animal Accomendation', and David Humes 'Of Justice'," in

Darwinism's influence on the bear in literature

It is not possible to discuss the relationship between human and non-human animals in the latter part of the nineteenth century without taking into account Darwin's tremendous influence, principally here the conclusion he reaches in *Descent of man*: "the difference in mind between man and the higher animals, great as it is, certainly is one of degree and not of kind."[21] Although Darwinism was on one level the most radical philosophical challenge to anthropocentrism, the registering of these implications was not immediate. Instead, the notion of evolutionary development, from the primitive to the higher, could be used to argue for a difference between animals and humans and between peoples. Although man was an animal, he was the highest animal, and the evolutionary doctrine could be used again to secure man's supremacy. Yet, animal studies researcher Carrie Rohan proposes that "[w]hat the literature of the late Victorian and modernist era reveals, however, is the lurking anxiety that this view of human privilege cannot be maintained."[22]

Pelle Molin's short story "A ring-dance while mother is waiting..." ("En ringdans medan mor väntar ..." (1897)) draws an analogy between bear and man as parents defending their

---

Kenyon Review, April 24 (2019). The association between animal-rights and social radicalism was more complicated in the US, where the Quakers were notably important in the abolitionist movement. In the US around the turn of the twentieth century, various discourses on animality could also be used with racist implications. As Michael Lundblad has shown, white people could claim their humanity through their care for animals, in relation to blacks who were then presented as more 'savage', wild and inhuman. See Michael Lundblad, *The Birth of a Jungle: Animality in the Progressive-era U.S. Literature and Culture* (Oxford: Oxford University Press, 2013), 20.

[21] Charles Darwin, *The Descent of Man, and Selection in Relation to Sex*. With an introduction by John Tyler Bonner and Robert M. May (1871; repr., Princeton: Princeton University Press, 1981), 105.

[22] Carrie Rohman, *Stalking the Subject: Modernism and the Animal* (New York: Columbia University Press, 2009), 5.

children.[23] Lagerlöf also proceeds analogically in "The Peace of God," ("Gudsfreden" (1899)) through a reference to the biblical narrative about the good Samaritan and the medieval convention of *Pax et treuga Dei*. Even though neither Lagerlöf nor Molin mention the animal-rights movement emerging in their own time, they seem to incorporate such a perspective in their writings. A few years later, Lagerlöf would openly comment on the bear's possible extinction in her famous book *The Wonderful Adventures of Nils* (1906). More specifically, for our present purposes, what is central here is that Molin and Lagerlöf create new ways of perceiving the bear.[24] In their short stories, the bear becomes someone who resembles the human, man's neighbor; bear and human are once more connected, rekindling their long mutual history.

Pelle Molin's "A ring-dance while mother is waiting…"

Pelle Molin (1864–1896) was an artist and a writer from Ångermanland on the northeast coast of Sweden. A journalist and writer of short stories, Molin died young, at the age of 32. All his stories are about the lives of small peasants or Sami in northern Sweden. His stories did not have the same religious undercurrent as Selma Lagerlöf's, though his way of depicting the relationship between humans and non-human animals shows an unusual sensitivity to animals' agency and emotional life. His short story, "A ring-dance while mother is waiting…" (1897) could be read as an example of the lurking anxiety that Rohan mentions; there is no real difference between man and

[23] Pelle Molin och Gustaf af Geijerstam, *Ådalens Poesi. Efterlämnade skrifter af Pelle Molin. Utgifvna och försedda med en lefnadsteckning öfver författaren af Gustaf av Geijerstam* (Stockholm: Wahlström & Widstrand, 1897). I am grateful to Professor Anders Öhman for pointing out Molin's bear story to me. For other readings of Molin, see also Anders Johansson, Anders Öhman, & Peter Degerman, (eds.), *Norrlandslitteratur: ekokritiska perspektiv* (Göteborg: Makadam, 2018)

[24] Lagerlöf seems to have had an interest in animal rights. She criticized Hazelius for keeping wild animals in captivity at Skansen. In ch. 38 of *The Wonderful Adventures of Nils,* Nils liberates the eagle Gorgo, and then rides on Gorgo's back when they escape together from Skansen.

bear, and the bear becomes a representation of 'bare life' in Agamben's sense.

It is a very dramatic and sad story about a man called Salmon. While running through the woods on a bright summer's night on his way to fetch the midwife, Salmon encounters a bear and becomes involved in a life-or-death struggle with the animal. Salmon's wife is about to give birth to their fourth child. He has two hours to make the roundtrip from his wife through the forest to the midwife, and in the meantime is full of anxiety that something will happen to the child, or even worse, to his wife, making their three children motherless. The outcome depends on him, how fast he can run. Then he hears a noise and understands that it is a bear. He has met and shot many bears, but never has he seen one so angry.

> But never before this night of suffering and distress and urgency had he seen the like of it. He could not explain this unimaginable rage ... and this stubborn running rascal, perhaps he was hunted and wounded, had he been robbed of his kids? No, there was not a single drop of blood in the brown hairs.[25]

Salmon hopes that the bear will lose interest in the hunt and leave. When this is not the case, he spots a tree to hide behind. He knows that if he is fast, he can keep the pine tree between himself and the bear at all times, thus avoiding the bear's attacks.

> A jump in half circle and Nalle rushed past, barely half a yard away. The lascivious leap ended with a sudden stop in the moss, where the nose plowed a little way. A noisy roar ... the moss was torn up when the bear quickly turned around ... it stood like a cloud ... and then he came again in blind anger ... hurriedly stopped by the tree, when he saw Salmon bend away

[25] All translations into English from the original Swedish of Molin's and Lagerlöf's texts are made by the author.
"Men aldrig förr än denna lidandets och nödens och brådskans natt hade han sett maken till denna. Han kunde icke förklara detta ofattliga raseri ... och denna envisa löpande kanalje, var han kanske jagad och sårad, hade man beröfvat honom ungarne? Nej, det fanns icke bloddroppe i de bruna håren." Molin, 65.

... now rushed after him, but could not keep the circle as narrow as Salmon; his body was too long ... and then he came back again so he shot back and forth at pointed angles ... made sharp twists and turns like a frightened pig ... threw about ... bumped ... roared so it slammed about it ... scratching the moss, so that the meager sandy ground looked up with elongated yellow eyes ... but always came to the side of Salmon. Twigs crumpled, and all the small stones rattled and shrieked.[26]

The fight, with the bear attacking and Salmon moving fast around the tree so that the bear misses him every time, is the core of the story. The fight goes on for a long time, with only occasional relief coming from Salmon's thoughts of his wife in the agonies of childbirth and the children at home: "And mother, who worked all evening with hers—and waited ... waited!"[27]

The bear's rage is incomprehensible. Why does the bear not leave him be? This seemingly illogical fury makes the bear more monstrous. In medieval moral theology, a distinction was made between vice and sin. Vice was rooted in the very nature of a person, and hard to repress or control. Sin, on the other hand, arose from free and voluntary conduct (sometimes inspired by the Devil), and was, therefore, an offense against God.[28] Given free will, one should be able to refrain from sin, correct oneself,

---

[26] "Ett hopp i half cirkel och Nalle susade förbi, knappt en half aln ifrån. Det förfelade språnget slutade med ett tvärstopp i mossan, däri nosen plöjde en liten väg. Ett larmande ryt ... mossan refs upp i tvärvändningen ... den stod som en sky ... och så kom han igen i blind ilska ... gjorde hastig halt invid trädet, då han såg Salmon vika undan ... rusade nu efter honom men kunde icke hålla cirkeln så snäf som Salmon; hans kropp var för lång ... och så bar det sig igen, att han sköt fram och tillbaka i spetsiga vinklar ... gjorde tvära vändningar och kast som en skrämd gris ... kastade om ... stötte emot ... röt, så att det slamrade om det ... klöste i mossan, så att den magra sandjorden tittade upp med aflånga gula ögon ... men kom alltid på sidan om Salmon. Kvistar knastrade, och alla små stenar rasslade och skreko." Molin, 64.
[27] "Och mor, som arbetat hela aftonen med sitt—och väntade .... väntade!" Molin, 65.
[28] Pastoureau, 178–179.

or, if a sin was committed, to confess. In medieval bestiaries, the bear was connected to vice. Animals did not commit sins, they were imperfect creatures, more or less vicious.

The bear, as Pastoureau points out, was for the Church Fathers and theologians of the Middle Ages the creature who had most vices. When during the thirteenth century the vices merged into the form of the seven deadly sins, as opposed to the seven virtues, each sin and virtue was associated with a certain number of animals. Lion, eagle, and horse were associated with virtue, while bear, fox, monkey, pig, and dog were always negatively connected with sin.[29] Worst of all was the bear, who is associated with five of the seven sins; lust, anger, gluttony, envy, and sloth: "From the thirteenth century, he was the star of this hateful bestiary, a sad fate for a wild animal who was once the king of the beasts."[30]

It is noteworthy, Pastoureau continues, that in the bestiary of the seven major sins, the two animals considered closest to humans, bear and pig, are the most devalued. Too close kinship with animals seems to be unbearable, and any such uncanny similarities are redressed through derogation, and in the case of the bear, extermination. The major monotheist religions, Pastoureau writes, "do not like animals that nature and culture have declared to be 'cousins' or 'relatives' of man. [...] It has never been a good idea to resemble human beings to close."[31]

In Pelle Molin's text, the bear's incomprehensible and ongoing blind rage, its small glowing eyes, turn it into a devilish beast, much in the same way as the bear was described in the medieval bestiaries.

> Nalle's small pungent eyes glowed. The fur of the back lay tight, flat, backward. He had drawn his ears near the head. There was something of ice-cold determination in this com-

---

[29] Pastoureau, 183.
[30] Pastoureau, 184.
[31] Pastoureau, 184.

rade in the forest. Without a moment's pause he chased the skinny settler [...].[32]

Its fury and ice-cold determination make the bear monstrous. At the same time, the passage, with the word "comrade", suggests that there is a human, and therefore moral, resemblance with this raging adversary in the forest. As Pastoureau suggests, the border between human and animal must be maintained, partly on moral grounds. A too close resemblance between human and animal would ascribe not only free will and the possibility of voluntary good conduct to the animal but also a moral obligation from human to animal. One cannot just hunt and kill such a creature.

So, the bear could not be killed by a human being unless it was made into a monster. A fact true both on the individual level in Molin's story as well as on the more overarching cultural level. When Salmon realizes that he has his knife with him, he aims at the bear and manages to inflict a wound on the animal. Salmon's act seals the battle. Now, one of them will die:

Now he knew that the game would not end until one of them lay cold and still. If the prospect of a peace settlement had been slight a little while ago, it was now null. It seemed clear now that it would be decided for Bear-Salmon whether he still was Bear-Salmon. Now, one of their lives would end, but hardly the bear's ... in such uneven battle. Salmon thought, "It is not I who will become a widower this night; it's mother who will be widowed ... mother, who is waiting for me."[33]

---

[32] "Nalles små stickande ögon glödde. Ryggens hår låg tätt, slätt, bakåtlagdt. Öronen hade han dragit intill hufvudet Det låg någonting af isande beslutsamhet hos denne kamrat i skogen. Utan ett ögonblicks uppehåll jagade han efter den magre nybyggaren." Molin, 65.

[33] "Nu visste han, att leken icke skulle ändas förr än en af dem låg kall och stilla. Hade utsikten till en uppgörelse i godo för en stund sedan varit ringa, var den nu ingen. Det syntes tydligt, att nu skulle det gälla för Björn-Salmon, om han ännu var Björn-Salmon. Nu skulle enderas lif spillas, men knappast björnens ... i sådan

They fight for a long time, repeatedly attacking each other, the bear with all its force and Salmon with his knife. In the end, he manages to kill the bear. Exhausted, Salmon falls asleep. He wakes up half an hour later when a bear cub, who had been hiding in the tree, falls in his lap. The reader, and Salmon, then understand that the bear was not a crazy aggressive male, but a female desperately trying to protect her child. Had Salmon chosen another tree to hide behind or looked up, just once, the whole tragedy could have been averted. Or, had he managed to see the resemblance between himself and the bear, then he would have understood that the cause of agitation was the same for the bear. The bear had acted in the same way as Salmon: struggling and fighting to protect her family, her child.

Throughout, the story is told from the angle of Salmon, except for this penultimate paragraph, which takes the perspective of the bear cub. It breaks up the anthropocentric viewpoint and accentuates the similarities between man and bear. This sudden switch in narrative perspective gives an agency to the animal, to the enemy's child, now an orphan:

> It is the bear's cub. He is uncertain of the importance of this deep silence after this long clamor. But he sees that mother made peace and the other too, and he feels the desire to get away from here. He has not been a little scared up here. Now he puts his paws next to the trunk and begins to slide down. It goes slowly at first…

> It was not a sensible man's gaze in Salmon when he was awakened by a heavy bundle which fell upon him. It was with him when he rushed to the village, something of a hunted quarry, a frightened grey tuft with something of the tail between his legs. There was nothing left of the night's hero, of

---

ojemn strid. Salmon tänkte: «det är icke jag, som blir änkling i natt; det är mor, som blir änka … mor, som väntar mig.» Molin, 69.

Bear-Salmon. It was only a starving settler, like a tree without twigs and alone, who ran for his poor life.[34]

When Salmon realizes what he has done, that he has killed the bear cub's mother, and that the bear cub now is in exactly that position Salmon himself fought so hard to avoid for his own children, he is filled with shame. He saw a monster where there was a mother with a child. He runs into the village like a scared dog or even worse, emasculated, like a "grey tuft with something of the tail between his legs."

Because he regarded the bear as a monster, the man himself was transformed into a monster, a shameful person. Thereby, both he and the bear become *fredlösa*, outlaws, that is *homo/ursus sacer*. As outlaws, as *homo/ursus sacer* they are an example of "bare life". Here, the border between man and animal is obliterated: "a condition in which everyone is bare life and a *homo sacer* for everyone else, and in which everyone is thus *wargus, gerit caput lupinum*", as Agamben writes.[35] Salmon is overwhelmed, not by a "lurking anxiety" as Rohan called it, but by full-blown angst in his realization that there is no difference between his children and those of the bear. In killing the bear, he has protected himself and his children, but at the cost of someone else's life, a poor little bear cub, who will now probably die of starvation. Bear and man are alike and thus have ethical responsibilities toward one another.

---

[34] "Det är björnhonans unge. Han är oviss på betydelsen af denna djupa stillhet efter detta långa larm. Men han ser, att mor gjort fred och den andre med, och han känner längtan att komma härifrån. Han har icke varit litet rädd häruppe. Nu sätter han tassarne intill stammen och börjar masa sig ned. Det går långsamt till en början....

Det var icke en vettig mans blick hos Salmon, då han väcktes af ett tungt bylte, som föll ned på honom. Det var hos honom, då han rusade i väg till bygden, något af ett jagadt vildbråd, en vettskrämd grå tuss med något af svansen mellan benen. Där fanns ingenting alls af nattens hjälte, af Björn-Salmon. Det var endast en svulten nybyggare, afkvistad och allena, som sprang för sitt fattiga lif." Molin, 74.

[35] Agamben, 64. The term *gerit caput lupinum* ("may he wear a wolfish head" / "may his be a wolf's head") was used in medieval English law to describe an outlaw, someone who could be killed without penalty.

The masculinization in the bear hunt, a notion very much present in both Molin's and Lagerlöf's stories, can be traced back to the Icelandic sagas, where, as Lena Rohrbach has shown in *Der tierische Blick: Mensch-Tier-Relationen in der Sagaliteratur*, encounters between man and animal are much more common than in other European literature from the Middle Ages.[36] The common encounter imagined with a bear is as hunter, a hunting that makes men more masculine.[37] Salmon is initially presented as a man who has killed many bears, but in the end—after killing the story's bear—he is described as a frightened creature who runs away with his tail between his legs. Killing a bear made him, in fact, lose his masculinity. As we shall see, Lagerlöf, who knew her Icelandic sagas by heart, depicts a similar process of emasculation in relation to an attempt to kill a bear.[38] In the end, both stories implode this close connection of masculinity and the bear-killings, when it turns out that men who kill or plan to kill bears in fact become emasculated in one way or another.

Selma Lagerlöf's "The Peace of God"

In Selma Lagerlöf's short story "The Peace of God" (1899), it is not only the ethical relationship with the bear, but the bear's moral agency, accentuated through the parable of the good Samaritan (Luke 10:25–37). Lagerlöf's story takes place in the intersection between the Old Nordic belief in the holiness of the bear, a post-Darwinist insight into animals' close connection to ourselves, and an animal rights perspective, which, with Christian roots, understands the bear as an endangered species.[39] In "Gudsfreden," Lagerlöf does this explicitly through a refer-

---

[36] Lena Rohrbach, *Der tierische Blick: Mensch-Tier-Relationen in der Sagaliteratur* (Tübingen: Francke, 2009).

[37] Rohrbach, 201–202.

[38] In her biography of Selma Lagerlöf Anna-Karin Palm shows how intensely Lagerlöf read the Icelandic sagas in her youth. Anna-Karin Palm, *"Jag vill sätta världen i rörelse": en biografi över Selma Lagerlöf* (Stockholm: Albert Bonniers förlag, 2019), chapter 2.

[39] Selma Lagerlöf, "Gudsfreden," *Drottningar i Kungahälla jämte andra berättelser* (Stockholm: Bonniers 1899), 252.

ence to *Pax et treuga Dei* and, specifically, to the dictum to love thy neighbor as thyself, as it was formulated in the Gospel of Luke.[40]

When Lagerlöf opens up the religious domain for the bear, a connection is made with the ancient belief that the bear is holy. An associative link, a cultural bridge one might call it, is made between the pre-Christian view of the bear as sacred and the twentieth century's endangered and protected bear. As Pastoreau has shown, up until the Middle Ages, the bear was the object of different cults across the European continent. In the Nordic region, the extolling of its sacred qualities went on much longer. In Finland, the traces of these bear ceremonies are very tangible and several songs in the *Kalevala* are today considered to be songs that were sung or recited next to the dead bear, often called "bear weddings."[41] Traces of these beliefs are also found in Sweden and occur into the eighteenth and nineteenth centuries. It seems as if the beliefs and ceremonies surrounding the bear could co-exist with the Christian faith.

Common to these ceremonies, e.g. how the bear was approached and how one behaved after the bear was killed, is the respect and reverence shown to the powerful animal. The bear must never be killed in its sleep during hibernation. If it is winter, the bear must be awakened and lured out of its den. The ceremonies were often called the bear's funeral feast, or, as

---

[40] The tradition from the Middle Ages was created in reaction to the constant fighting not only among the nobility, but noble men fighting also with everyone else. Peace was permanently proclaimed in certain buildings, as the church. And certain people like monks, clerics and women, cattle and horses, should always be protected by this peace. "The Truce of God" or *Treuga Dei* concerned only special periods and had its origin in Normandy in the city of Caen in the 11th century. The Truce of God peace was required throughout Advent, the season of Lent, and from the beginning of the Rogation days until eight days after Pentecost, and during certain days of the week. Lagerlöf's inclusion of the the wild animals in the category protected by the The Truce of God, was probably an accepted interpretation.

[41] Juha Pentikäinen, *Golden King of the Forest: the Lore of the Northern Bear* (Helsinki: Etnika, 2007). See also Håkan Rydving, "The 'Bear Ceremonial' and Bear Rituals Among the Khanty and the Sami." *Temenos* 46, no. 1 (2010): 31.

already mentioned, the bear's wedding. There is an oral eyewitness account from as late as 1890 in Sweden.[42]

Lagerlöf's story takes place on Christmas Eve in Ingmarsgården, the homestead of the rich Ingmarson family. The house is swept and cleaned until the very last minute, with the sauna heated so that everyone could take a bath before Christmas. The girl whose job it is to tie birch twigs for the sauna bath cannot properly perform her task since she has no thin sprigs with which to tie. As everyone is busy, old Ingmar Ingmarson decides to go out himself, and cut the sprigs. The wind blows, it snows intensely. The snowy wind makes old Ingmarson dizzy and on his way home he walks in the wrong direction, into the forest, instead of home over the fields. Lost in the woods, the reader follows a surprisingly long and scary description of how the old man walks in the blizzard in the woods, becoming increasingly tired while the dark descends upon him. Ingmarson understands that if he falls asleep, he will freeze to death. In the end, he gives up and crawls in under a heap of twigs. However, it turns out to be a bear's den.

> But when he pushed his body under the twigs, he felt that there was something warm and soft inside the pile. There must be a bear sleeping here, he thought. He felt how the animal was moving and heard how it was sniffing around in the air. He lay still anyway. He thought nothing other than that the bear could happily eat him. He could not take another step to get away from him. But the bear did not seem to want to do anythong to the one who sought protection under his roof during such a stormy night. He moved a little further down in his den as if to make room for the guest, and shortly afterwards he slept with steady, hissing breath.[43]

---

[42] Björklöf, 260.

[43] "Men då han sköt in kroppen under kvistarna, kände han, att därinne i högen låg något, som var varmt och mjukt. Här ligger visst en björn och sofver, tänkte han. Han kände hur djuret rörde sig och hörde hur det vädrade omkring sig. Han låg stilla i alla fall. Han tänkte intet annat än att björnen gärna kunde få äta upp

Old Ingmar Ingmarson is thus saved from freezing to death by the bear, who without harming him lets him share his den during the night. A true compassionate act.

While old Ingmarson is lost in the woods, everyone in his household wait at home, worrying; no one could do anything because of the storm. To calm everyone, Mrs Ingmarson reads from the Bible, and what she, more or less by coincidence, chooses to read is the story of the Good Samaritan:

> The old woman read and read and came to the question: "Who was his neighbor, who came before the robbers?" But before she had time to read the answer, the door opened and old Ingmar entered the room.
>
> "Mother, father is here," said one of the daughters, and it was never read out loud, that the man's neighbor was the one who had shown him mercy.[44]

So, the question of who the man's neighbor is, was never answered. Nor does anyone bother to ask the question when it is agreed that they must hastily find and shoot the bear, rather than celebrate Christmas in joy, now that father had returned to them. "Because it is so," says the text, "that the bear, it is a man's duty to slay, where and when he comes upon him. It is not possible to spare a bear, because sooner or later he gets taste for meat, and then he saves neither animal nor man."[45] But even

honom. Han orkade ej gå ett steg till för att komma undan honom. Men björnen tyckte sig väl ej vilja göra något åt den, som sökte skydd under hans tak under en sådan ovädersnatt. Han flyttade sig något längre ned i sin håla liksom för att ge rum åt gästen, och strax därefter sof han med jämna, susande andetag." Lagerlöf, "Gudsfreden," 256.

[44] Den gamla kvinnan läste och läste och kom till frågan:»Hvilken var nu hans nästa, som för röfvarena kommen var?» Men innan hon hunnit läsa svaret, sköts dörren upp och gamle Ingmar kom in i rummet.»Mor, far är här,» sade en af döttrarna, och det blef aldrig uppläst, att mannens nästa var den, som hade bevisat honom barmhärtighet. Lagerlöf, "Gudsfreden," 258.

[45] "Ty det är så, att björnen är det en mans plikt att fälla, hvar och när han råkar honom. Det går ej an att skona en björn, ty förr eller senare får han dock smak på kött, och då sparar han hvarken djur eller människa." Lagerlöf, "Gudsfreden," 258.

though she knows this injunction well, Mrs. Ingmarson is distressed, and she continues to search in the Bible.

But after they had gone to the hunt, the old Mistress of the house felt a great anxiety come over her and had taken to reading. Now she began to read about what was preached in the church this day, but she came no further than to this, "Peace on earth, and Goodwill to all Men!" She remained sitting, and stared at these words with her fading eyes, and from time to time she drew a heavy sigh. She did not read any further, but she repeated again and again with a slow and dragging voice: Peace on earth, and Goodwill to all Men!"[46]

Before she has even had time to formulate for herself what is amiss, the youngest son rushes in. He is very upset and can barely talk. She pats him on the cheek and holds him "as she has not done since he was a little boy." He breaks down and starts crying.

'I can understand that there is something about father,'
- 'Yes, but it is worse than that,' sobbed the son.
- 'Is it worse than that?' The man cried inconsolably, he knew not how to get power into his voice. Finally, he raised his coarse hand with his wide fingers and pointed to that, which she just had read.
- "Peace on earth, and Goodwill to all Men!"
- 'Is there anything about this?' she asked.
- 'Yes' he answered.
- 'Is there something about Christmas peace?'
- 'Yes.'
- 'You wanted to do an evil act this morning.'

[46] "Men sedan de gått bort till jakten, hade den gamla husmodern fått en stor ängslan öfver sig och hade tagit till att läsa. Nu började hon läsa om det, som den dagen predikades i kyrkan, men hon kom ej längre än till detta,»Frid på jorden, och människorna en god vilje!» Hon blef sittande och stirrade på dessa ord med sina slocknande blickar, och allt emellanåt drog hon en tung suck. Hon läste ej vidare, men hon upprepade gång på gång med långsam och släpande röst:»frid på jorden, människorna en god vilje!» Lagerlöf, "Gudsfreden," 259.

- 'Yes.'
- 'And God has punished us?'
- 'God has punished us.'[47]

Finally, he tells her what happened. They had found the den and charged the guns. As mentioned earlier, in the old bear ceremonies it was forbidden to kill a bear while it was asleep. It was an act of disrespect. Now old Ingmar Ingmarson and his sons intended to kill the creature who saved him *and* break the ancient taboo about killing a sleeping bear. An animal, more to the point, that Lagerlöf's contemporaries would have known to be endangered, no longer existing in Värmland, for example. And, on Christmas Eve itself, too, when peace is supposed to rule on earth! The violation can be indexed on many levels. The bear also literally strikes back: "he came straight on to the old Ingmar Ingmarson and gave him a blow over his head, which brought him down, as if he had been hit by lightning."[48] The bear does not care about the other hunters, he just kills old Ingmarsson, and then runs off into the forest.

Within the context of the story, God has punished Ingmar and his sons for not showing mercy to their neighbor. Realizing that they are the ones who have broken God's Peace, and therefore have been punished by God, Mrs. Ingmarson insists that her

[47] Jag kan förstå, att det är något med far,» sade hon.
- »Ja, men det är värre än så,» snyftade sonen.
- »Är det värre än så?» Karlen grät allt häftigare, han visste ej hur han skulle få makt med sin röst.
Slutligen lyfte han upp sin grofva hand med de breda fingrarna och pekade på detta, som hon nyss läst. -»Frid på jorden.» - »Är det något med detta?» frågade hon.
-»Ja,» svarade han.
- »Är det något med julfreden?»
- »Ja.»
- »Ni ville göra en ond gärning i morse.»
- »Ja.» - »Och Gud har straffat oss?»
- »Gud har straffat oss.» Lagerlöf, "Gudsfreden," 260.
[48] "han kom rakt emot den gamle Ingmar Ingmarson och gaf honom ett slag öfver hjässan, som fällde honom, såsom hade han träffats af blixten." Lagerlöf, "Gudsfreden," 260.

husband's funeral should be as low key as possible. The bear and the human both become *homo/ursus sacer* here. When Ingmarson and his son went out to kill the bear, they treated the bear as *fredlös*, as someone that could be killed but not sacrificed, as excluded from both profane and divine law. But, in the end it is old Ingmarson, punished by God and killed by the bear, and then deprived of having a high-status funeral, thereby expelling him from both the divine and profane order, who has become a *homo sacer*, a *fredlös*. Again, man and bear are interconnected, they both mirror each other and change places.

> But at Christmas, God has declared peace between animals and humans, and while the poor animal respected God's command, we broke it, and now it is we who face God's punishment. [Mrs Ingmarson says][49]

The bear becomes, in Lagerlöf's story, not only man's neighbor but a creature with a moral agency. In contrast to the humans, the bear has acted in accord with God's commandments. It is the bear who chooses to be a merciful Samaritan, and who also has the ability to see that thy neighbor can be someone who is different from oneself, even someone regarded as an enemy. Animals and people have always been a part of God's kingdom, but in Lagerlöf's story they become equal moral beings in mutual dialogue. Only that it is man who betrays the agreement with the animals and therefore is punished by God. By making bear and human equal moral beings before God, Lagerlöf rejects anthropocentrism, which places man, as an image of God, at the center of the universe.

As is often the case with Lagerlöf, her stories can be read both secularly and religiously. Read from a cultural-historical perspective, and framed in post-Darwinian terms, Lagerlöf here seems to undermine the evolutionary logic that says that man is

---

[49] "Men om julen har Gud satt fred mellan djur och människor, och det arma djuret höll Guds bud, men vi bröto det, och därför äro vi nu under Guds straff." Lagerlöf, "Gudsfreden," 262.

the crown of evolution and thus can do what he wants with more primitive beings. From an animal rights perspective, it is possible to read the story as an intervention in the political debates at the time, where in the Swedish newspapers of the 1890s it was possible to read the call "Don't let the bear be exterminated."[50]

When this story is related to older conceptions of the bear, such as in accounts where the bear was seen as omniscient, with the ability to understand human speech, we can see that Lagerlöf's representation follows a well established but forgotten history; her short story becomes an example of a bear who hears and knows everything.[51] That the bear is awake and hears how the hunters are gathering outside, that the bear understands what they are planning, and knows who the culprit is—it is only old Ingmarson the bear attacks—seems to testify to the notion that the bear understands human speech. Old Ingmarson has in every sense failed in respect to the bear, irrespective of whether the animal is regarded as sacred or man's neighbor in a Christian sense.

In the end, the bear and old Ingmarson share the same place in the universe, and the same condition of having become *fredlösa*, that is, *sacer* in Agamben's sense of being a hybrid between man and animal: "a realm of indistinction and of passage between animal and man, *physis* and *nomos*, exclusion and inclusion: the life of the bandit is the life of the *loup garou*, the werewolf, who is precisely neither man nor beast, and who dwells paradoxically within both while belonging to neither."[52]

Ursus sacer—bear death as bare life

As Ella Odsted has pointed out in her book from 1949 on werewolf-belief in Sweden there are strong beliefs concerning

---

[50] Quoted after Einar Lönnberg, *Björnen i Sverige 1856–1928* (Uppsala & Stockholm: Almqvist & Wiksell, 1929), 11.

[51] Björklöf, 270.

[52] Agamben, 63.

animal transformation into both wolf and bear in Swedish and Nordic folklore. In the northern part of Scandinavia shape-shifting occurs with bears rather than wolves, which means that in the North the werewolf is actually a werebear.[53] It is reflected in expressions like "run bear," "go bear," "go into bear shape," "turn into bear."[54] The human being who becomes *fredlös* is a hybrid of human and animal, a kind of shapeshifter, a werewolf, or rather a werebear. To quote Agamben again: "What had to remain in the collective unconscious as a monstrous hybrid of human and animal, divided between the forest and the city—the werewolf—is, therefore, in its origin the figure of the man who has been banned from the city."[55]

In the connection between *homo sacer*, the Germanic and Scandinavian concept of *fredlöshet/Friedlosigkeit* and were-wolves, pointed out by Agamben, the bear in its complex tradi-tion of werebears, holy bears, and bears as *fredlösa* with a bounty on their heads, can be understood as *ursus sacer*—and by exten-sion it can be regarded as a political category. For Agamben this original ban of the *homo sacer*, this *lychantropy*, is directly connected to the law and the city. Bare life or sacred life are both always present and always presuppose sovereignty. Agamben sees this in contrast to our modern way of representing the political realm in terms of citizens' rights, free will, and social contracts.[56]

---

[53] Ella Odstedt, *Varulven i svensk folktradition* (1948; repr., Täby: Malört, 2012), 95.

[54] In Swedish: *Löpa björn, gå björn, gå i björnhamn, vänd till björn.* The idea of self-transformation was most common in Jämtland, Härjedalen, Dalarna and Värmland, but also in Ångermanland. The shape shifter commonly turns into a wolf or a bear. In Dalarna and Värmland shape shifting can only be into bear. The most common causes of shape shifting were ravenousness, pleasure or revenge. The notion that some people can cast a spell on others in order to make them shapeshift into a predator exists all over Sweden. Odstedt, 63–65, 95.

Lagerlöf relates to this notion of humans magically turned into bears with the story of the bear from Gurlitta in the *The Saga of Gösta Berling*, which only a bullet made from a church-bell's metal can kill.

[55] Agamben, 63.

[56] Agamben, 64.

Agamben wants to reread Hobbes' and Rousseau's foundational myth of the city. According to Agamben, the city is not
founded on the citizen's free will. The state of nature, he writes,
is in truth a state of exception. It is not something founded
once and for all, but instead something continually operative
in the civil state in the form of sovereign decisions.[57] What is
more, the latter refers *immediately* to the life (and not the free
will) of citizens. Thus, it is life as such that appears as the
originary political element, the *Urphänomen* of politics, we can
say. Yet this life is not simply natural reproductive life, the zoē
of the Greeks, nor *bios*, a qualified form of life. It is, rather, the
bare life of *homo sacer and* the *wargus*, a zone of indistinction
and continuous transition between man and beast, nature and
culture.[58]

Not only is bare life the *Urphänomen* of politics, but it is so
in a "continuous transition between man and beast, nature and
culture." If we follow Agamben's argument on *homo sacer*,
politics and the city, further by returning to the picture of von
Rosen standing next to the dead bears, we can consider their
corpses, the *ursus sacer*, as in political terms. The dead bears are
displayed on the street outside von Rosen's home in Stockholm.
It happens to be on Strömgatan, facing the Royal castle, and the
parliament. The heads of the dead bears are pointing in the
direction of the sovereign. They are the city's *wargus*, the werebear, which, according to Agamben, as quoted above, is the
figure of the man who has been banned from the city. Expunged
of its once holy status, and killed for a bounty, the dead bears
facing the castle become the sign of that indistinguishable line
between human and animal, culture and nature. Bear death as
bare life. Von Rosen's violent act of exhibiting the dead bears in
the city in view of the King, also shows who has been banned
from the city and the culture. The bear. Michel Pastoureau

[57] Agamben, 65.
[58] Agamben, 65.

argued: "In killing the bear, his kinsman, his fellow creature, his first God, man long ago killed his own memory."[59] If the *urphänomen* of politics is an always already transgressed line between human and animal, between culture and nature, then the bear is as every bit political as humans. We do not need to transcend or question the anthropocentric paradigm, because the political realm is always already crossed, muted and mixed in a never-ending transition between man and beast. When considered as a political notion, *ursus sacer* reminds us that in bare life there is no difference between humans and animals. We share the same habitat, in nature as in the city.

References

Agamben, Giorgio. *Homo Sacer: Sovereign Power and Bare Life.* Translated by Daniel Heller-Roazen. 1995. Reprint, Stanford: Stanford University Press, 1998.

Armstrong, Philip. *What Animals Mean in the Fiction of Modernity.* London: Routledge, 2008.

Björklöf, Sune. *Björnen: i markerna & kulturen.* Möklinta: Gidlund, 2010.

Darwin, Charles. *The Descent of Man, and Selection in Relation to Sex.* With an introduction by John Tyler Bonner and Robert M. May. 1871. Reprint, Princeton: Princeton University Press, 1981.

Hagood, Caroline. "Animal Rights Versus Human Rights: Anna Sewell's *Black Beauty*, Paula Casal's 'Animal Accommodation', and David Humes 'Of Justice'." *Kenyon Review*, April 24, 2019.

Hollindale, Peter. "Plain Speaking: Black Beauty as a Quaker text," *Children's Literature* 28 (2000), 95–111.

Johansson, Anders, Anders Öhman och Peter Degerman (eds.). *Norrlandslitteratur: ekokritiska perspektiv.* Göteborg: Makadam, 2018.

Lagerlöf, Selma. *Gösta Berlings saga.* Stockholm: Albert Bonniers förlag, 1891.

Lagerlöf, Selma. *Nils Holgerssons underbara äventyr, band 2.* Stockholm: Albert Bonniers förlag, 1907.

Lagerlöf, Selma. "Gudsfreden," *Drottningar i Kungahälla jämte andra berättelser.* Stockholm: Albert Bonniers förlag, 1899.

Lindén, Claudia & Hans Ruin. "A Home to Die in: Hazelius, Skansen and the Aesthetics of Historical Disappearance," in *History unfolds: sam-*

---

[59] Pastoureau, 239.

tidskonst möter historia: Contemporary Art Meets History. Edited by Helene Larson Pousette. Stockholm: Historiska, 2017.

Lindén, Claudia. "The Bear as Man's Neighbour in Swedish Nineteenth-Century Fiction," in *Aesthetics of Protestantism.* Edited by Joachim Grage, Thomas Mohnike, Rohrbach, Lena. Forthcoming in 2022.

Lundblad, Michael. *The Birth of a Jungle: Animality in Progressive-era U.S. Literature and Culture.* Oxford: Oxford University Press, 2013.

Lönnberg, Einar. *Björnen i Sverige 1856–1928.* Uppsala & Stockholm: Almqvist & Wiksell, 1929.

Molin, Pelle and Gustaf af Geijerstam. *Ådalens Poesi. Efterlämnade skrifter af Pelle Molin. Utgifvna och försedda med en lefnadsteckning öfver författaren af Gustaf af Geijerstam.* Stockholm: Wahlström & Widstrand, 1897.

Odstedt, Ella. *Varulven i svensk folktradition.* 1948. Reprint, Täby: Malört, 2012.

Palm, Anna-Karin. *"Jag vill sätta världen i rörelse": en biografi över Selma Lagerlöf.* Stockholm: Albert Bonniers förlag, 2019.

Pastoureau, Michel, *The Bear. History of a Fallen King.* Cambridge: The Belknap Press of Harvard University Press, 2011.

Pentikäinen, Juha. *Golden King of the Forest: the Lore of the Northern Bear.* Helsinki: Etnika, 2007.

Preece, Rod and David Fraser. "The Status of Animals in Biblical and Christian Thought: A Study in Colliding Values." *Society & Animals* 8, no. 3 (2000), 245–263.

Rohman, Carrie. *Stalking the Subject: Modernism and the Animal.* New York: Columbia University Press, 2009.

Rohrbach, Lena. *Der tierische Blick: Mensch-Tier-Relationen in der Sagaliteratur.* Tübingen: Francke, 2009.

Rydving, Håkan. "The 'Bear Ceremonial' and Bear Rituals Among the Khanty and the Sami." *Temenos* 46, no. 1 (2010): 31.

Sewall, Anna. *Black Beauty. The Autobiography of a Horse.* London: Jerrold, 1877.

Sundqvist, Olof, *An Arena for Higher Powers: Ceremonial Buildings and Religious Strategies for Rulership in Late Iron Age Scandinavia,* Leiden: Brill, 2016.

"Truce of God," *Encyclopaedia Britannica* (accessed 01–02–2021).

Tünaydin, Pelin. "Pawing Through the History of Bear Dancing," *Frühneuzeit-Info* 24 (oct. 2013).

Tracing the Wolf in Hermann Hesse's *Der Steppenwolf*

Oscar von Seth

Harry Haller, the middle-aged, intellectual protagonist in Hermann Hesse's *Der Steppenwolf* (1927), is different from other people: *"He walked on two legs, wore clothes and was a human, but actually he was a wolf of the steppes."*[1] Harry is repeatedly described with the adjective *Fremdheit* (strangeness). For instance: "um den ganzen Mann herum [war] eine fremde und [...] ungute oder feindliche Atmosphäre."[2] ("the man was enveloped in a strange and [...] uncomfortable or hostile atmosphere.") His dual nature accentuates both his otherness and him being a wolf, an animal believed to be "the ultimate symbol of wilderness ...."[3] It signals that he is an untamed creature of the wild.

---

[1] All translations of Hesse's novel have been made by the article's author. German original: *"Er ging auf zwei Beinen, trug Kleider und war ein Mensch, aber eigentlich war er doch eben ein Steppenwolf."* Hermann Hesse, *Der Steppenwolf*, in *Sämtliche Werke. Band 4: Die Romane. Der Steppenwolf, Narziß und Goldmund, Die Morgenlandfahrt* (Berlin: Suhrkamp Verlag, 2001), 45.
Choosing not to use any of the existing English translations has two reasons. The first derives from Walter Benjamin's thoughts on translation as a sort of balancing act between transferring form, content, and meaning, where the latter is more important than linguistic exactness. (See Walter Benjamin, "The Task of the Translator." Translated by Harry Zohn, *The Translation Studies Reader*, ed. Lawrence Venuti [London: Routledge, 2000].) Drawing on Benjamin, the present translations do not aim at providing "linguistically elegant" renditions of Hesse's prose but rather serves the purpose of conveying *literal meaning* from the original text. The second reason is that at least four English translations of *Der Steppenwolf* have been published after Basil Creighton's first version in 1929, and all of them criticize or outright reject their predecessors. Comparing these varied translations with the interpretations made herein would, within the scope of this article, be too extensive a project.
[2] Hesse, 8.
[3] Steven H. Fritts, Robert O. Stephenson, Robert D. Hayes, and Luigi Boitani, "Wolves and Humans," in *Wolves: Behavior, Ecology, and Conservation* (Chicago: University of Chicago, 2003), 290.

Der Steppenwolf begins when Harry becomes a lodger in a bourgeois home in a city. His fragmented human-animal nature—namely, that he has "*a dual nature, one human and one wolfish*"⁴—makes it impossible for him to identify with conformist society, leading him to consider suicide. One evening, after having aimlessly wandered the streets, he finds a doorway in an alley leading to a "Magic Theater." Harry does not enter but instead meets a stranger who gives him a pamphlet entitled "Treatise of the Steppenwolf." The treatise, surprisingly, is an inquiry into Harry's own existence. It explains that he is "*an unsatisfied person.*"⁵ If he can learn to perceive himself as more than just wolf and man, however, he will reach the peaceful realm of the Immortals. The Immortals are artists like Goethe and Mozart who have transcended the mediocrity of life through humor.

Soon afterwards Harry meets the mysterious young Hermine. She teaches him how to dance and about sexual pleasure, indulgences with which he is unfamiliar. Similar to Harry's human-animal nature, Hermine has two sides to her. She is a gender-non-conforming character with fluid gender expressions, an aspect that will be addressed later in the article, since it is entwined with the protagonist's species duality.⁶ Through Hermine, Harry is acquainted with the prostitute Maria and the jazz musician Pablo. The novel culminates at a masked ball where Harry takes drugs supplied by Pablo, who brings him into the Magic Theater. In the theater hidden parts of Harry's personality are revealed and in an intricate, dream-like episode he discovers that Hermine has had sex with Pablo.

---

⁴ German original: "*zwei Naturen, eine menschliche und eine wölfische*," Hesse, 45.
⁵ German original: "*ein unzufriedener Mensch.*" Hesse, 45.
⁶ Hermine's fluid gender expressions—that she appears as both woman and man, and either can be labeled an *intersex person* or one whose gender expression is trans/non-binary—makes Hesse's choice of pronoun for her problematic. Although this aspect of the text merits further discussion, when discussing Hermine in this article the pronoun "she" will be used. In my upcoming monograph on Hesse's *Peter Camenzind* (1904) and *Der Steppenwolf* (due for publication in 2022) Hermine's gender-non-conformism receives greater attention.

Out of jealousy he kills her. For this crime and for having taken life too seriously, Harry is condemned by the Immortals. The novel ends with them all laughing at him and having now merged with Mozart, Pablo appears as one of the Immortals, waiting for Harry to join him.

This reading emphasizes *Der Steppenwolf*'s human-animal motif. While the research field on the authorship of Hermann Hesse (1877–1962) is substantial, few have given attention to *Der Steppenwolf*'s animal aspects.[7] From an animal studies angle Alexander Mathäs' research is a significant contribution. Mathäs argues that Hesse's novel "seeks to reveal the human dependence on an instinctual, subconscious nature beyond rational control, thus exposing the myth that individuals are superior to other living beings by virtue of their ability to rationally know themselves."[8] Drawing on Mathäs' argument the aim here is to "trace the wolf" in *Der Steppenwolf*. This means observing how the wolf appears in the text, as well as how the animality it brings to the narrative functions as a counterpoint to—and critique of—the anthropocentric paradigm, which regards humans as superior to all other animals.

Tierähnlichkeit and animality

Concerning how one "traces animals" in literature, Philip Armstrong—drawing on the work of John Simons—has written: "in seeking to go beyond the use of animals as mere mirrors for human meaning, our best hope is to locate the 'tracks' left by animals in texts, the ways cultural formations are affected by the materiality of animals and their relationships with humans."[9]

---

[7] For research on the novel's animal aspects, see David Gallagher, *Metamorphosis: Transformations of the Body and the Influence of Ovid's Metamorphoses on Germanic Literature of the Nineteenth and Twentieth Centuries* (Amsterdam: Rodopi, 2009), 326–338.

[8] Alexander Mathäs, *Beyond Posthumanism: The German Humanist Tradition and the Future of the Humanities* (New York and Oxford: Berghahn Books, 2020), 242.

[9] Philip Armstrong, *What Animals Mean in the Fiction of Modernity* (London: Routledge, 2008), 3.

Reading literary animals by giving attention to their tracks is, according to Armstrong, a notion with the purpose of challenging human-animal hierarchies and essentialist conceptions of species, as well as allowing animal agency—a stance shared by many in the critical animal studies field. Susan McHugh for instance writes: "Although animals abound in literature across all ages and cultures, only in rarified ways have they been the focal point of systematic literary study,"[10] suggesting that *literary animal agency* derives from acknowledging literary animals as more than proxies for human subjectivity. Also, Ann-Sofie Lönngren argues that even though we, as human beings, are incapable of completely escaping an anthropocentric worldview: "it is certainly possible to question the centrality of 'the human' in the humanities, to point out the consequences of this bias, and to employ theoretical concepts and methods according to which more-than-anthropocentric knowledge can be produced."[11]

Attempting to read the wolf in Hesse's novel exclusively as a "real" animal, however, poses somewhat of a challenge. *Der Steppenwolf* does not involve any clear-cut representations of an actual wolf. Rather, as the introductory quote shows, we are presented with an amalgamation of a human and an animal, the former of which is given wolf-like traits. The author's construction of Harry's animality is thus comparable with Theodor Adorno's concept *Tierähnlichkeit*, that is, humans' resemblance to animals. In Adorno's "Notes on Kafka" he perceives a conflict between the ultimate bourgeois concept of human dignity and the likeness between man and animal.[12] Recognizing our *Tierähnlichkeit* as humans—how we resemble animals—is, to Adorno, a means of addressing human beings' subjugation of other animals, as well as an appeal to find balance in this unequal

---

[10] Susan McHugh, *Animal Stories: Narrating Across Species Lines* (Minneapolis: University of Minnesota Press, 2011), 6.

[11] Ann-Sofie Lönngren, *Following the Animal: Power, Agency, and Human-animal Transformations in Modern, Northern-European Literature* (Newcastle upon Tyne: Cambridge Scholars Publishing, 2015), 22.

[12] Theodor W. Adorno, "Notes on Kafka," in *Prisms*, trans. Samuel and Shierry Weber (Cambridge, MA: The MIT Press, 1981), 270.

relationship. And, as Christina Gerhardt points out, animals are, to Adorno, a "condition of possibility not only for reading the self, humans, and culture but also for an unreadable other, alterity."[13] Gerhard follows Adorno and Max Horkheimer's contention in *Dialectic of Enlightenment* (1947) about animal otherness. "The idea of man in European history," they write, "is expressed in the way in which he is distinguished from the animal. Animal irrationality is adduced as proof of human dignity."[14] In *Der Steppenwolf*, however, the animal is *not* portrayed as irrational but as having intelligence and subjectivity, and a shared corporeality with a human. Hesse's novel therefore challenges the perception that humans are the superior species.

Interestingly, besides being conveyed thematically in *Der Steppenwolf*, *Tierähnlichkeit* can also be identified on a material level. Although Harry's physical body is that of a human being (he walks, for instance, "on two legs"), his animal characteristics are expressed through a couple of bodily wolf-like attributes: Harry "reached out his sharp-looking, short-haired head and sniffed around with his nose nervously …."[15] Harry's "sharp-looking head" reminds us of the pointy shape of a wolf's face and he is described as having: "short hair that flickered in shades of gray."[16] This mirrors the fact that while wolves can be both black and white most of them have mottled gray furs.[17]

Additionally, Harry often sniffs; an activity with animal-like connotations. At one point he is standing outside a jazz club full of people, contemplating whether or not to enter: "I stood there sniffing for a moment, smelled the bloody, bright music, vici-

---

[13] Christina Gerhardt, "The Ethics of Animals in Adorno and Kafka," *New German Critique*, no. 97 (2006): 160.

[14] Max Horkheimer and Theodor W. Adorno, *Dialectic of Enlightenment*, trans. John Cumming (New York: Continuum, 1989), 245.

[15] German original: "hatte seinen scharfen kurzhaarigen Kopf witternd in die Höhe gereckt, schnupperte mit der nervösen Nase um sich her …." Hesse, 8.

[16] German original: "ganz [kurzes] Kopfhaar, das hier und dort ein wenig grau flimmerte." Hesse, 8.

[17] L. David Mech and Luigi Boitani, *Wolves: Behavior, Ecology, and Conservation* (Chicago: University of Chicago, 2003), xv.

ously and lustfully sensing the atmosphere of these halls."[18] This example depicts the wolf as a threat to humans—as an antagonist—which corresponds to the ways with which wolves have historically been viewed. "In Western cultures," Garry Marvin states, "wolves, more than any other animal, have been emblematic of the wild and particularly of the dangerous and threatening qualities of the wild."[19] And Peter Arnds writes: "Though admired as a skillful predator by hunting and war-mongering societies, [the wolf] has also been feared as an animal that is able to kill and devour humans."[20] Harry/the wolf as humanity's antagonist is enhanced by having his status as an outsider continually emphasized. He is a shy but wild animal: "ein verirrtes Tier, das seine Umwelt nicht begriff …." (36) (a stray animal that did not understand his environment ….) Other characters' reactions convey that Harry exudes something animalistic, even though he "passes" for a human. But as David Gallagher points out, the reader must neither see the wolf in a literal sense, nor witness Harry's transformation between wolf and human to understand the significance of his animal nature.[21] The importance of "wolfishness" in Harry's characterization suggests that animality is key to understanding Hesse's text.

Because of two species merging in Harry—the wolf and the human being, one might say, co-constructed—the concept of animality as it is defined by Michael Lundblad is fruitful to draw on. Lundblad argues that rather than seeking to improve relationships between humans and non-humans, the emphasis in the field of animality studies "remains more on discursive constructions of animalities in relation to human cultural

---

[18] German original: "Ich stand einen Augenblick schnuppernd, roch an der blutigen grellen Musik, witterte böse und lüstern die Atmosphäre dieser Säle." Hesse, 38.

[19] Garry Marvin, *Wolf* (London: Reaktion, 2012), 7.

[20] Peter Arnds, *Lycanthropy in German Literature* (Houndmills, Basingstoke, Hampshire: Palgrave Macmillan, 2015), 1.

[21] Gallagher, 336.

politics ...."[22] Instead of focusing on "real" animals Lundblad suggests "animalities": "a set of dynamics that move beyond the human, to be defined as texts (broadly conceived, not just literary), discourses and material relationships that construct animals, on the one hand, or humans in relation to animals, on the other hand, or both."[23] Not tracing an *actual* animal in *Der Steppenwolf* but instead highlighting the discursive co-construction of the human and wolf within Harry is not to be seen as surrendering to anthropocentrism. As will be disclosed in this reading, what Hesse labels Harry's "wolfish nature" is never inferior to his "human nature." Actually, his animal side—the wolf—is elevated as an ideal.

Human-animal dualism

Scholarship has shown that Hesse's writings are characterized by dualisms that he attempts to synthesize.[24] In *Der Steppenwolf* one predominant dualism is between human and animal. This dichotomy is articulated through the juxtaposition of bourgeois culture and Harry Haller's outsider-status as a wolf. One could, of course, argue that the categories of "human" and "animal" are not really dual, since humans are also animals. Although as far as we know non-human animals are not concerned with the concept of bourgeois ideology. It is thus safe to assume that the bourgeoisie in *Der Steppenwolf* stands for the "human" whereas Harry represents what is "animal."

---

[22] Michael Lundblad, *Animalities: Literary and Cultural Studies Beyond the Human* (Edinburgh: Edinburgh University Press, 2017), 11.

[23] Lundblad, 1–2.

[24] One of Hesse's biographers, Walter Sorell, states that to Hesse "life consisted of a constant fluctuation between two poles, of a relentless oscillation between the two cornerstones of existence. He never tired of pointing to the duality of life since he never completely escaped from being pulled from one extreme to the other." (Walter Sorell, *Hermann Hesse: The Man Who Sought and Found Himself* [London: Oswald Wolff, 1974], 115.) And Wilbur B. Franklin asserts that in almost all of Hesse's writing "there is a longing to find a reconciliation of opposites, to discover an absolute behind the polarity in man's existence." (Wilbur B. Franklin, "The Concept of 'the Human' in the Work of Hermann Hesse and Paul Tillich.")

The bourgeoisie manifests itself as the norm with which the wolf's untamed otherness is measured, something to which Theodore Ziolkowski also alludes. With the wolf from the steppes, he claims, "Hesse was attempting to delineate his own specific situation: that of a man who felt himself to be so cut off from the world of normal people that he was like a wolf among the lambs of bourgeois society because his very existence threatened their ideals, beliefs, and way of life."[25] An iteration of this is visible in Hesse's novel when the protagonist moves into the neat, bourgeois home.[26] When the landlady and her nephew talk about Harry, she says: "Here it smells of cleanliness and order, and a welcoming, civilized life [...] He looks like he is no longer used to that and has missed it."[27] But Harry does not miss such a life. He is proud to be "*completely cut off from the bourgeois world*"[28] and although he grew up in a middle-class home, he has revolted against it. Harry believes himself to be someone who rises above "*the petty norms of average life*"[29] but he is, simultaneously, strangely drawn to bourgeois settings. Choosing to stay in a clean apartment in an urban environment, rather than remaining in nature, indicates that Harry is ambivalent about where he belongs.

The bourgeois culture surrounding Harry illuminates the conditions of his status as *Sonderling* (outsider), *Einsiedler* (hermit), or better yet, lone wolf. This is a point that resonates with Giorgio Agamben's thoughts on the *homo sacer* (Latin for "the sacred or *accursed* man" in ancient Roman law). In

---

[25] Theodore Ziolkowski, *The Novels of Hermann Hesse: A Study in Theme and Structure* (Princeton, N.J.: Princeton University Press, 1965), 179.

[26] Ziolkowski points out that *Der Steppenwolf* is "more overtly autobiographical than any of Hesse's other fiction. Almost every detail in the characterization of Harry Haller—from his sciatica and eyeglasses and general physical appearance to his reading habits and political views—is drawn from Hesse's own life and person." (Ziolkowski, 179.)

[27] German original: "Es riecht hier bei uns nach Sauberkeit und Ordnung und nach einem freundlichen und anständigen Leben ... Er sieht aus, wie wenn er daran nicht mehr gewöhnt wäre und es entbehrt hätte." Hesse, 10.

[28] German original: "*gänzlich außerhalb der bürgerlichen Welt*," Hesse, 53.

[29] German original: "*die kleinen Normen des Durchschnittslebens*," Hesse, 53.

Agamben's work the *homo sacer* comes into being in "a zone of indistinction between the human and the animal" and this creature is "a man who is transformed into a wolf and a wolf who is transformed into a man ...."[30] Agamben explains that the *homo sacer* has, from medieval times, been considered an outlaw. Banned from the city, he can be killed with impunity. The *homo sacer* is *friedlos* (without peace), which is a suitable description for Harry Haller. Although Hesse's novel is set inbetween the two World Wars, Harry is in a perpetual war with himself. The human and the wolf within him are in "*endless bitter enmity with each other*"[31] and Hesse even uses the *friedlos* term to describe Harry's species: "*Die friedlosen Steppenwölfe* ...."[32] Harry is thus perceived as an outlaw. Suspicious and threatening, he even avoids the police: "The man's wariness of seeming suspicious to the police matched his strange and otherworldly appearance."[33]

In light of Harry's fear of the law he does, on the one hand, embody the *homo sacer* perfectly. On the other hand, as Arnds asserts, iterations of the wolf in German literature are more complex than Agamben suggests.[34] *Der Steppenwolf* is a prime example of this complexity because while there are similarities between the *homo sacer* and Harry Haller (they are labeled outsiders, outlaws, and "wolf-men"), there are also divergencies. The *homo sacer* is banned from the city and forced to live in the woods. Harry remains, on the contrary, within city limits. The human part of his human-animal nature makes this a possibility. Since Harry passes for a human, he is not at risk of being killed

---

[30] Giorgio Agamben, *Homo Sacer: Sovereign Power and Bare Life*, trans. Daniel Heller-Roazen (Stanford, CA: Stanford University Press, 1998), 106. Editors' note: Concerning Agamben's concept *homo sacer*, see also Claudia Lindén's chapter in this volume.

[31] German original: "*ständiger Todfeindschaft gegeneinander*," Hesse, 46.

[32] Hesse, 57.

[33] German original: "Gerade zu dem Unvertrauten und Fremden, das der Mann an sich hatte, schien mir diese Scheu vor der Polizei allzu gut zu passen, um nicht als verdächtig aufzufallen." Hesse, 9.

[34] Arnds, 2.

by the city inhabitants. Instead he contemplates taking his own life, thus fulfilling the promise of what Agamben calls "the Ban" himself. Moreover, Harry is not a forest wolf, which according to Arnds is the more conventional version of this animal in German literature: "Being a wolf of the steppes and not of the forest (*Waldwolf*) may be a significant detail in connection with [Haller's] lack of patriotism, with Haller's un-German, if not foreign nature."[35] In a German context the word "steppe," which refers to ecoregions in Eurasia characterized by desolate, grassland plains without trees, is foreign. The word also connotes perceptibility, since on a steppe there are no trees to hide behind. We are, apparently, encouraged to truly observe the Steppenwolf-part of Harry's nature and to identify with the outsider who rejects bourgeois conformism.

In German literature the wolf as a metaphor, Arnds writes, is a reflection of "bourgeois anxieties about crime, vagrancy, invasion, and idleness …."[36] In Hesse's novel there are examples of all these fears: The landlady's nephew notices Harry's apprehension toward the police (crime); Harry is homeless and has a nomadic lifestyle (vagrancy); the fact that Harry passes for a "normal" bourgeois human makes him an infiltrating threat to that society (invasion); and since his purpose in the world of the bourgeois is unclear—that he, an intellectual, prefers to contemplate in solitude rather than partake in bourgeois sociality—may, in fact, be regarded as a threat to modernist conceptions of progress (idleness). Harry is, accordingly, labelled "asocial," and "a strange, wild […] creature from another world […]."[37]

As we have seen, Harry has little reverence for the norms of the bourgeoisie. He is able to tolerate the middle-class because he is not a part of it: "I also appreciate the contrast between my life—my lonely, loveless and haunted, thoroughly messy life—

---

[35] Arnds, 103.
[36] Arnds, 8.
[37] German original: "ungesellig"; "ein fremdes, wildes […] Wesen aus einer anderen Welt […]." Hesse, 7.

and this family-like, bourgeois environment."[38] Although throughout history, the wolf has often been regarded a threat to humans, Arnds states that it has also been a bearer of superior characteristics such as valiancy and nobility.[39] This vacillation between antagonistic and idealized Other is integral to the figure of Harry Haller. What sets him apart from human culture is that he desires "enjoyment, experience, ecstasy and elevation,"[40] and especially the final expression, elevation, suggests that Hesse uses the animal part of Harry as a means of illuminating transcendence from the one-sidedness and mediocrity of human life.

Wilbur B. Franklin argues that since Hesse's writing "dwells in the inner, subjective experiences of his heroes" and focus less on interpersonal relationships, it is useful in defining what is human.[41] Franklin equates what it means to be human with the ability to *think*, which is a common characteristic in Hesse's heroes. *Der Steppenwolf* is an exception, however, since it attempts to demarcate what it might mean to be an animal. In the novel Hesse posits the animal as the "thinker." Harry Haller/the wolf is portrayed as an intellectual whose philosophical aptitude supersedes other humans, whom he labels "monkeys."[42] It is interesting that Hesse uses monkeys as a symbol for the futility of being human. Even though primates are generally regarded intelligent, humans described as monkeys can be seen in two ways. Monkeys can function as signifiers of the animal side of man—that man, too, is an animal—but in *Der Steppenwolf* they primarily represent the "unevolved" human. Hesse's text conveys that humans, like primates, may be intelligent, have high levels of cognition, possess language, and are able to solve problems, but Harry's wolf-nature represents a more evolved sort of being. It does, therefore, establish a hier-

---

[38] German original: "ich habe auch den Kontrast gern, in dem mein Leben, mein einsames, liebloses und gehetztes, durch und durch unordentliches Leben, zu diesem Familien- und Bürgermilieu steht." Hesse, 29.

[39] Arnds, 1.

[40] German original: "Wonne, Erlebnis, Ekstase und Erhebung," Hesse, 32.

[41] Franklin, 77.

[42] German original: "Affen," Hesse, 13.

archy among non-human animals wherein primates are categorized as an unevolved species. In light of the novel's frequent use of the "N-word" as a derogatory label for black, "uncultivated" individuals who prefer jazz music to Mozart—and repeatedly are labelled "monkey-like"—the text's idealized conception of the *white* wolf-man is problematic.[43]

Also, labelling the wolf "ideal" has other troubling discursive implications since in Nazi Germany wolves were greatly revered and from the beginning of the Second World War, lycanthropic folklore was revitalized by Nazi's who upheld the mythical figure of the werewolf as a representation of German purity and strength.[44] Nazi U-boats were referred to as "wolf packs" and Hitler gave three of his headquarters wolfish names, among them *Wolfsschanze* (Wolf's Lair) in East Prussia.[45] Also, "Adolf" is derived from *Athalwolf*, an Old High German name meaning "noble wolf" which may account for why Hitler referred to himself as a wolf—his favorite pseudonym—on several occasions during the war.[46] Additional troubling connections between *Der Steppenwolf* and Nazi ideology are pointed out by Andrew Hollis who suggests that Hesse's writings are characterized by political ambiguity since the author himself was a pacifist and anti-nationalist whose work was still read by many of his adversaries, that is, people whose political and ideological convictions bordered on National Socialism.[47] *Der Steppenwolf's* wolf-theme in particular makes Hesse's political ambiguity visible. Harry Haller may be openly critical of nationalism but in the early twentieth century when the novel was written, German

[43] For further reading on the troubling depictions of black individuals in *Der Steppenwolf*, see chapter 3 in Mark Christian Thompson, *Anti-Music: Jazz and Racial Blackness in German Thought Between the Wars* (Albany: State University of New York Press, 2018).

[44] Eric Kurlander, *Hitler's Monsters: A Supernatural History of the Third Reich* (New Haven, CT: Yale University Press, 2018), 278–281.

[45] Marvin, 75–78.

[46] Marcel Atze, *"Unser Hitler": Der Hitler-Mythos im Spiegel der Deutschsprachigen Literatur nach 1945* (Göttingen: Wallstein, 2003), 385.

[47] Andrew Hollis, "Political Ambivalence in Hesse's 'Steppenwolf,'" *The Modern Language Review* 73, no. 1 (1978): 110.

wolf-man narratives actually tended to give voice to national conservative ideas.[48] Although Hesse's intention was likely not to promote aggressive nationalism there are indications in *Der Steppenwolf* that his protagonist considers the *Bürger* (common man) expendable: "*a few million more or less do not matter, they are substance, nothing else.*"[49] Harry's view of the middle-class is contrasted with his own elevated wolf-nature. Also, the ominous reference to "*a third Reich*"[50] for those who can outgrow bourgeois mediocrity is certainly problematic in the wake of the Nazi reign. Today's readers should bear in mind, however, that Hesse wrote his novel before Hitler began to publicly idealize wolves. Any discursive correlations between the two should thus not reflect negatively on the author. Hesse was, in fact, writing about wolves already in 1907 when he authored a short story about a wolf who is hunted and killed—a story that predates Hitler's public reverence for the animal with decades.

It is evident so far that a great deal of ambivalence surrounds the wolf as a symbol. Hesse's *Der Steppenwolf* conveys an array of associations, from Nazi icon to *friedlos* outcast and, as we shall see in the following, its wolf-man is also associated with *queerness*.

Queerness in the wolf

When "queer" is understood as a signifier of that which disrupts normative conceptions of gender and sexuality, the wolf-part of Harry accentuates a connection between animality and queerness in *Der Steppenwolf*. As George Chauncey points out (albeit

[48] Axel Goodbody, "Wolves and Wolf Men as Literary Tropes and Figures of Thought: Eco- and Zoopoetic Perspectives on Jiang Rong's *Wolf Totem* and Other Wolf Narratives," in *Texts, Animals, Environments. Zoopoetics and Ecopoetics* (Freiburg i. Br.: Rombach, 2019), 318–319. Goodbody lists Hermann Löns' *Der Wehrwolf* (1910) and Ernst Wiechert's *Der Totenwolf* (1924) as wolf-man narratives conveying national conservatism.

[49] German original: "*es kommt auf ein paar Millionen mehr oder weniger nicht an, sie sind Material, sonst nichts.*" Hesse, 66.

[50] German original: "*ein drittes Reich*," Hesse, 57.

in a North American context), the term "wolf" was frequently used in the early twentieth century within the context of male same-sex acts. Wolves, Chauncey writes, were men who "abided by the conventions of masculinity and yet exhibited a decided preference for male sexual partners."[51] The correlation between wolves and homosexuality is also alluded to by Freud in his 1918 study of "the Wolf-man," a latent homosexual. It even manifests itself in the werewolf,[52] of which Phillip A. Bernhardt-House writes: "The werewolf is generally seen as a 'hybrid' figure of sorts—part human and part wolf—and its hybridity and transgression of species boundaries in a unified figure is, at very least, unusual, thus the figure of the werewolf might be seen as a natural signifier for queerness in its myriad forms."[53] The werewolf—wolf-man—is an iteration of the *homo sacer* and while the *homo sacer* has no overtly queer characteristics, its status as an *outlaw* mirror the fact that homosexuality was illegal in Germany until as late as 1994.

That Harry is an outsider can, on the one hand, be seen as a self-made choice by an elitist intellectual. On the other hand, as exclusion from normative society because of his norm-challenging wolf-man nature: "my life is sort of unusual, I exist somewhere in the margin,"[54] he explains. In contrast to the humans around him, Harry's animality makes him a norm-breaker and

---

[51] George Chauncey, *Gay New York: Gender, Urban Culture, and the Making of the Gay Male World, 1890–1940* (New York: Basic Books, 1994), 87.

[52] The research field on the mythology of werewolves is too vast and varied to be accounted for in full here. For further reading, see, e.g., Montague Summers' groundbreaking study from 1933 in which historical documents and folklore from throughout Europe are examined: Montague Summers, *The Werewolf in Lore and Legend* (Mineola, N.Y.: Dover, 2003). Further reading on werewolves in literature can be found in Brian J. Frost, *The Essential Guide to Werewolf Literature* (Madison: University of Wisconsin Press, 2003), wherein the werewolf myth is traced from its origins in superstitious beliefs to its iterations in contemporary horror and fantasy fiction.

[53] Phillip A. Bernhardt-House, "The Werewolf as Queer, the Queer as Werewolf, and Queer Werewolves," in *Queering the Non/Human* (Aldershot, Hampshire: Ashgate, 2008), 159.

[54] German original: "ich lebe so etwas abseits, etwas am Rande," Hesse, 18.

this is enhanced by the novel's queer aspects. The similarities between Harry's human-animal nature and Hermine's gender non-binarism connotes queerness in and around both of them. In one of the few analyses of Hesse's literature wherein queerness is emphasized, Craig Bernard Palmer states: "In addition to being both real and symbolic, Hermine is also simultaneously male and female and thus can bond with Harry on both the homosocial and heterosexual level."[55] Palmer argues that Hermine's gender fluidity opens up for a form of male bonding that allows Harry to express repressed homoerotic urges. "By fulfilling Harry's homosocial needs in her female persona," he writes, "she is able to bypass the shame associated with those needs by men."[56] Since Hermine also introduces Harry to Pablo, she facilitates the same-sex desire hinted at in their interactions. Although Harry declines a sexual invitation from Pablo, one of the hidden traits revealed in the Magic Theater is Harry's latent homosexuality. During this surrealistic episode Harry observes several iterations of himself in a mirror; one of them is "a young, elegant fellow [who] threw himself, laughing, at Pablo, embraced him and ran away with him."[57] Harry clearly has a latent desire for men.

Hermine as a facilitator for same-sex desire is underscored by the fact that her most significant purpose appears to be as a *teacher* to the protagonist. Not only does she teach Harry how to dance but also, by pairing him with the prostitute Maria— with whom Harry, in accordance with Hermine's directives, engages sexually—she "schools" him in sexual practice. As a wolf, Harry's sexual engagement with Maria is curious since among wolves the common social formation is a male and a female with the intent to *breed*—a heterosexual *reproductive*

---

[55] Palmer, Craig Bernard. "The Significance of Homosexual Desire in Modern German Literature." Missouri: Washington University St. Louis, 1997. Published online [accessed 03-02-2021].

[56] Palmer, 20.

[57] German original: "ein junger eleganter Kerl, sprang dem Pablo lachend an die Brust, umarmte ihn und lief mit ihm davon." Hesse, 169.

unit.[58] But neither Harry nor Maria express desire to mate long-term or have children; their sex is recreational, "for fun." The wolf-part in Harry thus rejects his species-specific heterosexual breeding convention, a rejection that is mirrored by the human part of him: "*he knew neither family life nor social ambition* [...]."[59] Harry calls his previous family life "zusammengebrochen" (69) (collapsed) and the vague hints of a distant girl with whom he has an uncommitted relationship does not indicate an ambition to procreate. Harry's status as a lone wolf is thus emphasized. At the same time, he needs Hermine to teach him how to have sex with Maria—in a sense Hermine "tames" and socializes him—which challenges the conception that heterosexuality comes more "natural" than other sexualities. The fact that a figure like Hermine, who transcends normative conceptions of gender, is the educator in these specific topics makes visible the queer implications of *Der Steppenwolf*. Hermine and Harry—queerness and animality—work in tandem to disrupt normative notions of reproductive heterosexuality.

To Harry, however, his potential for queerness also provokes anxiety. This is apparent when he murders Hermine and since she is a gender non-conformist, her murder is, in reality, a "crime of passion" with transphobic overtones. However, while she can be regarded as Harry's "mirror-image," her death can be seen as a symbolic representation of Harry's suicide.[60] Ralph Freedman, among others, argues that "the characters [in *Der Steppenwolf*] are intricate mirrors for one another."[61] Hermine says to Harry: "I am a sort of mirror for you [...]."[62] Also, Hermine demands from Harry that he kills her: "You will follow

[58] Mech and Boitani, 1–2.

[59] German original: "*er [kannte] weder Familienleben noch sozialen Ehrgeiz [...].*" Hesse, 53.

[60] Cf. Andreas Kiryakakis, *The Ideal of Heimat in the Works of Hermann Hesse* (New York: Peter Lang, 1988), 138.

[61] Ralph Freedman, *Hermann Hesse: Pilgrim of Crisis. A Biography* (London: Cape, 1979), 287.

[62] German original: "ich [bin] wie eine Art Spiegel für dich [...]." Hesse, 106.

my command and *kill me.*[63] Her command clearly mirrors Harry's own suicidal contemplations. Therefore, when Hermine is read as Harry's reflection, her murder becomes an expression of Harry's internalized homo- and transphobia. In the murder of Hermine we see Harry's fear of his own fragmented nature, as well as his fear of the fluid, queer sexuality he himself possesses. This is one explanation of Harry's homophobic hesitation toward Pablo and his reluctance to accept Pablo's sexual advances.

Conclusion

The aim of this reading has been to trace the wolf in *Der Steppenwolf.* In the introduction it was suggested that the novel's protagonist has a dual nature that accentuates otherness. It was argued that being half man, half wolf—an animal that is regarded the ultimate symbol of the wild—signals that Harry is an untamed creature. The analysis has shown that the wolf in Hesse's complex novel vacillates between an idealized and antagonistic image. Its multifaceted and contradictory implica-tions are also stressed by Alexander Mathäs who argues that "the Steppenwolf, as a symbol with manifold meanings, stands for 'the Animal' in general, and as such for the human other, in that it both distinguishes itself from the human but also embodies it. The Steppenwolf, on the one hand, marks the uncivilized abject, and on the other a purportedly more genuine, uncorrupted human nature worthy of preservation."[64] If we recall the previ-ously quoted passage by Adorno and Horkheimer about how human beings in European history have "distinguished them-selves *from animals,"* Hesse reverses this assessment—in *Der Steppenwolf* it is an animal that distinguishes itself *from humans.*

In elevating the wolf, *Der Steppenwolf,* on the one hand, can be said to criticize the anthropocentric paradigm. Moreover, it offers an expanded concept of diversity and inclusivity that

---

[63] German original: "Du wirst meinen Befehl erfüllen und *wirst mich töten."* Hesse, 108.

[64] Mathäs, 244–245.

moves beyond the human-wolf binary: "*The division of wolf and man, instinct and spirit, through which Harry seeks to understand his fate is a great simplification [...] Harry does not consist of two beings, but of hundreds, of thousands.*"[65] This quote suggests that Hesse advocates peaceful co-existence and kinship between human beings and wolves, as well as other animals. On the other hand, elevating the wolf conveys a hierarchy among non-human animals. Monkeys, which are compared to the peripheral black people in the novel, represent a lower, unevolved animality that the wolf within Harry has "distinguished himself from." Based on the comparison between racial blackness and a low form of animality, the protagonist comes across as racist. In reproducing racist stereotypes and promoting racial inequality to foster "wolf-agency" in *Der Steppenwolf*, its anthropocentric critique is thus arbitrary. Harry's racism combined with his internalized and external trans- and homophobia makes him profoundly unsympathetic. While he himself embodies queerness (such as a latent desire for men) the murder of Hermine accentuates fear of his own fluid, queer sexuality. What is evident, conclusively, is that Harry is disgusted by everyone, including himself. His disgust for others is primarily articulated in his feelings for the bourgeoisie, but Harry's elitism is equally visible in his reverence for Mozart, Goethe and the Immortals, and further contrasted with his disdain for jazz. Mark Christian Thompson argues that in *Der Steppenwolf* jazz is equated with racial blackness and he also suggests that blackness is an element of the protagonist's multifaceted identity: "To represent race and near-vestigial blackness in Haller," Thompson writes, "Hesse simply figures his 'inner crisis' as that between man (European, German) and animal (black, jazz, recalling that both blackness and jazz were considered bestial before, during, and well beyond the 1920s)."[66]

---

[65] German original: "*Die Zweiteilung in Wolf und Mensch, in Trieb und Geist, durch welche Harry sich sein Schicksal verständlicher zu machen sucht, ist eine sehr große Vereinfachung ... Harry besteht nicht aus zwei Wesen, sondern aus hundert, aus tausenden.*" Hesse, 59–60.
[66] Thompson, 62.

Harry fears what is black within himself and if we recall the example of him "sniffing" outside a jazz club, contemplating whether or not to enter, he *lustfully* senses the atmosphere" inside. This indicates ambivalence. Sensing the atmosphere of the club makes Harry acknowledge the depth of his otherness and not entering—because of his racism—echoes his internalized trans- and homophobia.

In light of Harry Haller's racist, elitist and phobic tendencies, his only redeeming feature is perhaps his self-loathing. His fear of his own complex nature makes him *friedlos,* without peace, and his "war-like" internal struggle—his intense self-hatred—comes to fruition in his repulsion for others. At the end of the novel, when Pablo and Mozart appear as the same person, we see an iteration of what Harry aspires to be. If he can finally learn to perceive himself as more than just a wolf and a man—that is, to synthesize into "not two beings, but hundreds, *thousands"*—he will be allowed to enter the peaceful realm of the Immortals. For Harry, achieving peace is thus more than synthesizing his humanity and animality. Rather, the synthesis for which he craves is between a myriad of contradictions.

References

Adorno, Theodor W. "Notes on Kafka." In *Prisms*, 243–271. Translated by Samuel and Shierry Weber. Cambridge, MA: The MIT Press, 1981.

Agamben, Giorgio. *Homo Sacer: Sovereign Power and Bare Life.* Translated by Daniel Heller-Roazen. Stanford, CA: Stanford University Press, 1998.

Armstrong, Philip. *What Animals Mean in the Fiction of Modernity.* London: Routledge, 2008.

Arnds, Peter. *Lycanthropy in German Literature.* Houndmills, Basingstoke, Hampshire: Palgrave Macmillan, 2015.

Atze, Marcel. *"Unser Hitler": Der Hitler-Mythos im Spiegel der Deutschsprachigen Literatur nach 1945.* Göttingen: Wallstein, 2003.

Benjamin, Walter. "The Task of the Translator." Translated by Harry Zohn. In *The Translation Studies Reader*, 15–25. Edited by Lawrence Venuti. London: Routledge, 2000.

Bernhardt-House, Phillip A. "The Werewolf as Queer, the Queer as Werewolf, and Queer Werewolves." In *Queering the Non/Human*,

159–183. Edited by Noreen Giffney and Myra J. Hird. Aldershot, Hampshire: Ashgate, 2008.

Chauncey, George. *Gay New York: Gender, Urban Culture, and the Making of the Gay Male World, 1890–1940*. New York: Basic Books, 1994.

Franklin, Wilbur B. "The Concept of 'the Human' in the Work of Hermann Hesse and Paul Tillich."

Freedman, Ralph. *Hermann Hesse: Pilgrim of Crisis. A Biography*. London: Cape, 1979.

Freud, Sigmund. *The 'Wolfman'* [*From the* History of an Infantile Neurosis]. Translated by Louise Adey Huish. London: Penguin Books, 2010.

Fritts, Steven H., Robert O. Stephenson, Robert D. Hayes, and Luigi Boitani. "Wolves and Humans." In *Wolves: Behavior, Ecology, and Conservation*, 289–316. Edited by L. David Mech and Luigi Boitani. Chicago: University of Chicago, 2003.

Frost, Brian J. *The Essential Guide to Werewolf Literature*. Madison: University of Wisconsin Press, 2003.

Gallagher, David. *Metamorphosis: Transformations of the Body and the Influence of Ovid's Metamorphoses on Germanic Literature of the Nineteenth and Twentieth Centuries*. Amsterdam: Rodopi, 2009.

Gerhardt, Christina. "The Ethics of Animals in Adorno and Kafka." *New German Critique*, no. 97 (2006): 159–178.

Goodbody, Axel. "Wolves and Wolf Men as Literary Tropes and Figures of Thought: Eco- and Zoopoetic Perspectives on Jiang Rong's *Wolf Totem* and Other Wolf Narratives." In *Texts, Animals, Environments. Zoopoetics and Ecopoetics*, 307–324. Edited by Frederike Middelhoff, Sebastian Schönbeck, Roland Borgards, and Catrin Gersdorf. Freiburg i. Br.: Rombach, 2019.

Hesse, Hermann. *Der Steppenwolf*. In *Sämtliche Werke. Band 4: Die Romane. Der Steppenwolf, Narziß und Goldmund, Die Morgenlandfahrt*, 5–203. Edited by Volker Michaels. Berlin: Suhrkamp Verlag, 2001.

Hollis, Andrew. "Political Ambivalence in Hesse's 'Steppenwolf'." *The Modern Language Review* 73, no. 1 (1978): 110–118.

Horkheimer, Max and Theodor W. Adorno. *Dialectic of Enlightenment*. Translated by John Cumming. New York: Continuum, 1989.

Kiryakakis, Andreas. *The Ideal of Heimat in the Works of Hermann Hesse*. New York: Peter Lang, 1988.

Kurlander, Eric. *Hitler's Monsters: A Supernatural History of the Third Reich*. New Haven, CT: Yale University Press, 2018.

Lundblad, Michael. *Animalities: Literary and Cultural Studies Beyond the Human*. Edinburgh: Edinburgh University Press, 2017.

Lönngren, Ann-Sofie. *Following the Animal: Power, Agency, and Human-animal Transformations in Modern, Northern-European Literature.* Newcastle upon Tyne: Cambridge Scholars Publishing, 2015.

Marvin, Garry. *Wolf.* London: Reaktion, 2012.

Mathäs, Alexander. *Beyond Posthumanism: The German Humanist Tradition and the Future of the Humanities.* New York and Oxford: Berghahn Books, 2020.

McHugh, Susan. *Animal Stories: Narrating Across Species Lines.* Minneapolis: University of Minnesota Press, 2011.

Mech, L. David and Luigi Boitani. *Wolves: Behavior, Ecology, and Conservation.* Chicago: University of Chicago, 2003.

Palmer, Craig Bernard. "The Significance of Homosexual Desire in Modern German Literature." Missouri: Washington University St. Louis, 1997. Published online [accessed 03–02–2021]

Sorell, Walter. *Hermann Hesse: The Man Who Sought and Found Himself.* London: Oswald Wolff, 1974.

Summers, Montague. *The Werewolf in Lore and Legend.* Mineola, N.Y.: Dover, 2003.

Thompson, Mark Christian. *Anti-Music: Jazz and Racial Blackness in German Thought Between the Wars.* Albany: State University Of New York Press, 2018.

Ziolkowski, Theodore. *The Novels of Hermann Hesse: A Study in Theme and Structure.* Princeton, N.J.: Princeton University Press, 1965.

Killing Animals to Spare Them

Karin Dirke

In the late 19th century a sentimental verse, The horse's prayer, was circulated in Swedish schools and animal welfare organizations. The verse, of unknown origin, was distributed in various versions by animal welfare societies in the western world around the turn of the century. The poem was a reflection of Anna Sewell's story *Black Beauty* (1877), told from the perspective of the horse, in first person.[1] The horse asks the human to treat it kindly and to recognize the sacrifice of the animal.

> [...]
> I carry you, I pull you,
> I only live for you.
> You know I can't
> speak of my suffering
> but God will reward you.
> At last,
> when my strength is gone,
> take my life
> in the least painful way.[2]

The ending of the verse is a nexus of the 19th century paradoxical relation to animals, i.e. their suffering and death. The loyalty and work of the horse is the point of departure of the poem, though its final solution is the killing of the animal. While having its

[1] The verse is widely known in western horse culture, though I have been unable to unravel the details of its origin. Editors' note: Concerning Sewell's *Black Beauty* see also Sune Borkfelt's and Claudia Lindén's chapters in this volume.

[2] This author's translation from the version of the poem appearing in Anne Hedén, Ulrika Milles och Moa Matthis (eds), *Över alla hinder: en civilisationshistoria* (Bonnier, Stockholm, 2003). The Swedish version reads as follows: "[...] jag bär dig, jag drar dig/ jag lever endast för dig/ Du vet att jag inte kan/ tala om min nöd/ Men Gud skall belöna dig/ Till sist, / då mina krafter är slut,/ tag mitt liv/ på minst plågsamma sätt."

roots in the nineteenth century, the poem has since been reproduced and circulated widely.

This chapter concerns the nineteenth century view of the
suffering and death of animals and how it was tackled by animal
protectionists. The chapter sets out to investigate how ultimately, animal protection resulted in the killing of animals. The
empirical example and focus of the chapter is the writings of a
poet, newspaper maker and horse slaughterer—Karl Johan
Ekeblad (1817–1895)—active in Stockholm, Sweden, in the
middle of the nineteenth century.

Ekeblad's time period was characterized by great change in
Sweden, just like in the rest of Europe. Sweden was in the midst
of industrialization, a process that brought with it worker's
protests and organization. Politically, there was also a shift in
Sweden resulting in the establishment of a two-chamber parlia-
mentary system. The transformation of political power during
the nineteenth century, described by Michel Foucault as the
development of biopower, the "power to make live and let die",
can be amply illustrated by Ekeblad's political mission.[3] While
Foucault himself did not include animals in his analysis, scholars
following him have shown how the concept of biopower can be
expanded to the agricultural and indeed the non-human world
of food production.[4] In the following I will discuss how the
"power to make live and let die" was played out in nineteenth
century animal protection, and how the death of animals was
understood. Animals were used to discuss the discipline of the
lower classes, becoming, as it were, proxy objects for this
mission.

The animal welfare movement, which emerged in Sweden
and in the rest of Europe during the nineteenth century, considered the love of animals to be the most significant and
altruistic form of affection. At the same time, the foremost
method for expressing such love was to kill animals. This chap-

---

[3] As a point of comparison, see the discussion of the biopolitical contests in British
romanticism Ron Broglio, *Beasts of Burden: Biopolitics, Labor, and Animal Life in
British Romanticism* (State University of New York Press, 2017).
[4] Broglio, 8.

ter explores the ideas underpinning these measures. How and why did death become the animal welfare movement's best method for saving animals?

The slaughterer

The horse slaughterer Karl Johan Ekeblad was a remarkable figure in the city crowd of Stockholm. Fredrika Bremer, the well-known philanthropist and women's rights activist, wrote about him in her essays. Crippled by an accident at an early age, Ekeblad was noted both for his bodily appearance and for his unusual combination of livelihood: poetry, newspaper making and slaughter.[5] In 1849, following the worker uprisings of 1848, he published the newspaper *Folkbladet*. It was royalist in content, offering a message of reconciliation and anticommunism, aimed at the working class. He also published romantic poetry and several pamphlets on the care of horses and how to relieve poverty by serving horse meat to the poor. There are great similarities in style between Ekeblad's poetry and his nonfictional writing. Both are predominantly romantic, sentimental and royalist. His overall aim was to mediate his conservative, yet socially aware, message to the general public. Ekeblad strived to express sympathy with the working class, while discouraging them from revolutionary tendencies. He was supported by the upper class and was later discovered to have, in exchange for payment, provided the superintendent with information about the atmosphere among the workers.[6] Ekeblad's mission was class bridging; while he often directed his ideas to the upper class, his aim was to change the behavior of the working classes.

In 19th century Stockholm, the occupation of slaughterer was considered a brutal identity. The act of slaughtering was often performed in the city center. Before possibilities for refrigeration, the most efficient way to preserve fresh meat was to keep it

---

[5] Fredrika Bremer, "Mitt Fönster 1855," in *Skisser, uppsatser och poem* (Stockholm; Beijers 1912), 34.

[6] John Björkman, *"Må de herrskande klasserna darra." Radikal retorik och reaktion i Stockholms press, 1848–1851* (Möklinta: Gidlunds förlag 2020), 192–193.

alive. Therefore, animals were driven into the city center to be slaughtered close by the meat markets. In this way both animals, and their death, had prominent visibility in the city. People could see the animals, hear and smell their death. The slaughterer was viewed with contempt. The work of the butcher was demanded yet at the same time despised. At the bottom of social hierarchy was the horse slaughterer. Horse slaughter was traditionally seen as the lowest form of butchery, comparable to the work of the executioner. Horse meat was believed to be taboo and was not fit for consumption. Therefore, dead horses' bodies were considered to be a waste, at best used as bait for the purpose of killing carnivores.[7]

Despite all this, Ekeblad was a respected character in mid-century Stockholm. Bremer described Ekeblad as a moral paragon, as a character and as an animal friend. She admired him for his passion for animals and his mission to protect them from suffering. Ekeblad's plight for animal welfare made him prominent among men, stated Bremer. He was one of very few men, she wrote, who took an interest in animals and their wellbeing, just like many women of his time.[8] When Ekeblad was active as a horse slaughterer, animal welfare as an organized movement had not yet been established in Sweden. However, there was a lively movement in England for the defense of animals. Laws had been established in England to protect animals, and in 1824 the first Society for the Protection of Animals was founded. This association which soon gained the interest of queen Victoria and would later become the RSPCA.[9]

---

[7] Brita Egardt has written about horse slaughter from an ethnological point of view in her dissertation *Hästslakt och rackarskam: en etnologisk undersökning av folkliga fördomar* (Stockholm: Nordiska muséet, 1962). How the horse's body was used as bait is discussed in Bergström, Dirke, Danell "The Wolf War in Sweden during the Eighteenth Century—Strategies, Measures and Leaders" in *A Fairytale in Question: Historical Interactions Between Humans and Wolves* (Cambridge: White Horse Press, 2015), 57–78.

[8] Bremer, 34.

[9] Harriet Ritvo, *The Animal Estate: the English and Other Creatures in the Victorian age* (1987; repr., Penguin, London, 1990), 129.

For Fredrika Bremer, the protection of animals was linked to a wider movement of philanthropy with its roots in England. In a footnote in her text about Ekeblad, Bremer notes that Sweden has since accepted a law for the protection of animals (1857).[10] Standing on the city square, where she would often spot him, Bremer described Ekeblad as a rare figure, an original and an unusual character. Bremer understood Ekeblad's low-ranking status as a slaughterer. She explicitly contrasted it to his elevated position as an animal friend, and moral paragon. Her discussion of him aimed at highlighting the contrast between his high moral standards and his low social rank. Issues of status and social order in general became central to the discussions about animal welfare. Ekeblad is, Bremer concluded, a horse slaughterer by profession but a horse lover in mind. He helps both the animals that suffer and the humans who agonize from witnessing cruelty; and even though, as Bremer states, he has been laughed at and despised, Ekeblad kept on campaigning for the welfare of horses.[11]

Ekeblad was well known in Stockholm at the time. He was talked about not only for his poetry and his political engagement but primarily for his campaign for getting people to accept eating horse meat. Promoting the consumption of horse meat became an especially important issue for Ekeblad. In pamphlets and in practice he argued for the consumption of tastey and wholesome horse meat. Ekeblad's idea was that if the horse received a value as dead meat, it would encourage people to treat them well, feed them and then kill them, rather than work them to death under a rider or in front of a carriage. Overworked draught horses were obviously a common sight on the streets of the city.

Ekeblad's starting point was eminently practical. He imagined that many edible and useful products were to be found in people's surroundings, if only they could gain knowledge of their utility by letting go of their prejudices. He suggested dif-

---

[10] Bremer, 33.
[11] Bremer, 33.

ferent kinds of lichen to be used by poor people for food. The aim was to encourage people to collect whatever nature had to offer, rather than to burden the poor relief. This would also promote good morals, Ekeblad argued.[12] He suggested that the children of the poor should be taught to collect lichen, and went so far as to print recipes for how to cook them. He argued in a similar way for the eating of horse meat. The traditional prejudices against the practice, in the form of a catholic taboo against eating horse, were seen as a hinderance. In the same way the prejudice against eating fruits, mushrooms and lichen stopped people from using the products of nature, Ekeblad argued.[13] Horse meat, mushrooms and lichen, Ekeblad imagined, could be consumed by lower classes though they were not intended for the well to do. The aim was thus both to fight poverty and to promote the welfare of horses. Ekeblad wrote:

> All begging would end and all poverty be banished, if the morally better and educated people all over the nation would enter a great and holy covenant, and with warmth and love attempt to convince the poor man, that nature provides him with the means of an honest livelihood without him having to be a burden to his fellow men.[14]

Such was Ekeblad's mission: disciplining the lower classes to make use of food from nature, including horse meat. The idea was to facilitate the moral improvement of the poor by putting them to work. The unarticulated aim, but obvious starting point,

---

[12] Karl Johan Ekeblad, *Hjelp i nöden, eller råd till allmogen, att under swåra år och wid smärre tillgångar till föda för sig och husdjuren anwända några helsosamma och födande wildt wäxande naturalster, på hwilka å landet finnes ymnig tillgång, och som utan penningar kunna anskaffas äfwen af den fattigaste*, 2. betydligt tillökta och förb. uppl., (Lundberg, Stockholm, 1847).

[13] Ekeblad, *Hjelp*, 18.

[14] Ekeblad, *Hjelp*, 52. Author's translation. Swedish original: "Allt tiggeri skulle kunna afskaffas och all nöd afhjelpas, om de bättre och bildade öfwerallt i riket ingingo ett stort och heligt förbund, att med wärma och kärlek söka öfwertyga den fattige, att naturen sjielfmant gifwer honom medel till ärlig bergning utan att han behöfwer ligga medmenniskor till last."

was to uphold the status quo. Ekeblad's struggle was conservative at the core. Horse meat was a wasted resource that should be used, he reasoned. For charity, Ekeblad himself cooked soup from horse meat and offered it to the poor.

Death as a savior

Not only did the horse meat feed the poor, it also gave the horse a value outside its ability to work. Thus, for Ekeblad, the commodification of horses' bodies was a way of protecting them. Killing horses instead of working them to death meant their passing would come earlier, before becoming ill and overworked. The idea of death as a *savior* was a supposition. This idea—death as the solution to the problem of an intolerable life—grew in the nineteenth century, particularly in relation to animals. Just like in the poem, "The Horse's prayer", the idea was that animals accepted to work for humans if they were treated well, and would be killed before their life became unbearable.

The basis for this idea can be found in Jeremy Bentham's writings. In the revolutionary year of 1789 he stated, in a famous footnote to his *An Introduction to the Principles of Morals and Legislation,* that animals do have interests but they cannot premeditate death, and therefore do not fear it. Passing away is thus not harmful to animals. Provided their death is quick and painless it can, on the contrary, contribute to the total happiness in the world. With death, an animal's suffering is ended while its body provides meat and other products for humans. By including animals in his theory of the maximization of happiness, as well as stating that animal lives lacked intrinsic value, Bentham established the theoretical and moral grounds for killing animals. The focus was instead directed to the suffering of animals, which was to be limited by all means necessary. In his famous footnote concerning animals, Bentham states: "[…] the question is not: Can they *reason*? nor, Can they *talk*? but can they *suffer*?"[15] Bentham has been championed by animal welfare

---

[15] Jeremy Bentham, *An Introduction to the Principles of Morals and Legislation* (Athlone Press: London, 1970), 283n.

societies as a forerunner of ideas concerning the moral treatment of animals.

To kill in order to relieve suffering is a good example of what Foucault speaks about as biopower. Foucault describes the biopolitical rule as the power to make live and to let die. The "let die" part of biopower, however requires a distinction of bodies, a set of tools to distinguish whose life is livable and whose is not.[16] Animals were useful in this way because they had hitherto always been considered to be different.[17] Ekeblad, and for that matter the whole animal welfare movement, argued that animals should be protected *because of* and not despite their difference to humans. Precisely because they lacked linguistic ability, democratic rights or power, animals were worthy of protection.[18] Therefore, the argument worked in two ways: on the one hand, asking for liberation and the recognition of the necessity of animal welfare, but on the other hand strongly anchoring animal protection in the existing social order.[19] The argument counteracted any radical ideas of likeness between human and animal as well as any ideas of animals having rights to claim. Underpinning the allegation was an unarticulated threat, directed to both animals and the lower classes: stay submissive or you will no longer be worthy of our help.

Contrary to the poor, animals did not complain. This aspect was obvious in Ekeblad's writings. The silence, or muteness of animals was emphasized and was a ubiquitous topic in the animal protection rhetoric.[20] This aspect was especially remarkable in Ekeblad's texts regarding the suffering of horses. Because

[16] Christine Bierman and Becky Mansfield, "Biodiversity, Purity, and Death: Conservation Biology as Biopolitics," *Environment and Planning D: Society and Space* 32 (2014), 257–273.

[17] This was of course about to change, with the publication of Darwin's *Origin of the Species* in 1859.

[18] Susan Pearson, "Speaking Bodies, Speaking Minds: Animals, Language, History," *History and Theory* 52 (2013), 91–92.

[19] Per-Anders Svärd (2015) has convincingly argued for how the continuing exploitation of animals in society requires the animal welfare regime.

[20] Karin Dirke, *De värnlösas vänner: den svenska djurskyddsrörelsen 1875–1920* (Stockholm: Almqvist & Wicksell International, 2000), 155–158.

of its muteness the horse is worthy of better treatment, Ekeblad argued.[21] Hierarchy, class and difference permeated his writings. While highlighting the human's superior intelligence, he underlined the usefulness of animals. Clearly, for Ekeblad, animals had been created as submissive and low-ranking beings. Animals work for us, Ekeblad stated, and we should therefore treat them with kindness.[22] The demand for benevolence increases since animals lack the ability to speak for themselves. The possibility for animals to express their suffering has not been provided by humans, and this makes their misery greater.[23] Historian Susan Pearson discusses the nineteenth century debate on animals and language. She demonstrates how animal protectionists of that time linked linguistic ability to democratic rights. While her point of departure is the American animal welfare movement, the discussion is highly applicable in a European context. Pearson links ideas about animals' inability to use language to a larger nineteenth century debate about the origins of language.[24] When, for example, the American writer Harriet Beecher Stowe wrote about animals she emphasized their lack of speech. Animals were considered by Beecher Stowe to be "hapless" because of their inability to speak or write. Pearson states that for "protectionists, animals' inability to speak rendered moral obligation as linguistic surrogacy." However, according to Pearson, some protectionists contested the idea of animal speechlessness, arguing for a broader definition of language including other ways of communicating with animals. Yet, both positions were similar in noting linguistic ability to be the significant difference between human and animal. The idea of linguistic capability as defining what is essentially human was thus well established in the nineteenth century.[25]

---

[21] Karl Johan Ekeblad, "*Om kreaturens suckan,*" *en vördnadsfull skrivelse till några av vårt lands utmärktaste medborgare* (Stockholm, 1863), 4.

[22] Ekeblad, "*Om kreaturens suckan,*" 3.

[23] Pearson, "Speaking Bodies, Speaking Minds," 92.

[24] Pearson, "Speaking Bodies, Speaking Minds," 91–108.

[25] Pearson, "Speaking Bodies, Speaking Minds," 91–93, quotations from 92, quotation of Beecher Stowe from Pearson.

In Ekeblad's writings, however, the main focus of his argument is not the ability of the animal to speak, but the human's ability to *listen*. No matter what linguistic abilities the animals possesses, for communication with humans to happen it requires that the human is attentive to it. This would happen only if the human was, Ekeblad argued, properly (morally speaking) equipped. Therefore, the argument was focused on human betterment, rather than animal liberation. Animals were, according to Ekeblad, made for the sake of humans. Despite that they lack the ability to speak, animals can communicate with "good and honorable" people with the "silent language of the moist eye."[26] Thus, people need to be good and honorable in order to hear the animals' plight. This sentimental language, the emphasis on the subordination of animals and the human debt towards animals, were all typical for the early animal welfare movement's mobilizations.

Ekeblad argued for a teleological and evolutionary thinking, according to which everything strives towards an increasing degree of moral perfection. This perfection, according to Ekeblad, consists of "spiritual capacities" which meant being morally perfect, hard-working, thankful and righteous.[27] All these traits were, in nineteenth century western culture, expressed with the concept of *civilization*. The level of civilization was measured in relation to humans. Therefore, those animals perceived to be closer to humans were, by Ekeblad and many others of his time, considered to be more civilized than others. This was also the reason why horses were deemed particularly deserving of human kindness. Ekeblad emphasized the utility of horses. Due to its hilly landscape, the slaughterer argued, Sweden would never have a railway system as extensive as other countries. Therefore, there will always be need for horses and we are obliged to treat them well.[28] If we mistreat our horses, he continued, it will render us heathen, just like the pre-

[26] Ekeblad, "*Om kreaturens suckan*," 3. Translations of this text by the author. Swedish original: "fuktiga ögats tysta språk"
[27] Ekeblad, "*Om kreaturens suckan*," 4. Swedish original: "andliga förmögenheter"
[28] Ekeblad, "*Om kreaturens suckan*," 5.

Christians who offered horses to the gods. The key in Ekeblad's argument is Christian civilization and moral betterment. Treating horses well will mean improving humans, making them more civilized.

The problem Ekeblad was attempting to address concerned the selling, rather than the killing of worn-out horses.[29] He was not concerned with the commodification of the horse's body, but rather wanted to change how it was done. Death, he thought, would relieve the horse of its worthless life. The power to decide whose life is worth living and whose is not was obviously and unquestionably placed in the hands of humans, at least as far as Ekeblad was concerned.

The early animal welfare movement also depended on the idea of death as a savior. When the first nationwide animal welfare society in Sweden started its operations in 1875, slaughter was an important topic that needed addressing. Animal protectionists intensively engaged in methods to kill animals. Slaughter, they argued, was generally not performed in an animal friendly manner. Therefore, the aim of the animal welfare organization was to professionalize the business of killing animals. Technology, and a focus on death occurring swiftly and painlessly, was thus a central preoccupation. They bought different types of slaughter apparatuses to test their function. Everything from slaughter masks for killing cattle, the euthanizing machine "Blixt" for smaller animals, to the popular "poultry guillotine" were tried under supervision of the veterinarians engaged in these societies. The guillotine was donated by the society to be erected on the city square in order to kill poultry bought on the market. Finally, the Swedish Women's Society for the Protection of Animals organized a euthanasia establishment where pets could be killed under veterinarian supervision.[30] The death of animals was thus the main method

---

[29] Ekeblad, "*Om kreaturens suckan*," 6.

[30] I have discussed the Swedish animal welfare movement's ideas about slaughter in my dissertation, *De värnlösas vänner*, 188–213. The poultry guilliotin in the city square is mentioned in the newspaper *Arbetet* 1903–07–06, 3.

of the animal welfare movement. Ekeblad's horse slaughtering business was noted by the animal welfare movement and he was awarded a medal from the Swedish society for the Protection of Animals in the end of the 19th century for his achievements in animal welfare.[31]

The dead animal and the morally perfect human

If the foundation and consequence of the arguments for animal protection were a way of conserving the existing social order, why then take the trouble to argue about animals? Biopolitical power works on populations rather than individuals. While the attention was directed toward individual animals, relieving them from intolerable life, the movement's overall target was to improve and control the behavior of humans. The 19th century struggle for an animal's right to die was primarily aimed at the moral welfare of humans. The overall mission was to educate humans, to make them morally better.

Within a biopolitical framework the rule pertaining to animals becomes generalized, affecting the wider human population. The aim of saving animals from suffering was thus not merely to stop people from acting cruelly but also to protect humans from being exposed to their pain. The idea that human morals would be harmed by witnessing cruelty was ubiquitous. Bremer's references to the horse slaughterer were in line with this. The focus was on lifting humans from uncivilized darkness, disciplining them to care for animals. Humans were visualized as the culmination of evolution, the highest of all living beings, but at the same time they needed help in progressing on the moral ladder. The argument continuously highlighted difference; not all humans were equally moral. Essentially, such ideas had their derivation in the philosophy of Immanuel Kant. Kant did not mention animals in his writings. However, in his later published lectures on ethics, this topic had a certain prominence. Kant argued that animals do not have rights and that

---

[31] Uno Willers, "Karl Johan Ekeblad" in *Svenskt biografiskt lexikon*, band 8 (1949), 608.

humans therefore have no obligations towards them. All the same, there are similarities between humans and animals. When exposed to pain animals react like humans and can obviously experience it. Therefore, there is an indirect reason neither to mistreat animals nor to witness cruelty to animals. To do otherwise is to risk desensitization. Being unresponsive when confronted with animal suffering could lead to an indifference in front of human agony.

In his lectures Kant referred to a series of well-known pictures, *The four stages of cruelty*, by the English artist William Hogarth (1697–1764). Hogarth's pictures were immensely popular and were widely circulated. They illustrated the stages of descending into moral depravity. The discipline in them was obvious.[32] Hogarth made several narrative series of prints which illustrated how one despicable behavior led to another, finally resulting in the perpetrator being severely punished by his own degradation. In *The Four Stages of Cruelty* it is cruelty to animals that leads the main character Tom Nero (appropriately given the tyrannical emperor's name) to destruction. The last picture shows the anti-hero in the anatomical theatre, being dissected while the tortured dog from the first picture escapes with Tom Nero's heart in his mouth.[33] The pictures were reproduced at quite a low cost and were intended to be distributed widely to the general public.[34] The aim was to focus on animal cruelty as an introduction to moral depravity leading to death and despair.

Horses and class

The Swedish discussion on animals', and particularly horses' suffering, was a mirror of the morale in Hogarth's prints and ultimately the ethics of Kant. The first time an animal protection law was discussed in Sweden—in the house of nobility, 1844—

[32] Ronnie Lippens, "The Light of High Modern Discipline: Viewing the Birth, Life and Death of the Disciplinary Society in William Hogarth, Joseph Wright of Derby and Edward Hopper," *Law and Humanities* 8, no. 1 (2014), 7.

[33] James A. Steintrager, "Monstrous Appearances: Hogarth's 'Four Stages of Cruelty' and the Paradox of Inhumanity" i *The Eighteenth Century* 42, no. 1 (2001), 59.

[34] Steintrager, "Monstrous Appearances," 60.

horses were the principal focus. A law protecting animals as property already existed; it was prohibited to mistreat someone else's animal to the extent that it was no longer usable. There were, however, no limits to what one could do to one's own animals. Among the nobility it was now proposed that animals should be protected from abuse. The animals in mind were primarily draught-horses, transporting goods and people in the city. Class was an obvious starting point here. Those abusing horses were thought to emanate from the lower class. Just like in the second stage of cruelty in Hogarth's series, where Tom Nero has become a coachman, and abuses his horse, it was primarily carters who were accused of animal abuse.[35] Class was a clear undercurrent in the discussion. The animal abuser was described as uncivilized, of a lower class and insensitive. The proposal for a law protecting animals was, however, on this occasion, not passed in the Swedish parliament.

Suffering

In his argument, Ekeblad played with a tender aspect of the nineteenth century relationship with death. The main point was neither death in itself, nor the horse's right to life, but, as discussed earlier, the suffering of the horse. Just like in Hogarth's prints there was a mix of criticisms targeting the showing of cruelty, yet at the same time explicitly articulating the same cruelty. While condemned, the suffering was emphasized and articulated with an almost lustful sentimentality in Ekeblad's writings:

> When the horse, whether dead or slaughtered is not perceived as valuable, greed, together with betrayal and cruelty thinks it is rightful to abuse him to the end, so long as there remains at least one drop of blood left, or still a living piece of meat to gnaw on. The weaker, the more miserable the creature is, the heavier the rogue's lead whip lands on the wound-covered skin which is dried to the meatless, battered bones. Enduring

[35] Dirke, *De värnlösas vänner*, 66.

horrible cursing, being pulled by the reins, endlessly whipped, sold from one rascal to another – buyers who often have the most heartless livelihoods, relentlessly trying to deceive each other; as the result of all these hardships, the animal gets no rest until its powerlessness weighs down under its tormentor's scourge.[36]

Both Ekeblad and Fredrika Bremer thus expressed ideas about Christianity, suffering and death typical for the 19th century. Here suffering became the lynchpin of the argument. When Bremer praised Ekeblad in her essay, she primarily pointed to how he had moved suffering away from public view:

[...] we no longer see here in Stockholm such starving, skinny horses carrying burdens by which at any moment they are weighed down, as we had done so, with disgust and sorrow, a few years back. Honor to the Christian horse friend![37]

Conclusion

There are several paradoxes in the way 19th century animal protectionists thought about suffering and death. On the one side there was, during the century, an easily swayed sentimentality, discussed widely in scholarly work concerning art, literature and philosophy of the period. Not only one's own suffering was cherished and articulated but also, and in parti-

---

[36] Ekeblad, "*Om kreaturens suckan,*" 6–7. Author's translation. Swedish original: "När han såsom död eller slagtad icke ansetts vara af något värde, har snikenheten i förening med svek och grymhet, trott sig ega rätt att till det yttersta misshandla detta djur, så länge en bloddroppa finnes qvar att utpressa eller en lefvande köttsmula att gnaga. Ju svagare, ju eländigare kreaturet är, desto tyngre faller skojarens blypiska på den sårhöljda huden, som är fasttorkad vid de köttlösa, mörbultade knotorna. Under ohyggliga eder, betselryckningar och tallösa piskrapp går den gamle hästkraken ur den ene skojarens hand i den andres, och som desse idkare af det hjertlösaste näringsfång söka i svek öfverlista hvarandra, får djuret ingen hvila förr än det maktlöst dignar under sin plågares gissel."

[37] Bremer, 34. Author's translation. Swedish original: "[...]vi se icke mer i Stockholm så utsvultna, utmagrade hästar, släpande på bördor, under hvilka de hvart ögonblick hålla på att digna, såsom vi så ofta med avsky och sorg sett där för några år tillbaka. Heder åt den kristne hästvännen!"

151

cular, the pain of others. The struggle to diminish hardships in society brought about social movements for philanthropy, abolitionism and animal welfare. These movements attracted, and were upheld by, women. At the same time there was an attempt to eliminate cruelty and suffering from public view, because of its desensitizing effects. Cruelty of all sorts should be removed from the public sphere in order to spare people from moral depravity. The propaganda against suffering, including its sentimental expressions, became filled with an emphasis on pain of all sorts. That is, the sentimental opinion-makers who wanted to ban visible suffering from the public sphere, at the same time filled a discursive space with talk of pain, suffering and death.

In a biopolitical struggle to make live and let die, animals—horses in particular—were relieved of their life. This had two purposes: (i) to save humans from witnessing the hardships of animals, and (ii) to promote moral perfection among people. While upholding and emphasizing difference, pain and suffering was to be eliminated from public view.

In his discussion of Foucault, Agamben and Esposito, Cary Wolfe argues that the modern, industrial breeding and killing of animals for consumption—what is called factory farming—is a fundamental aspect of modern biopolitics, making live and letting die, which will not let itself be regulated by laws concerning animal welfare.[38] Indeed, anti-cruelty laws seem to be a necessary component for the continuation of managing meat production.[39] In this respect there is a historical continuum between the early arguments for animal welfare and current debates on vegetarianism/veganism and animal protection. Ekeblad, rooted to his own time, advanced his arguments before laws existed concerning animal welfare. He positioned, and played out, three aspects in his argument: horse welfare; the abolition of poverty, and raising the morals of (poor) people. Of the three, analysis suggests that the moral discipline of humans

[38] Cary Wolfe, "Before the Law: Animals in a Biopolitical Context" in *Law, Culture and the Humanities* 6, no. 1 (2010), 8–23.
[39] See Svärd.

is the superior claim. Though horse welfare and the abolition of poverty were sought by Ekeblad, both, according to the logic of his own argument, required the moral education of the lower classes. The idea of the animal's intrinsic value, as well as the further claim that it has any claims or rights, did not enter into his argument. The animal was never anything but a commodity to the animal protectionists of the mid nineteenth century.

The horse slaughterer Karl Johan Ekeblad in manifold ways embodied the complexities of the western 19th century public sphere. Being—bodily as well as socially—potentially outcast, he argued from the position of a recluse. Yet, his message was completely in line with conserving power, maintaining the biopolitical rule of making live and letting die. Just like in The horse's prayer, Ekeblad's claim was speaking for the animal, listening to its appeal, but only hearing it begging to be killed.

References

Bergström, Roger, Karin Dirke & Kjell Danell. "The Wolf War in Sweden during the Eighteenth Century—Strategies, Measures and Leaders" in Masius, Patrick & Sprenger, Jana (ed.), *A Fairytale in Question: Historical Interactions between Humans and Wolves*, White Horse Press, Cambridge, 2015, 57–78.

Bierman, Christine & Becky Mansfield, "Biodiversity, purity, and death: conservation biology as biopolitics" in *Environment and planning D: Society and Space* 32 (2014), 257–273.

Björkman, John, *"Må de herrskande klasserna darra" Radikal retorik och reaktion i Stockholms press, 1848-1851*. Möklinta: Gidlunds förlag, 2020.

Bremer, Fredrika, "Mitt Fönster 1855" i *Skisser, uppsatser och poem*. Stockholm; Beijers 1912.

Broglio, Ron, *Beasts of Burden: Biopolitics, Labor, and Animal Life in British Romanticism*, State University of New York press, 2017.

Dirke, Karin, *De värnlösas vänner: den svenska djurskyddsrörelsen 1875–1920*, Almqvist & Wiksell International, Diss. Stockholm: Univ., Stockholm, 2000.

Egardt, Brita, *Hästslakt och rackarskam: en etnologisk undersökning av folkliga fördomar*. Stockholm: Nordiska muséet, 1962.

Ekeblad, Karl Johan, *Hjelp i nöden, eller råd till allmogen, att under swåra år och wid smärre tillgångar till föda för sig och husdjuren anwända några helsosamma och födande wildt wäxande naturalster, på hwilka å landet finnes ymnig tillgång, och som utan penningar kunna anskaffas äfwen af den fattigaste* 2. betydligt tillökta och förb. uppl., Lundberg, Stockholm, 1847.

Ekeblad, Karl Johan, *"Om kreaturens suckan," en vördnadsfull skrivelse till några av vårt lands utmärktaste medborgare*, Stockholm, 1863.

Hedén, Anne, Ulrika Milles & Moa Matthis, *Över alla hinder: en civilisationshistoria*, Bonnier, Stockholm, 2003.

Lippens, Ronnie, "The Light of High Modern Discipline: Viewing the Birth, Life and Death of the Disciplinary Society in William Hogarth, Joseph Wright of Derby and Edward Hopper" in *Law and Humanities*, 8, no. 1 (2014).

Pearson, Susan, "Speaking Bodies, Speaking Minds: Animals, Language, History" in *History and Theory*, December 2013, 91–108.

Ritvo, Harriet, *The Animal Estate: the English and Other Creatures in the Victorian Age*. 1887. Reprint, Penguin: London, 1990.

Steintrager, James A, "Monstrous Appearances: Hogarth's 'Four Stages of Cruelty' and the Paradox of Inhumanity" in *The Eighteenth Century* 42, no. 1 (2001).

Svärd, Per-Anders, *Problem Animals: A Critical Genealogy of Animal Cruelty and Animal Welfare in Swedish Politics 1844–1944*. Stockholm University, Stockholm, 2015.

Willers, Uno, "Karl Johan Ekeblad" in *Svenskt biografiskt lexikon*, band 8, 1949.

Wolfe, Cary, "Before the Law: Animals in a Biopolitical Context" in *Law, Culture and the Humanities* 6, no. 1 (2010), 8–23.

Names and Namelessness in Animal Narratives

Sune Borkfelt

> The first morning, Romochka gave the puppies names. He surveyed them proudly. Brown, black, white, grey. All his! Then another day he gave them other names. Then he forgot their names and forgot that he had ever looked at them as a boy looks at puppies.
>
> Eva Hornung, *Dog Boy* (2009)[1]

At one point early in her novel about a young boy who is adopted by a pack of feral dogs, Eva Hornung briefly touches upon the complications of naming. Still identifying as someone on the human side of a human/animal binary, and affected by cultural ideas about human-dog relations, Romochka (whose own name echoes the Roman myth of Romulus and Remus) goes about the Adamic task of naming the puppies recently born into the pack. As in the biblical tale of Adam naming the animals in Genesis, naming is tied to both dominion and creation.[2] After initially naming them, Romochka "survey[s]" the puppies "proudly" as a creator of their identities and consequently looks at them with a sense of ownership ("All his!"). Eventually, however, he forgets the names and, as he becomes further integrated into the pack, the dogs are instead referred to through relational signifiers such as 'Grey Brother,' 'White Brother,' and 'Black Sister.'

Perhaps easily overlooked in the context of the novel's overall plot, Hornung's short passage on naming points to the importance of what we do when we name and to the potential effects of naming on our relations with other animals. Names are representations; irrespective of whether they are connected directly to

[1] Eva Hornung, *Dog Boy* (London: Bloomsbury, 2010), 19.
[2] Cf. Sune Borkfelt, "What's in a Name?—Consequences of Naming Non-Human Animals," *Animals* 1, no. 1 (2011), 118–119.

characteristics of those named (thus emphasizing these characteristics over others) or their application to particular individuals is entirely arbitrary, they always have the power of representations. Or, as I have written elsewhere, "[a] name is a representation and can therefore potentially carry all the values, ideas, perceptions and conceptions carried by representations and have the array of potential consequences, which can ensue from representation."[3] Thus, "we may do favours or disservice to places and beings (human and non-human) when we name them"—a fact that has had and continues to have real-world consequences for our relations with nonhuman animals.[4]

Naming gives us the possibility of talking about something or someone in concrete terms, and hence it helps mould future perceptions of those named. Therein lies both its usefulness and its power. Or, as Grant W. Smith puts it, "[i]f I tell my friend that this is my dog *Fido*, my friend will see Fido from a slightly different angle."[5] But how do the functions and power dynamics of naming work in fiction, and specifically in literary depictions of nonhuman animals, where the author creates the characters and naturally, continually affects our ideas of them? So far, neither literary onomastics nor literary animal studies have paid any kind of systematic attention to the names of nonhuman characters. Through both theoretical explorations and literary examples in this chapter, I aim to bring together these fields to start creating a theoretical basis for discussing what might be called literary animal onomastics and to argue, ultimately, that we might want to start paying more attention to the literary techniques, the power dynamics, and the ethics of naming nonhuman animal characters in literary fiction.

---

[3] Borkfelt, 117.

[4] Borkfelt, 117.

[5] Grant W. Smith, "Theoretical Foundations of Literary Onomastics," in *The Oxford Handbook of Names and Naming*, edited by Carole Hough (Oxford: Oxford University Press, 2016), 305.

Literary uses of proper names

In order to start a theoretical discussion of nonhuman animal names in literary fiction, it is necessary to first revisit some of the theory regarding literary names as such, and explore how this may be relevant to the specifics of nonhuman characters' names.

Studying literary onomastics is hardly a straightforward undertaking. As one scholar of names in children's literature states, "the names of fictive characters comprise a heterogeneous and dynamic category of names" and "the categorisation and considerations of names in literary works become extremely complex" for a number of reasons.[6] The literary realm offers a multitude of different kinds of stories and thus of characters, whose names may depend on such things as their individual nature, specific purposes, and genre conventions. For instance, "imaginary characters often receive imaginary and semantically loaded name[s], whereas realistic persons commonly have conventional and neutral name forms."[7]

It is perhaps useful to think about names in literary fiction in terms of two closely connected and key questions: (i) from where do the names derive their meaning? and (ii) what are the potential effects of the names in, as well as beyond, the narrative in question? In relation to the former, one key discussion in literary onomastics thus concerns the degree to which the proper name derives its meaning from the context, that is, from the fictional narrative itself. Roland Barthes, for instance, considered that as a

> sign, the proper name offers itself to an exploration, a deci-
> pherment: it is at once a "milieu" (in the biological sense of
> the term) into which one must plunge, steeping in all the
> reveries it bears, and a precious object, compressed, em-
> balmed, which must be opened like a flower. In other words,
> if the Name ... is a sign, it is a voluminous sign, a sign always

[6] Yvonne Bertills, *Beyond Identification: Proper Names in Children's Literature* (Åbo: Åbo Akademi University Press, 2003), 233–234.
[7] Bertills, 233.

157

pregnant with a dense texture of meaning, which no amount of wear can reduce, can flatten, contrary to the common noun, which releases only one of its meanings by syntagm.[8]

For Barthes, names thus carry more potential for meaning than other nouns; they are "pregnant with a dense texture of meaning" because context can make them carry multiple meanings at once, or interchangeably. With the common noun, the context will help determine one exact meaning, whereas the proper name can simply have meanings added on top of each other as context is added. Names, Barthes observed, are "in effect, *catalyzable*;" and "can be filled, dilated, the interstices of [their] semic armature can be infinitely added to."[9] Thus, not only does the narrative add context to the proper name of a given character as the reader learns more about that character, but meanings may also shift with new readers, since the name's "semic spectre" is "variable in time, according to the diachrony of its reader."[10]

As Yvonne Bertills rightly points out, while Barthes's view acknowledges some of the importance of personal names for texts, it also leaves names without "independent meaning," since their meanings are always "supplied by context."[11] Barthes's focus is mainly on realist writing where, he argues, the author needs to choose names so that there is "a kind of natural affinity between signifier and signified;" the relation between the name and that which it signifies is "based on a relation of *imitation*."[12] In other words—unlike, for instance, in the above example from Eva Hornung's *Dog Boy*—the power is removed from the name, which merely represents its object as precisely as possible.

It may be, of course, that the character helps determine the name, because a name is sought that corresponds to particular characteristics, but the opposite may also be true, and reducing

---

[8] Roland Barthes, "Proust and Names" [1967] in *New Critical Essays*, trans. Richard Howard (Berkeley: University of California Press, 1990), 59–60.

[9] Barthes, 61 (emphasis original).

[10] Barthes, 61.

[11] Bertills, 235.

[12] Barthes, 62.

naming to a process of imitation, or of catching the essence of its object, is problematic. For one thing, as Bertills argues, "the relationship between the semantic aspects of the name and the character ... often has specific functions in the narrative" and "the name often concretely describes, characterizes or suggests ... information about the character."[13] Experienced readers of works by Charles Dickens, for example, would likely agree, and names in the fantasy genre also often contribute their own meaning to characters or affect the relation between characters and readers.[14] Frederick M. Burelbach, for instance, sees names in literature as regulators of distance or proximity between characters and readers. Thus, Burelbach argues that a nickname "acts ... to narrow the distance between the character and the audience," while "[n]ames that are too obviously meaningful or unusual will tease the readers into thought, thrusting them out of the fictional world into a realm of critical appreciation and analysis."[15]

Surely, what Burelbach points out is a relevant effect also for animal narratives, and it would be worth knowing more about how names may distance us from nonhuman animal experiences by breaking our immersion in narratives written from nonhuman points of view. This is relevant not least because both naming and immersion have been suggested as avenues for engendering empathy with characters in literary narratives.[16]

---

[13] Bertills, 235–236.

[14] See Bertills 235–236. On names in Dickens see, e.g., John A. Stoler, "Dickens' Use of Names in *Hard Times*," *Literary Onomastics Studies* 12, no. 1 (1985), 153. Stoler suggests that the sounds in names used by Dickens often bring forth associations even without any kind of literal meaning to them.

[15] Frederick M. Burelbach, "Names as Distance Controllers in Literature," *Literary Onomastics Studies* 13, no. 1 (1986), 173–175.

[16] Suzanne Keen, *Empathy and the Novel* (Oxford: Oxford University Press, 2007), 28, 76 and 94. Keen suggests the potential effect of naming for character identification may play a role in narrative empathy, and also argues that due to our willing immersion in it "fiction does disarm readers of some of the protective layers of cautious reasoning that may inhibit empathy in the real world." Vera Nünning, *Reading Fictions, Changing Minds: The Cognitive Value of Fiction* (Heidelberg: Universitätsverlag WINTER, 2014), 102. Nünning argues convinc-

Thus, if we want to explore the potential effects of narratives in engendering more caring attitudes toward animals, we might want to take a closer look at the naming practices in such narratives. On the other hand, as Burelbach also argues, names that create a certain distance may work well for narratives where authors may aim for "intellectual consideration of the philosophical issues rather than emotional involvement with the character," which might well seem relevant to works trying to highlight specific ethical or political aspects of human/nonhuman relations.[17]

Another consequence of Barthes's ideas about imitation and derivation of meaning from the context is that—by overly emphasizing the relation between the name and the particular character—it runs the risk of glossing over political aspects of the act of naming and the various ways in which names may be used to colonize, dominate, belittle (or aggrandize), and objectify those named.[18] Albeit somewhat vaguely, Barthes does arguably acknowledge that the context, which may provide meaning to a name, can come from aspects of a text that bring forth readers' connotations to the name, but there is no consideration of how such connotations may, for instance, further negative attitudes to groups or beings, which the named characters might be read as representing. This may be of particular relevance when those named are already marginalized from ethical concern, as is mostly the case for nonhuman animals, or where human others are implicitly marginalized through comparisons to nonhumans made in the names of either human or nonhuman characters. Think, for instance, of the implicit exoticism and connotative connections to non-Christian Indian traditions found in the names of animals in Kipling's *Jungle*

ingly that whereas "we are unlikely to remain passive for an extended period of time" in real-life situations, i.e. we might act or walk away, being immersed in fiction can give us a more "extensive and intensive practice of empathic feelings" over prolonged periods of time.

[17] Burelbach, 175.

[18] For more on these political and ethical aspects of naming in relation to other animals outside literature, see Borkfelt, "What's in a Name?"

Books (1894–1895), meant to evoke the work's Indian setting and characters within a particular Western, imperialist imaginary.[19] Through connotative connections to the practices of native humans in India, names such as 'Shere Khan' and 'Kaa the Rock Python' arguably not only help to stereotype non-western animal species, but also lend credence to readings that treat the stories as pure allegory. In such narratives, the names may thus work as part of a particularly anthropocentric anthropomorphism, which can distract from what the stories (also) have to say about animals.[20]

Types of names, types of naming

In the context of literary animal names, it is worth exploring the connections between anthropomorphism and naming a little further. It is not difficult to grasp the argument that naming *per se* is an exercise of anthropomorphism, and some have expressed concern about the dangers of humanizing other animals through naming.[21] Yet, possibly depending on the specific name, it may also be seen as an acknowledgement of the individual subject, that is, more of a de-objectification than an act of humanizing as such. For instance, building on work by Stacey K. Sowards, communications researcher Tema Milstein connects naming to Frans de Waal's notion of "animalcentric anthropomorphism," which "emphasizes both continuities and discontinuities with humans."[22] Thus, naming practices that

[19] Rudyard Kipling, *The Jungle Books* (Oxford: Oxford University Press, 1998). On the animals of *The Jungle Books* in the imperial imaginary, see, e.g., Jopi Nyman, *Postcolonial Animal Tale from Kipling to Coetzee* (New Delhi: Atlantic Publishers, 2003), 38–55.

[20] For more on Kipling's animal stereotypes, see Sune Borkfelt, "Colonial Animals and Literary Analysis: The Example of Kipling's Animal Stories," *English Studies* 90, no. 5 (2009), 557–568.

[21] Frank Nuessel, *The Study of Names: A Guide to the Principles and Topics* (Westport CT: Greenwood Press, 1992), 116. See also Borkfelt, "What's in a Name?" 123.

[22] Tema Milstein, "Nature Identification: The Power of Pointing and Naming," *Environmental Communication* 5, no. 1 (2011), 5. Stacey K. Sowards, "Identification through Orangutans: Destabilizing the Nature/Culture Dualism," *Ethics and*

attempt to carry out such animalcentric anthropomorphism may be said to highlight individual subjects without the implication that this makes them human as such, but *with* the implication that they have much in common with humans—a sentiment that seems highly applicable to many contemporary literary depictions of nonhuman animals.

As Milstein argues, identification practices applied to nature and animals can subvert linguistic practices that tend to place all agency with humans acting towards an objectified nature.[23] Naming through animalcentric anthropomorphism might then be seen as recovering animals as subjects, meaning that naming comes to imply an agency that lies with the nonhuman animals—rather than with something human that the animals are meant to symbolize. This is significant not just because it can play a part in depicting other animals *as* nonhuman subjects in their own right (a key focus for literary animal studies), as opposed to what John Simons calls "displaced metaphors for the human," but also because agency may play a vital role in sparking empathy for literary characters.[24] In her seminal work on narrative empathy, Suzanne Keen thus specifically remarks on how "character identification routinely overcomes" what she sees as "the significant barrier of species difference," likely because "empathy may be swiftly activated by a simple sign of an active agent."[25] As she writes, "[m]erely naming a character may set readers' empathy in motion."[26] Thus, if names manage to be animalcentric, in the sense that it is clear to the reader that they signify living nonhuman beings, they may help pave the way for empathy with animals through literary depictions.

An example of such animalcentric anthropomorphic naming is found in Barbara Gowdy's *The White Bone* (1998). Told from

the Environment 11, no. 2 (2006), 45–61. Frans de Waal, *The Ape and the Sushi Master* (New York: Basic Books, 2001).

[23] Milstein, 5.

[24] John Simons, *Animal Rights and the Politics of Literary Representation* (London: Palgrave, 2002), 6.

[25] Keen, 68.

[26] Keen, 68–69.

the perspective of elephants, *The White Bone* is a novel that attempts to radically transform anthropomorphism to make it less anthropocentric. This includes a language adapted to the novel's nonhuman perspectives, and as a consequence also different naming practices.[27] Indeed, the novel starts with the renaming of the novel's protagonist, Mud, as she is given—and resists—her "cow-name" She-Spurns, after her first mating.[28] As readers eventually learn, female elephants are given one name at birth and then re-named by the elder females in their family once they have mated. In this way, the novel at once draws attention to the exercise of power in naming (due to Mud's resistance to it) and to the idea that names must fit with elephant *umwelten* and epistemologies. For example, "[a] cow calf who comes into the world at the unusual hour of high noon—the hour when all things have become so diminutive that they fail to throw a shadow—is called either Tiny or Speck," and the names of grown females refer to their actions (She-Demands, She-Measures, She-Soothes, She-Screams etc.), thus directly implying agency, and specifically emphasizing female agency, which fits the fact that elephants live in matriarchal groups.[29]

While the naming practices of Gowdy's elephants alter or reinvent anthropomorphic traditions, as do other aspects of the novel, they also offer a high degree of individuality for the novel's characters. Arguably, this is generally part of an added potential for names in literature. As others have pointed out, real-world names, whether applied to humans or nonhumans,

---

[27] Barbara Gowdy, *The White Bone* (London: Flamingo, 2000). For a more general analysis of how Gowdy's novel deals with anthropomorphism and otherness, see Sune Borkfelt, "Non-Human Otherness: Animals as Others and Devices for Othering," in *Otherness: A Multilateral Perspective*, edited by Susan Yi Sencindiver, Maria Beville and Marie Lauritzen (Frankfurt am Main: Peter Lang, 2011), 148–151.

[28] Gowdy, 3.

[29] Gowdy, 8. By contrast, male elephants in the novel keep the names given to them at birth.

are prone to a certain degree of recycling.[30] While literary names may of course follow similar conventions, they need not do so, even if genre conventions or a wish for realism may set certain limits. Thus, when it comes to names, there is a "greater degree of prosodic inventiveness in literature" than in real life.[31] Thus, depending on genre conventions, authors can create names for which readers have no connotations from previous uses. Indeed, one might argue that because there is perhaps fewer formal restrictions to nonhuman animal names in the first place, compared to human names, authors might even create a greater level of individuality for nonhuman animals in narratives where human names need to conform to a sense of realism. As Barthes has argued, the realist writer is not "free to invent the names he likes, but [...] obliged to invent them 'properly'."[32] Yet, we might well ask what freedoms from such 'properness' authors may have or take when it comes to naming animal characters, not just outside of genres that need to convey a sense of realism, but in general. As Gowdy's elephant names demonstrate, such freedoms can be taken in ways that heighten a sense of nonhuman animals' individualities and attempt to subvert previous anthropocentric literary naming practices. Indeed, the fact that some of the female elephants attempt to resist their names in favour of keeping their birth names further emphasizes this sense of individuality, as it leads to discussions on the appropriateness of a particular name for a certain individual.[33]

Of course, authors also often choose names for animals exactly because they come with particular connotations or lend themselves to particular symbolic uses. This is always significant, since characters' names inevitably become part of their characterization, to a greater or lesser extent.[34] Consider, for

---

[30] Bertills, 43. Katharina Leibring, "Animal Names," in *The Oxford Handbook of Names and Naming*, edited by Carole Hough (Oxford: Oxford University Press, 2016), 617.

[31] Smith, 296.

[32] Barthes, 67.

[33] Gowdy, 19–22.

[34] See, e.g., Bertills 51–56.

instance, the example of the tiger Richard Parker in Yann Martel's bestselling novel *Life of Pi* (2001), a novel that plays around with names in a number of ways.[35] In the story itself, we are told that the name Richard Parker is due to "a clerical error" in which the tiger is confused with the hunter who trapped him, and the anthroponymic qualities of the name are important for a number of statements in the novel, especially for purposes of irony or narrative impact.[36] However, Martel borrows the name from Edgar Allan Poe's *The Narrative of Arthur Gordon Pym of Nantucket* (1838), which—like *Life of Pi*—is a tale of sea-voyage and shipwreck, in which Richard Parker is the first to suggest cannibalism among four men lost at sea.[37] Given that Martel's novel essentially revolves around how a boy, alone in a lifeboat with a tiger and a few other animals, avoids being eaten as they float around the Pacific Ocean, this is surely significant, and suggests reading the novel's animals allegorically so that the story becomes one of cannibalism rather than of human-animal relations. In this sense, while the name Richard Parker certainly helps make the tiger stand out as an individual in the narrative, it also might be said to help distract attention away from more animal-centred readings of the novel.[38]

---

[35] Yann Martel, *Life of Pi* (Edinburgh: Canongate, 2003). For a more detailed discussion of naming in the novel, see Don L. F. Nilsen, "Onomastic Play and Suspension of Disbelief in Yann Martel's *Life of Pi*," *Onoma* 40 (2005), 115–124.

[36] Martel, 132–133. Nilsen, 116–117.

[37] Edgar Allan Poe, *The Narrative of Arthur Gordon Pym of Nantucket and Related Tales* (Oxford: Oxford University Press, 1998), 90. Ironically, Poe's novella also features a dog named Tiger, who strangely disappears from the narrative along the way without explanation.

[38] To be clear, I am not arguing that Martel's novel does not have this allegorical layer (it clearly does) nor even that this is not dominant (though this is debatable). Rather, it is part of the novel that it negotiates with the reader about the balance between such a 'human' reading and a more animal-centred one, and the literary background to the name Richard Parker clearly functions as an argument for reading the novel's animals as metaphors for humans. However, not least through its extensive discussions on the nature of zoos, on animal training, on anthropomorphism and zoomorphism etc., *Life of Pi* has a great deal to say about human-nonhuman animal relations, which should not be wholly dismissed or ignored in favour of an allegorical reading.

It is worth noting how names given to animals by other characters in literary narratives reflect not just on those named, but also on those doing the naming. The clerical error that causes the naming of Richard Parker is clearly a humorous stab at the Indian bureaucracy the clerk represents, and among Gowdy's elephants Mud and her friend Date Bed suggest the elder females wish to antagonize the younger ones with the names they choose for them as they mature.[39] In this way, names can also come to signify something about the relations between characters and thus the degree to which a certain character does or does not belong with the other characters that surround him or her. Anna Sewell's classic *Black Beauty* (1877) is arguably such a tale, in which names are used to indicate both relations and belonging. As the novel's equine protagonist-narrator is acquired by varying owners, and his trials and fortune consequently shift over the course of the novel, he goes from being called Darkie, to Black Beauty, to Black Auster, to Bayard, to Blackie, to Old Crony, before finally re-acquiring the old name of Black Beauty as the book reaches its happy conclusion.[40] In this way, the narrative can be read as the life journey of a horse through shifting identities in order to come home to the name that truly defines him, namely the one indicated by the novel's title. Hence, the narrative signals through its onomastics that its protagonist is still out of place and has not quite arrived home, even in the instances when interim owners or caretakers are portrayed positively. That the name of Black Beauty is significant is also indicated in the relative care with which it is initially chosen:

> "Well, my dear," she said, "how do you like him?"
> "He is exactly what John said," he replied; "a pleasanter creature I never wished to mount. What shall we call him?"
> "Would you like Ebony?" said she. "He is black as ebony."

[39] Gowdy, 21–22.
[40] Anna Sewell, *Black Beauty* (London: Penguin, 1994), 4, 20, 94, 141, 199, 209, 212. Editors' note: Concerning Sewell's *Black Beauty* see also Karin Dirke's and Claudia Lindén's chapters in this volume.

"No, not Ebony."

"Will you call him Blackbird, like your uncle's old horse?"

"No, he is far handsomer than old Blackbird ever was."

"Yes," she said, "he really is quite a beauty, and he has such a good-tempered face and such a fine, intelligent eye—what do you say to calling him Black Beauty?"

"Black Beauty—why yes, I think that is a very good name. If you like it shall be his name," and so it was.[41]

The dialogue reflects that he is not named lightly. He cannot be reduced to the one characteristic of 'Ebony', nor can he have the recycled name of 'Blackbird'; instead, his name—though primarily aesthetic—comes from reflection on not just his beauty, but also his temper and intelligence, before the final "and so it was" of the equine narrator implies how the name seems to be nearly a fact of nature to him; it is a name in and to which he belongs. Thus, in Sewell's novel, the right humans can name a horse correctly, while naming is simultaneously tied to the exercise of power as names change with transferrals of ownership, at times signalling a loss of identity and dignity that the equine protagonist does not deserve. Conversely, the right name signals a sense of belonging also evident in its Victorian entwinement with ideas of English nationality when the coachman tells the stable boy that the "master and mistress had chosen a good sensible English name for [the horse], that meant something, not like Marengo, or Pegasus, or Abdallah."[42]

Empowerment and namelessness

As a first-person narrator, Black Beauty can potentially let the reader know his feelings about his name(s) or object as he sees fit, just as Gowdy's anthropomorphic elephants—told from a third-person perspective—are able to object in dialogue. Other animal characters, without such anthropomorphic abilities, have less of an option. Yet, instances of unnaming and nameless-

[41] Sewell, 19–20.
[42] Sewell, 20.

ness can form similarly, or even more powerful, responses to the sense of power and ownership implied by naming.

Helen Humphreys's *Wild Dogs* (2004) is told from a variety of human first-person perspectives, centring on six people tied together by the fact that their dogs choose to run wild and form a pack in the woods at the edge of a city. The six meet at the edge of the woods, and call out to the dogs, "uttering the human names that used to belong to them."[43] The novel thus continually negotiates questions of belonging, both in the sense of ownership and in the sense of being in the right place, as well as negotiating the balance between reading the dogs as symbolic and as real. As Alice, the first narrator, tells us, "[l]ove is like those wild dogs" and "[t]he wild dogs are real. They are out there, beyond the safety of the streets and houses, beyond the lights of the city. And one of those wild dogs is mine."[44] Like love, the dogs are difficult to pin down (or perhaps the other way around), and names are significant in this negotiation of autonomy and belonging. While we learn the names of the dogs in the first chapter, it is also clear from early on that these names matter only to the humans. In the words of Alice, their relations to the dogs are "about belonging. Once we belonged with those dogs, belonged to them, and now that they've left us we don't know who we are."[45] In Humphreys's novel, names—human and nonhuman—mean something only relationally, and the fact that the dogs do not return when their names are called can be read as a rejection of both certain forms of relation and of ownership, and an empowerment of those who choose to walk away, to not belong to the name or the one calling the name.

This empowering move of giving back unwanted names is placed even more centrally in Ursula Le Guin's classic short story "She Unnames Them" (1985). Here, the story is told from the perspective of Eve (though her name, crucially, never appears in the story) as she unnames all the animals, as well as

[43] Helen Humphreys, *Wild Dogs* (London: Maia Press, 2005), 12.
[44] Humphreys, 11.
[45] Humphreys, 12.

herself, as an empowering move to counter Adam's original naming of them all in Genesis.[46] While the story is clearly allegorical and concerns itself mostly with the generic labels of species, its politics of (un)naming are real and equally relevant to the names of individuals, as the implied domination is potentially similar. Marian Scholtmeijer observes correctly that the story "hinges upon the overthrow of language as the agent of reality," but it is specifically the power of patriarchy and anthropocentrism to define—to name—others that the woman and animals reject in Le Guin's story, thus empowering themselves to create new kinds of relations.[47] As the woman tells us, after their unnaming the animals "seemed far closer than when their names had stood between myself and them like a clear barrier."[48] The power dynamics of naming have stood in the way of proper understanding, because every being was always viewed through the lens of that initial representation.

For both Humphreys's dogs and Le Guin's woman and animals, it is the rejection of names, which comes to raise animals out of being passive objects, revealing them as active agents. Essentially, such unnaming can thus perform similar functions to those of the animalcentric anthropomorphic naming practices seen in Gowdy's *The White Bone*, and authors can also choose not to name nonhuman characters to signal a degree of independence or preserve a sense of mysticism from which an animal may draw some of its power.[49]

---

[46] Genesis 2.20–23. Ursula Le Guin, "She Unnames Them," in *Buffalo Gals and Other Animal Presences*, 194–196 (London: Victor Gollancz, 1990). Editors' note: Concerning Ursula Le Guin see also Michael Lundblad's and Amelie Björck's chapters in this volume.

[47] Marian Scholtmeijer, "The Power of Otherness: Animals in Women's Fiction," in *Animals and Women: Feminist Theoretical Explorations*, edited by Carol J. Adams and Josephine Donovan (Durham: Duke University Press, 1995), 255.

[48] Le Guin, 195.

[49] An example of this is arguably Julia Leigh's *The Hunter* (1999), in which the protagonist hunts the unnamed last female thylacine, who gains much of her power over his imagination from her elusiveness and anonymity. Julia Leigh, *The Hunter* (London: Faber and Faber, 2000).

Conclusion

Names, namelessness, and acts of naming (and unnaming) are a part of what and how literary narratives communicate about other animals and our relations with them. This is hardly insignificant. Just as one can argue—as does Grant W. Smith—that "the function and meaning of names lie at the very heart of literature," so one might argue that names and practices of naming strike at the heart of the politics of animal representation.[50] The choices of whether to name, and how, do after all create the basis for further representation, and can play a crucial role in how fictional animals relate to, or resemble, the real, living creatures that surround us, as well as the effort (or lack of effort) and understanding with which we approach the interspecies connections we form with other animals. Through the (re)application of theory on names and naming, and a number of exemplifications from different works of fiction, I have attempted to show how the politics, ethics, and power dynamics of naming are central to depictions of nonhuman animals in literary narratives, while they also fulfil different narrative functions. As I have discussed, names and naming in animal narratives can play a significant part in how works of literature tackle such issues as distance and proximity, anthropomorphism, stereotyping, belonging, empowerment, and narrative empathy, as well as the ever-important negotiation between the traditional urge to read animal narratives allegorically or symbolically, and the kinds of readings that insist on the importance of animals as more than mere metaphor.

My review of the issues here is, however, hardly exhaustive; there are undoubtedly numerous literary examples, contexts, and theories concerning our relations with nonhuman animals that might be used to explore the issues of names and naming further, or in which the role of naming might be highlighted to provide new insights into the literary techniques and politics of representing those relations. It is my hope that the present

[50] Smith, 295.

chapter may, for some, provide a starting point or a stepping-stone in such explorations.

References

Barthes, Roland. "Proust and Names." In *New Critical Essays*, 55–68. Translated by Richard Howard. Berkeley: University of California Press, 1990.

Bertills, Yvonne. *Beyond Identification: Proper Names in Children's Literature*. Dissertation. Åbo: Åbo Akademi University Press, 2003. http://bibbild.abo.fi/ediss/2003/BertillsYvonne.pdf.

Borkfelt, Sune. "Colonial Animals and Literary Analysis: The Example of Kipling's Animal Stories." *English Studies* 90, no. 5 (2009): 557–568.

---. "Non-Human Otherness: Animals as Others and Devices for Othering." In *Otherness: A Multilateral Perspective*, 137–154. Edited by Susan Yi Sencindiver, Maria Beville and Marie Lauritzen. Frankfurt am Main: Peter Lang, 2011.

---. "What's in a Name? – Consequences of Naming Non-Human Animals." *Animals* 1, no. 1 (2011): 116–125.

Burelbach, Frederick M. "Names as Distance Controllers in Literature." *Literary Onomastics Studies* 13, no. 1 (1986): 171–182.

de Waal, Frans. *The Ape and the Sushi Master: Cultural Reflections of a Primatologist*. New York: Basic Books, 2001.

Gowdy, Barbara. *The White Bone*. London: Flamingo, 2000.

Hornung, Eva. *Dog Boy*. London: Bloomsbury, 2010.

Humphreys, Helen. *Wild Dogs*. London: Maia Press, 2005.

Keen, Suzanne. *Empathy and the Novel*. Oxford: Oxford University Press, 2007.

Kipling, Rudyard. *The Jungle Books*. Edited by W.W. Robson. Oxford: Oxford University Press, 1998.

Le Guin, Ursula. "She Unnames Them." In *Buffalo Gals and Other Animal Presences*, 194–196. London: Victor Gollancz, 1990.

Leibring, Katharina. "Animal Names." In *The Oxford Handbook of Names and Naming*, 615–627. Edited by Carole Hough. Oxford: Oxford University Press, 2016.

Leigh, Julia. *The Hunter*. London: Faber and Faber, 2000.

Martel, Yann. *Life of Pi*. Edinburgh: Canongate, 2003.

Milstein, Tema. "Nature Identification: The Power of Pointing and Naming." *Environmental Communication* 5, no. 1 (2011): 3–24.

Nilsen, Don L. F. "Onomastic Play and Suspension of Disbelief in Yann Martel's *Life of Pi*." *Onoma: Journal of the International Council of Onomasteic Sciences* 40 (2005): 115–124.

Nuessel, Frank. *The Study of Names: A Guide to the Principles and Topics*. Westport, CT: Greenwood Press, 1992.

Nünning, Vera. *Reading Fictions, Changing Minds: The Cognitive Value of Fiction*. Heidelberg: Universitätsverlag WINTER, 2014.

Nyman, Jopi. *Postcolonial Animal Tale from Kipling to Coetzee*. New Delhi: Atlantic Publishers, 2003.

Poe, Edgar Allan. *The Narrative of Arthur Gordon Pym of Nantucket and Related Tales*. Edited by J. Gerald Kennedy. Oxford: Oxford University Press, 1998.

Scholtmeijer, Marian. "The Power of Otherness: Animals in Women's Fiction." In *Women and Animals: Feminist Theoretical Explorations*, 231–262. Edited by Carol J. Adams and Josephine Donovan. Durham: Duke University Press, 1995.

Sewell, Anna. *Black Beauty*. London: Penguin, 1994.

Simons, John. *Animal Rights and the Politics of Literary Representation*. London: Palgrave, 2002.

Smith, Grant W. "Theoretical Foundations of Literary Onomastics." In *The Oxford Handbook of Literary Onomastics*, 295–309. Edited by Carole Hough. Oxford: Oxford University Press, 2016.

Sowards, Stacey K. "Identification through Orangutans: Destabilizing the Nature/Culture Dualism." *Ethics and the Environment* 11, no. 2 (2006): 45–61.

Stoler, John M. "Dickens' Use of Names in Hard Times." *Literary Onomastics Studies* 12, no. 1 (1985): 153–164.

Artistic Intervention II

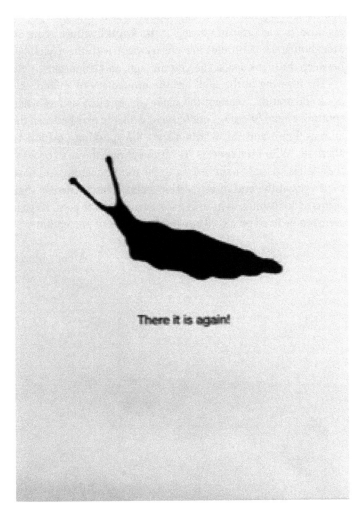

Emma Kihl: *There it is again!*, ink drawing, 2021

Reflection

Ratatǫskr member Emma Kihl is the artistic editor of this volume, but she is also an artist in her own right. In her earlier work she has explored the history and agency of the A4-sheet, and in her ongoing PhD project about Agneta Enckell's poetry and also as a lecturer in writing at the Royal Institute of Art in Stockholm, she continues her engagement with the exchanges between the blank space, the graphic sign, and language.

The drawing of the snail has the immediacy of a children's book illustration, evoking the naive joy most of us feel when spotting a snail (if not on our lettuce). Still, the play between the animal figure and the words allows the speaking position to alternate. Who is talking? Is "it" in the phrase the snail or what the snail is seeing? Snails belong to the mollusc family and have their eyes at the end of retractable stalks. This particular snail seems to be rushing, in its own pace, away from the page. Its gaze seems to be fixed on a goal beyond our scope of perception.

Amelie Björck

FEELING AND THINKING ACROSS
SPECIES AND SCALES

Lungs and Leaves:
Ecosystemic Imaginaries and the Thematics of
Breathing in Finnish Environmental Poetry

Karoliina Lummaa

I want to produce oxygen[1]

Who is speaking in the aphoristic single verse poem by Raisa Marjamäki cited above? The subject might not even be human. The poem expresses an urge to accomplish something that only beings with chlorophyll in their systems are able to do: produce oxygen. Autotrophs tend not to speak, however. The poem combines a verbal wish with a vegetal capability and, in so doing, celebrates photosynthesis as something generally desirable. If the wish is likened to human speech, the poem also ties together the chemically and biologically interlinked processes of breathing—the intake of oxygen and release of carbon dioxide—and photosynthesis—the process of using light energy to convert carbon dioxide, water, and minerals into oxygen and sugars.[2] A breather wishes to become a photosynthesizer.

Marjamäki's poem exemplifies a specific yet consistent motif in Finnish environmental poetry: breathing. During the 1970s, after Rachel Carson's *Silent Spring* (1962) had become widely known in Finland, some poets described silent, poisoned birds gasping for air and dying from pesticide ingestion. At the same time, poets writing about urban environments linked city life to

---

[1] Author's translation. Finnish original reads: "Haluan tuottaa happea." Raisa Marjamäki, *Ei kenenkään laituri* (No one's dock), (Helsinki: Poesia, 2014), VI sheet. Marjamäki's book consists of loose sheets bound together with two rubber bands inside two loose cardboard covers. The pulpy and rubbery, loose materiality of the book enhances its aphoristic, collage-like, and ambiguous environmental poetics.

[2] John King, *Reaching for the Sun: How Plants Work* (Cambridge: Cambridge University Press, 1997).

industrialization, noting how the air was becoming polluted and therefore heavy for both humans and non-humans to breathe. The role of plants as oxygen producers was also recognized, but generally nature writing focused on anthropogenic environmental problems.[3] Nowadays, environmental poetics are often more oriented toward systemic functions and processes in nature, such as biodiversity and climate change. Poets also examine and speculate about physical processes and bodily functions that tie creatures together with their environments, such as breathing or photosynthesis.

For the poets discussed in this essay—Raisa Marjamäki (b. 1987), Olli Heikkonen (b. 1965), Jouni Tossavainen (b. 1958), and Olli-Pekka Tennilä (b. 1980)—breathing exemplifies the chemical and anatomical openness of the body to its environment, and also refers to the processuality of physical existence. Simultaneously, the poets' focus on breathing highlights the physical performance and bodily experiences of individual organisms. In the works of these poets, breathing is typically connected to physical movement and vocal communication (calling, singing, speaking, hissing, growling, etc.), but, in some poems, breathing is also described as an activity that alters the organism's physical environment. Thus, a simple motif expands into wider environmental thematics touching upon various interrelated subjects: experience, communication, and relations between organisms and their environments.

The thematics of breathing also evoke some theoretically interesting questions about animality, human-animal relations, and the relationships between beings and their environments. Through evolution, each animal species has acquired its own physiological and behavioral characteristics, as well as its own ways of acting in and on its environment. Within human-animal studies, ecocriticism, and related critical discussions of the non-human, these characteristics have been addressed with

---

[3] Karoliina Lummaa, *Poliittinen siivekäs. Lintujen konkreettisuus suomalaisessa 1970-luvun ympäristörunoudessa* (Jyväskylä: Jyväskylän yliopisto, 2010).

conceptualizations such as the animal other or the non-human other.[4] As the otherness of animals refers first and foremost to difference and differentiation from the human, the concept of the animal other raises a myriad of epistemological as well as ethical questions: otherness remains beyond the scope of human experience and understanding, but otherness may also lead to subjugation and abuse.[5] However, otherness also refers to differences among different types of animals. Scholars interested in the species-specific abilities and capabilities of animals have approached otherness by utilizing the concept of *Umwelt*, introduced by Baltic-German ethologist Jakob von Uexküll.[6] The epistemological, ethical, and ethological-biological perspectives of animal otherness are fruitful in reading poems about breathing, but the poems also hold a view of animals and the non-human that highlights these beings' environmental agency and intersecting abilities and characteristics. Animals, trees, and humans in these poems are all breathers; interacting and environment-altering beings whose species-being is under constant reconfiguration.

In line with human-animal studies, ecocriticism, and post-humanism, multispecies studies focus on the material-semiotic and natural-cultural agencies and meanings of the non-human;

---

[4] Serpil Oppermann and Serenella Iovino, "Introduction: The Environmental Humanities and the Challenges of the Anthropocene," in *Environmental Humanities: Voices from the Anthropocene* (London: Rowman and Littlefield, 2017); Aaron M. Moe, *Zoopoetics: Animals and the Making of Poetry* (Lanham, Maryland: Lexington Books, 2014).

[5] Cary Wolfe, "In the Shadow of Wittgenstein's Lion: Language, Ethics, and the Question of the Animal," in *Zoontologies: The Question of the Animal* (Minneapolis: University of Minnesota Press, 2003); Matthew Calarco, *Zoographies: The Question of the Animal from Heidegger to Derrida* (New York: Columbia University Press, 2008).

[6] Jakob von Uexküll, *A Foray into the Worlds of Animals and Humans: with a Theory of Meaning*, trans. Joseph D. O'Neil (Minneapolis: University of Minnesota Press, 2010). On the concept of *Umwelt*, see, e.g., Ron Broglio, *Surface Encounters: Thinking with Animals and Art* (Minneapolis: University of Minnesota Press, 2011); Maria Olaussen, "Seeing the Animal Otherwise: An Uexküllian Reading of Kerstin Ekman's The Dog" in *Affect, Space and Animals* (London: Routledge, 2016).

but with an emphasis on coexistential relations across and beyond taxonomic differentiations and the nature/culture-divide.[7] All the aforementioned approaches are further entangled with new materialist thinking, which broadens the idea of agency to all kinds of matter and processes.[8] These fields and frameworks have raised attention to the ways in which non-human animals affect human environments and sustain ecological processes we need for our survival. Concepts of non-human environmental (or ecological) agency and interspecies relations are especially relevant to my analysis.

In this essay, I am interested in the ways in which the functions, activities, and abilities of non-humans are connected to the ecosystemic frameworks of poems written by Marjamäki, Heikkonen, Tossavainen, and Tennilä. I ask: how are the thematics of breathing and photosynthesis—the aerial functions of beings equipped with lungs, leaves, or tracheae—connected to non-human otherness, multispecies relations, and ecology?

Since scientific terminology and knowledge are frequently utilized by the poets I will discuss, as well as by contemporary environmental poetry more generally, and moreover since scientific knowledge guides our understanding of the non-human and influences artistic and cultural imaginaries of the non-human, I will foreground scientific terms and ideas in my analysis. The importance of biological and ecological terminology and knowledge in nature writing has been recognized by ecocritics.[9] On the other hand, the idea of neutrality and objectivity in ecological science has also been challenged.[10] My

---

[7] E.g., Thom van Dooren, Eben Kirksey, and Ursula Münster, "Multispecies Studies. Cultivating Arts of Attentiveness," *Environmental Humanities* 8, no. 1 (2016); Serpil Oppermann and Serenella Iovino, "Introduction." See also Frederike Middelhoff and Sebastian Schönbeck, "Coming to Terms: The Poetics of More-than-Human Worlds," in *Texts, Animals, Environments: Zoopoetics and Ecopoetics* (Freiburg: Rombach Verlag, 2019), 11–16, 26–27.

[8] Serpil Oppermann and Serenella Iovino, "Introduction."

[9] E.g., David W. Gilcrest, *Greening the Lyre: Environmental Poetics and Ethics* (Reno: University of Nevada Press, 2002), 12–18.

[10] Ursula K. Heise, *Imagining Extinction: The Cultural Meanings of Endangered Species* (Chicago: The University of Chicago Press, 2016); Ronald Sandler,

focus will be on the ways in which ecosystemic thinking and biological knowledge are utilized, thematically and rhetorically, to configure interspecies relations in poetry.

The cold breath in the woods

Don't take my name in vain,
for I'll come when you call.
I come through forests,
scrape moss and bark with my antlers,
mute birdsong with my breath, blow
wet leaves and moldered needles in the air.
I raise my nostrils to the wind,
the resins and rowan berries, I smell human longing.
Why do they long for me, my antlers
are bony and bring but pain. Why do they
build power lines, pave the forest path.
My hooves puncture the asphalt
and my eyes soak up the light.
Don't invite me
to the shade of your apple trees. Don't come
to the darkness of my forest.
Don't come. The roots will cling to your feet,
thorn bushes will tear your skin.[11]

"Techno-Conservation in the Anthropocene: What Does It Mean to Save a Species?" in *The Routledge Companion to the Environmental Humanities*, eds. Ursula K. Heise, Jon Christensen and Michelle Niemann, 72–81 (London: Routledge, 2017).

[11] Translation by Maria Lyytinen. Finnish original: "Älä lausu minun nimeäni turhaan, / sillä minä tulen kun kutsut. Tulen metsien läpi, / sarveni raapivat sammalta ja kaarnaa, / minun hengitykseni salpaa lintujen laulun, nostaa ilmaan / märät lehdet ja maatuneet neulat. / Kohotan sieraimet tuuleen, / pihkat ja pihlajanmarjat, haistan ihmisten ikävän. / Miksi he minua kaipaavat, minun sarveni / ovat luiset ja tuovat vain kipua. Miksi he / vetävät voimalinjaa, miksi päällystävät metsätien. / Minun sorkkani puhkovat asvaltin / ja silmäni imevät valon. / Älä kutsu minua / omenapuidesi katveeseen. Älä tule / minun metsäni pimeyteen. / Älä tule. Juurakot takertuvat jalkoihisi, / piikkipensaat repivät ihosi rikki." Olli Heikkonen, *Jäätikön ääri* (The edge of the glacier) (Helsinki: Tammi, 2007).

Many of the poems in Olli Heikkonen's *Jäätikön ääri* present the movements, thoughts, and aspirations of an elk (*Alces alces*). In the beginning of the book, the elk arrives from the deep and dense forest and spreads its cold breath around. When the elk first emerges from the forest and visits the speaker's yard, it is definitely an animal from another realm, more related to pines than to apple trees, more to moss and lichen than to rhubarb leaves or the grass of the speaker's garden.

Moving between the forest and the yard, the elk acts as a mediator between the two worlds. This distinction between the natural realm of forests and the cultural realm of human dwellings is a focal topic in humanistic scholarship on forests. In his seminal work, *Forests: The Shadow of Civilization*, Robert Pogue Harrison examines the history of the Western imagination of forests, showing how "the forest remains a margin of exteriority with respect to civilization."[12] Finnish environmental philosopher Tere Vadén differentiates *the forest, the yard*, and *the house* as three dimensions of experience. At first glance, this seems reminiscent of Giambattista Vico's mid-eighteenth century idea of a forest clearing as the point of departure for the primary cultural institutions of religion, matrimony, and for the burial of the dead.[13] Vadén, too, designates the realm of the house as the space for order and common customs. The yard is kept as a border between the primordial forest (adhering only to its own laws) and the house. The forest supplies the basis for all structures (material and semiotic) required in building a house and the ways of living of the house; and the yard's function is to keep these two realms separate. Unlike in Vico's myth, however, the forest of Vadén's thinking represents a way of experiencing or perceiving the world, and it has a language which precedes the language of the house and the yard. The language of the

---

[12] Robert Pogue Harrison, *Forests: The Shadow of Civilization* (Chicago: The University of Chicago Press, 1992), 201.
[13] Harrison, 3–13.

forest is the raw or untamed flow of experience, unbound by the structures of the house.[14]

The precedence, primordiality, and non-human originality of the forest's language resonates with Heikkonen's elk as it presents itself to the speaker: "Sink your fingers into the darkness of my fur, / for I am the crowned light of the forest. / My crown are the roots / which draw strength from raw soil."[15] The elk is firmly rooted in and empowered by the soil of the forest, and in its antlers, it carries the light—symbolizing the ability to see and know one's way in the depths of the forest. Through its breathing and the spreading of its breath throughout the forest, the elk is affecting its surroundings: "My breath / penetrates birds' plumage / and coats ferns with frost."[16] It even knows how to read the signs and symbols of humans, as it calls itself "the scent of a young forest marked for cutting."[17]

Somewhat surprisingly, the elk also expresses a wish to be more human-like. The poem *My ears keep turning* describes the elk's trembling skin, vocal chords, and jaws: "I have the vocal chords of an ungulate / and jaws tired from chewing, I cannot take / this lichen, these pine seedlings, time after time."[18] The scientific term for a hooved mammal, i.e. "ungulate," repeated mentions of an herbivorous diet, and various other physical characterizations of the elk build a consistent picture of a real animal. In Heikkonen's poems, the elk also transgresses species boundaries by transforming into a tree. The barky transformation intensifies the elk's position as a mediator, messenger, or representative of the forest in a physical, experiential, and per-

---

[14] Tere Vadén, *Kaksijalkainen ympäristövallankumous* (Tampere: Rohkean reunaan, 2010), 12–32.

[15] Translation by Maria Lyytinen. Finnish original: "Upota sormet minun turkkini pimeyteen, / sillä minä olen metsän kruunattu valo. / Minun kruununi on juurakko / joka imee voimaa raa'asta mullasta." Heikkonen, 10.

[16] Translation by Maria Lyytinen. Finnish original: "Minun hengitykseni / lävistää lintujen höyhenpeitteen / ja kuorruttaa saniaiset huurteella." Heikkonen, 10.

[17] Translation by Maria Lyytinen. Finnish original: "Nuoren leimikon tuoksu." Heikkonen, 10.

[18] Author's translation. Finnish original: "Minulla on sorkkaeläimen äänihuulet / ja puremisesta väsyneet leuat, en jaksa / aina tätä jäkälää, näitä männyntaimia." Heikkonen, 11.

haps also spiritual sense. Heikkonen's elk is a poetic hybrid. It is an animal transgressing and mediating the realms of the forest, the yard, and the house (literally and metaphorically); and an animal foraging for plants and lichen, losing its antlers, and sensing its enormous and strong herbivorous body. It smells of its habitat, of sylvan foliage and soil. The elk delivers an environmental message as it laments the way forests are managed. Its all-encompassing breath expresses the ways things affect and alter one another.

Multimorphism

During the last two decades, as the physical and ecological aspects of climate change and the forest's role in regulating carbon balance have been introduced to the wider public, the climate and forests have changed in poetry as well. Like scientists, some poets approach trees as machine-like creatures regulating climate through aerosol production, photosynthesis, and carbon storage. In *Kuusikirja*, a collection of poems accompanied by an essay on the Finnish literary and cultural history of trees and forests, Jouni Tossavainen explores the manifold meanings of forests and their uses, with a special emphasis on spruce trees (*Picea abies*). The following excerpt is from a poem alluding to the ecological, economic, religious, and emotional meanings of spruce trees. Sitting in a tree on a windy night, listening to its humming and rustling and smelling its resin, the speaker suddenly realizes what the tree is doing:

> [--]
> A branchy tree in the wind:
> an enormous suction pump. A big tree, the Great Spruce
> hugs a vast armful of air and water.
> Because of its long fibers, this sacred tree is precious

wood, cheap timber, because branches are ugly eye holes.[19]

The tree is sucking carbon dioxide from the air, releasing aerosols and oxygen, and pumping water upward through its mighty trunk. Back in time, this enormous tree would have been treated as sacred. Now, its value is measured as raw material for the forestry industry. The branches that carry the speaker and rub against the trunk (like hands against the body) leave ugly eye-like holes once the tree is cut for industrial use.

Trees have been a prominent motif throughout the history of Finnish poetry. Often, they are represented anthropomorphically, and are referred to with the gender-neutral human pronoun 'hän' rather than 'se' (i.e., 'it', referring to objects and non-human beings). Their likeness to humans stems from their upright posture, branches reminiscent of out-stretching limbs, relatively long lifespan, and tendency to grow in groups. Trees also have metabolism; they are able to process information, and live in symbiotic relationships with microbes and other life-forms.[20] These physiological, ecological, and ecosemiotic characteristics pave the way for the environmental and even techno-mechanistic imaginaries relevant to contemporary environmental poetry about trees. The following two fragmental poems by Olli-Pekka Tennilä show trees in a somewhat futuristic light:

The tree is the technology of the future.[21]

---

[19] Author's translation. Finnish original "[...] Oksainen puu tuulessa: / mahtava pumppu- ja imulaite. Suuri puu, Isokuusi, / halaa suuren sylin ilmaa ja vettä. / Pitkien syidensä takia tätä uhripuuta pidetään kalliina / kuitupuuna, halpana tukkina, koska oksat ovat rumia silmän reikiä." Jouni Tossavainen, *Kuusikirja* (The Spruce tree book), (Helsinki: Like, 2008, 56).

[20] King, *Reaching for the Sun*.

[21] Author's translation. Finnish original: "Puu on tulevaisuuden teknologia." Olli-Pekka Tennilä, *Yksinkeltainen on kaksinkeltaista* (Simple is twofold / Yellow alone is yellow together) (Helsinki: Poesia, 2012), 87.

If one could see what efficient machines trees are,
one would not be able to see anything else from all the puffing.[22]

Tennilä's environmental poetics are very much informed by the science of ecology, which he combines with philosophical reflections on sense perception, language, and interspecies relations. In the poems quoted above, the functions of trees are described in technological terms. At first glance, it might seem that Tennilä is claiming that trees are like machines, but in the context of his poetry the comparison between trees and machines works the other way around, as well. Trees are the original climate technology based on osmosis, photosynthesis, evaporation, and aerosol production and release. The efficient, complex functions of trees, and the appropriateness of these functions not only to the individual tree but also to the ecosystem (local and planetary), justify comparisons to machines and technology. Indeed, the technological imagery of trees presents them as functional entities in systemic relationships with their environment (rather than as singular machines). This functionality and systematicity is enhanced by the ecological framework of the poems about trees as machines.

The connections among breathing or photosynthesizing human bodies, animal bodies, plant bodies, and machines, we have seen in Marjamäki's, Heikkonen's, Tossavainen's and Tennilä's poems evoke a strong awareness of ecological interconnection. In Heikkonen's elk poems, the focus is on non-human breathing as something that happens in the sylvan realm, spreading coldness and life-sustaining power; but the elk is also "an infallible machine" and "a ticking messenger."[23] Tossavainen's and Tennilä's trees resemble humans and machines and serve definite ecological purposes. The identities and qualit-

---

[22] Author's translation. Finnish original: "Jos voisi nähdä, miten tehokkaita koneita puut ovat, / ei siltä tupruamiselta enää muuta voisi nähdä." Olli-Pekka Tennilä, *Ontto harmaa* (Hollow grey), (Helsinki: Poesia, 2016), unpaged.
[23] Translation by Maria Lyytinen. Finnish original "Erehtymätön koneisto"; "Tikittävä viestintuoja." Heikkonen, 10.

ies, or abilities, of the elk, humans, and trees remain partly open. Rather than anthropomorphism or zoomorphism, this ambiguity might be characterized as *multimorphism*.[24] The bodily functions and forms of non-human and human animals, plants, and machines serve as intersecting frames of reference and as models for perceiving, configuring, and writing about the elk and the trees. As a rhetorical device, multimorphism also calls into question what is human.

Raisa Marjamäki's poetry is yet another example of this interspecies openness related to the consumption or production of oxygen:

> When I was eight years old I still dreamt of
> having been accepted as a plant."[25]
>
> I want to produce oxygen[26]

The two fragments quoted above express a wish to become plant-like, either in a social context, i.e, recognized by others as a plant, or in a functional, agential sense. The quotation marks in the first fragment seem to present it as a piece of writing or speech, as the words of a human speaker. The allusion to humans is fortified, since the age of eight years is implied to be an age where unexpected things are "still" dreamt of.

As I claimed in the beginning of this essay, nothing in the second fragment necessarily indicates that the wish is a human one, but the speakers in poetry—even in environmental poetry—can quite easily be assumed to be humans. The following fragment challenges this assumption, however:

---

[24] On the contested concept of anthropomorphism, see Stewart Elliott Guthrie, *Faces in the Clouds: A New Theory of Religion* (New York: Oxford University Press, 1993); Moe, 17–18.

[25] Author's translation. Finnish original: "Kahdeksanvuotiaana haaveilin vielä että minut / hyväksyttäisiin kasviksi." Marjamäki, VI sheet.

[26] Author's translation. Finnish original: "Haluan tuottaa happea." Marjamäki, VI sheet.

a continuous, persistent prayer
photosynthesis[27]

This poem can be read as a metaphor equating prayer and photosynthesis. Photosynthesis is something that happens continuously and persistently, and, when read together with Marjamäki's other poems regarding plants and about the anxiety brought about by environmental change, it is quite easy to interpret photosynthesis as a prayer of hope. However, there are problems with the metaphorical interpretation. To whom is the prayer directed? What is the content or message of the prayer? Perhaps, then, prayer and photosynthesis are not the same thing, but, rather, simultaneous acts that have the same purpose or goal: the continuation of life. Both prayer and photosynthesis are acts directed at and conducted in the presence of light (physical or spiritual), emphasizing their life-supporting, even metaphysical, power.

Multimorphism is a rhetorical device that redistributes agencies and abilities across species boundaries. This is possible when the species, or at least the types of beings, are named or otherwise identified. Often, beings are described in a detailed manner, through typical behavior or bodily features, for example. While remaining a rhetorical and poetic device, multimorphism, in its simultaneous flexibility and specificity, is based on an interspecies creativity widely recognized by the environmental humanities. Poetry scholar Aaron M. Moe writes about the ability of animals to discover new forms "through an attentiveness to another species' bodily *poiesis*."[28] While bodily poiesis characterizes the behavior and communication of all types of animals (Moe mentions humpback whales as an example), for Moe it is also the basis of zoopoetics, the making of poetry by humans and non-humans.[29] Human writing about

---

[27] Author's translation. Finnish original: "Jatkuvasti sitkeästi toteutuva rukous / fotosynteesi." Marjamäki, IX sheet.
[28] Moe, 10, italics original.
[29] Moe, 10–11.

animals (and trees, I might add) is enabled by attentiveness to the bodily poiesis of all these other species. Environmental philosophers Deborah Bird Rose and Thom van Dooren have used the concept of multispecies ethos as an alternative to the biological concept of species. Multispecies ethos refers to a species' biocultural and embodied way of being that makes it both distinct from other species and open to them in co-existence and co-becoming.[30] The compassionate elk transgressing the limits of forest and garden; the spruce tree carrying a human and hugging air and water to produce oxygen; and the human wanting to photosynthesize are all poetic representations of interspecific bodily poiesis and multispecies *ethe*.

To Breathe, to Speak

Cellular respiration is one of the vital functions of living organisms. In cellular respiration, the body uses oxygen to break down food for energy, while carbon dioxide is produced as a waste product. Breathing is a means of importing oxygen into the system and removing carbon dioxide from it. How breathing occurs varies: insects such as bees do not have lungs. They have openings on the sides of their bodies called spiracles, where air enters into tubes (*tracheae*) that lead it throughout the body.[31] It may be difficult to imagine this type of breathing where the air flows through the body from multiple openings and tubes. And yet this is just one dimension of otherness in bees. They have their own, highly developed system of communication, for example, and moreover their metabolism and material realities are unique. In all their peculiarity and ecological importance,

---

[30] Deborah Bird Rose and Thom van Dooren, "Encountering a More-than-Human World: Ethos and the Arts of Witness," in *The Routledge Companion to the Environmental Humanities*, eds. Ursula K. Heise, Jon Christensen, and Michelle Niemann, 120–128 (London: Routledge, 2017).

[31] Pekka Borg, *Mehiläinen. Ekologia ja hoito* (Helsinki: Suomen Luonnonsuojelu Tuki, 1993).

bees have garnered growing interest among writers, literature
scholars, and environmental philosophers.[32]

Bees (*Apis mellifera*) and beekeeping are central motifs in
Tennilä's collection *Yksinkeltainen on kaksinkeltaista*. With
bees, Tennilä explores the conditions of life at various scales: the
microscopic realities of insects, the intricate connections
between diverse forms of life, and the questions of communication and signification. A subtle connection between pollina-
tion and breathing is suggested in the following poem:

> To breathe tropical, intense breathing air:
> of another lifeform,
> of a city formed by the swarm, a whirling tissue of insects.
> It rises upwards and stains yellowish everything along its
> path.[33]

The poem seems to introduce a different world altogether:
allusion to the tropics implies heat, and the words "city" and
"whirling tissue" refer to multitudes of insects. In another poem
about beekeeping, the speaker describes the insides of a beehive
as a "nanoclimate." In the poem quoted above, the speaker has a
peculiar experience of breathing air that has already passed
through these tiny beings. Everything is colored yellow, to imply
the presence of pollen, honey, and wax. The strange materiality
of bee life is explored in the following poem, as well:

> Humming. Interruptions in breathing. Vicissitudes. In time

[32] Kate Rigby, "Piping in their Honey Dreams': Towards a Creaturely Ecopoetics,"
in *Texts, Animals, Environments: Zoopoetics and Ecopoetics*, eds. Frederike
Middelhoff, Sebastian Schönbeck, Roland Borgards, and Catrin Gersdorf, 281–293
(Freiburg: Rombach Verlag, 2019); Susan McHugh, "Cross-Pollinating: Indigenous Frictions and Honeybee Fictions," in *Texts, Animals, Environments: Zoopoetics and Ecopoetics*, eds. Frederike Middelhoff, Sebastian Schömbeck, Roland
Borgards, and Catrin Gersdorf, 295–306 (Freiburg: Rombach Verlag, 2019).

[33] Author's translation. Finnish original: "Hengittää trooppista, kiihkeää
hengitysilmaa: / toisen eliömuodon, / parven muodostaman kaupungin, pölyävän
hyönteissolukon. / Se nousee ylöspäin ja värjää matkallaan kaiken kellertäväksi."
Tennilä, *Yksinkeltainen on kaksinkeltaista*, 66.

substances like resin and colophony. Suggestions between
light and shadow. Repeating points. Likenesses. Places where
something has stayed. Parts embalmed inside. Loops inten-
sifying into speech.[34]

The enigmatic lines suggest a multitude of associations between
sonic and visual phenomena and substances capable of change
and enclosure. As hardy, yellowish, complex substances of
vegetal origin, resin and colophony bear some resemblance to
beeswax and honey. All these materials are capable of enclosing
things within themselves, embalming parts, as it were.

The poems about bees are also poems about breathing, and
breathing, in turn, is connected to speaking and signification. In
the poem quoted above, something named as "loops" intensifies
into speech. One can think of "loops" as the complex movements with which bees communicate the locations of specific
plants to one another. Another poem about bees breathing and
speaking begins with the verses "Nothing signifies before it
slowly starts to signify. / First, speech becomes audible. First,
humming, interruptions in breathing."[35] The emergence of
meanings, i.e., of the signification of words or gestures, is a
process that humans tend to address conceptually, as a semiotic
phenomenon. Tennilä's poetry about bees points to the possibility of understanding the physical dimension of signification:
of speech transforming the rhythm of breathing, of wings and
legs forming a message that others are capable of deciphering as
information.

In contemporary environmental poetry, and especially in the
context of the thematics of breathing, it is interesting that both
Heikkonen's elk and Tennilä's bees are, albeit implicitly,

[34]Author's translation. Finnish original: "Huminaa. Hengityksen katkoksia.
Käänteitä. Ajan oloon / pihkamaisia ja hartsimaisia aineita. Valon ja varjon
keskistä / ehdottelua. Toistuvia kohtia. Kaltaisuuksia. Kohtia joihin on jääty. /
Sisään balsamoituja osia. Silmukoita yltymässä puheeksi." Tennilä, *Yksinkeltainen
on kaksinkeltaista*, 55.

[35] Author's translation. Finnish original: "Ei mikään merkitse ennen kuin alkaa
hitaasti merkitä. / Ensin puhe alkaa kuulua. Ensin kohinaa, hengityksen
katkoksia." Tennilä: *Yksinkeltainen on kaksinkeltaista*, 54.

expressing a need or a desire for communication. The elk has "the vocal chords of an ungulate" and is therefore unable to speak, but through its visits and its cold breath it affects its surroundings. The bees live in a tropical, yellow warmth quite unfathomable for humans, and still their life evokes allusions to communication and even speaking. The possibility of speaking is, on some level, present in Marjamäki's plant poetry, as well, as photosynthesis is connected to praying and plant-being and oxygen production are things that other-than-plants wish to accomplish.

Interspecies communication and the relationship between human language and the non-human are complicated subjects that have attracted plenty of interest from diverse fields of research.[36] In the poems discussed in this essay, speaking is connected to a larger network of actions or capabilities related to breathing—and breathing, as we have already learned, is connected to photosynthesis, movement, and the consumption of food or nutrients and water. However, breathing also has more philosophical or spiritual dimensions, relating to life and death.

Speaking, in the sense of language use, is often regarded as something primarily (or solely) human. In the context of interspecies histories, this conception seems rather narrow. Everything we now consider particularly human and particularly cultural were once things that developed in all kinds of interactions across species borders. Here, we are reminded of Tere Vadén's philosophy of forests. The language of the forest possesses all the intricate connections between lifeforms and forms of life prior to the human order of the house: "the forest's language may be more refined, more complicated, more skillful, more communal, more historical (oral tradition, everyday speech constantly pausing and with almost no structure whatso-

---

[36] Timo Maran, Dario Martinelli, and Aleksei Turovski, eds., *Readings in Zoo-semiotics* (Berlin: De Gruyter Mouton, 2011); Moe, *Zoopoetics*.

ever, poetry)," writes Vadén.[37] Robert Pogue Harrison presents an opposing conception of language. For Harrison, human speech is an act accentuating the difference between humanity and the rest of the world. Reading Thoreau's *Walden*, Harrison builds his own conception of humanity as separate from nature and dependent on language, or *logos*, as 'relation'. Harrison writes: "Human speech is in every case a confession of longing and finitude, no matter what it says or does not say or even cannot say. We speak our death to one another."[38] This conception of speech is connected to Harrison's idea of humans destined to dwell *in relation to* nature, rather than *in* nature. For Harrison, then, human language always marks the separation between humanity and nature.

The connections between breathing, speaking, and communication are subtle in Tennilä's bee poetry. Bees and humans, as well as other breathers, function and interact in ways that are difficult, if not impossible, to describe in definite ways. As Vadén suggests, poetry may come close to the language of the forest. This is one way to conceptualize the ambiguous and open-ended poetics of breathing in Tennilä's writing—a conceptualization that applies to the other poets I have discussed in this essay, as well. Poetic language may carry non-human influences and, in that sense, represent "the language of the forest."[39] Interestingly, the use of scientific knowledge and terminology does not contradict the imaginative openness and fluidity of poetic language, but may even support it as the poets rhetorically and thematically address diverse aspects of non-human life.

In this essay, I have discussed this openness as an instance of multimorphism, i.e., of the rhetorical entwinings of charac-

---

[37] Author's translation. Finnish original: "[...] metsän kieli voi olla myös talon kieltä hienostuneempaa, monimutkaisempaa, taidokkaampaa, yhteisöllisempää, historiallisempaa (suullinen perinne, arkipäiväinen lähes rakenteeton ja katkeileva puhe, runous)." Vadén, 31.

[38] Harrison, 230.

[39] Moe, *Zoopoetics*; Kadri Tüür, "Bird Sounds in Nature Writing: Human Perspective on Animal Communication," *Sign Systems Studies* 37, no. 3–4 (2009); Karoliina Lummaa, *Kui trittitii! Finnish Avian Poetics* (Helsinki: The Finnish Academy of Science and Letters, 2017).

teristics, abilities, and agencies across species differences. Regarding the thematics of breathing, a multimorphic network of meanings emerges among diverse types of animal and plant bodies and machines; between speaking and breathing, but also between breathing and photosynthesis. In Marjamäki's, Heikkonen's, Tossavainen's and Tennilä's poems, the metabolic, physical, and semiosic activities of animals, plants, and other beings are presented in contexts that are mythical, philosophical, sensual, and also scientific. With breathing and photosynthesis as the focal points of my analysis, I hope to have shown the importance of biological knowledge and ecosystemic thinking in the poetry of these authors.

The shared bodily experiences and the imagined and desired coalescences of abilities across species in contemporary environmental poetry may be read as expressions of a heightened sense of coexistence: humans, animals, and plants share the same environment, and their lives depend on the same ecological processes. Another way of interpreting these accounts of sharing and coalescences is to read them as a negation of the old, guilt-driven opposition of disastrous humanity and suffering nature.[40] A new way of relating to the non-human is actively sought, and it is fueled by a need for belonging, coexistence, and sharing—not separation. "I want to produce oxygen," as the statement of a human-animal speaker, is a telling expression of this poetic wish.

References

Borg, Pekka. *Mehiläinen. Ekologia ja hoito.* Helsinki: Suomen Luonnonsuojelun Tuki, 1993.

Broglio, Ron. *Surface Encounters: Thinking with Animals and Art.* Minneapolis: University of Minnesota Press, 2011.

Calarco, Matthew. *Zoographies: The Question of the Animal from Heidegger to Derrida.* New York: Columbia University Press, 2008.

---

[40] The guilt- and fear-driven anxious environmentalist poetics of earlier decades in Finland established a clear moral division between humans and nonhuman nature, the former neglecting and openly and ruthlessly abusing the latter (Lummaa, *Poliittinen siivekäs*).

Gilcrest, David W. *Greening the Lyre: Environmental Poetics and Ethics.* Reno: University of Nevada Press, 2002.

Guthrie, Stewart Elliott. *Faces in the Clouds: A New Theory of Religion.* New York: Oxford University Press, 1993.

Harrison, Robert Pogue. *Forests: The Shadow of Civilization.* Chicago: The University of Chicago Press, 1992.

Heikkonen, Olli. *Jäätikön ääri.* Helsinki: Tammi, 2007.

Heise, Ursula K. *Imagining Extinction: The Cultural Meanings of Endangered Species.* Chicago: The University of Chicago Press, 2016.

King, John. *Reaching for the Sun: How Plants Work.* Cambridge: Cambridge University Press, 1997.

Lummaa, Karoliina. *Poliittinen siivekäs. Lintujen konkreettisuus suomalaisessa 1970-luvun ympäristörunoudessa.* Jyväskylä: Jyväskylän yliopisto, Nykykulttuurin tutkimuskeskus, 2010.

Lummaa, Karoliina. *Kui trittitii! Finnish Avian Poetics.* Translated by Jaakko Mäntyjärvi, Emily Jeremiah, and Fleur Jeremiah. Helsinki: The Finnish Academy of Science and Letters, 2017.

Maran, Timo, Dario Martinelli, and Aleksei Turovski, eds. *Readings in Zoosemiotics.* Berlin: De Gruyter Mouton, 2011.

Marjamäki, Raisa. *Ei kenenkään laituri.* Helsinki: Poesia, 2014.

McHugh, Susan. "Cross-Pollinating: Indigenous Frictions and Honeybee Fictions." In *Texts, Animals, Environments. Zoopoetics and Ecopoetics,* edited by Frederike Middelhoff, Sebastian Schönbeck, Roland Borgards, and Catrin Gersdorf, 295–306. Freiburg: Rombach Verlag, 2019.

Middelhoff, Frederike and Sebastian Schönbeck. "Coming to Terms: The Poetics of More-than-Human Worlds." In *Texts, Animals, Environments: Zoopoetics and Ecopoetics,* edited by Frederike Middelhoff, Sebastian Schönbeck, Roland Borgards, and Catrin Gersdorf, 11–38. Freiburg: Rombach Verlag, 2019.

Moe, Aaron M. *Zoopoetics: Animals and the Making of Poetry.* Lanham, Maryland: Lexington Books, 2014.

Olaussen, Maria. "Seeing the Animal Otherwise: An Uexküllian Reading of Kerstin Ekman's The Dog." In *Affect, Space and Animals,* edited by Jopi Nyman and Nora Schuurman, 80–94. London: Routledge, 2016.

Oppermann, Serpil and Serenella Iovino. "Introduction: The Environmental Humanities and the Challenges of the Anthropocene." In *Environmental Humanities: Voices from the Anthropocene,* edited by Serpil Oppermann and Serenella Iovino, 1–21. London: Rowman and Littlefield, 2017.

Rigby, Kate. "Piping in their Honey Dreams': Towards a Creaturely Ecopoetics." In *Texts, Animals, Environments: Zoopoetics and Ecopoetics*, edited by Frederike Middelhoff, Sebastian Schönbeck, Roland Borgards, and Catrin Gersdorf, 281–293. Freiburg: Rombach Verlag, 2019.

Rose, Deborah Bird and Thom van Dooren. "Encountering a More-than-Human World: Ethos and the Arts of Witness." In *The Routledge Companion to the Environmental Humanities*, edited by Ursula K. Heise, Jon Christensen, and Michelle Niemann, 120–128. London: Routledge, 2017.

Sandler, Ronald. "Techno-Conservation in the Anthropocene: What Does it Mean to Save a Species?" In *The Routledge Companion to the Environmental Humanities*, edited by Ursula K. Heise, Jon Christensen, and Michelle Niemann, 72–81. London: Routledge, 2017.

Tennilä, Olli-Pekka. *Yksinkeltainen on kaksinkeltaista. Tekstisiruja.* Helsinki: Poesia, 2012.

Tennilä, Olli-Pekka. *Ontto harmaa.* Helsinki: Poesia, 2016.

Tossavainen, Jouni. *Kuusikirja.* Helsinki: Like, 2008.

Tüür, Kadri. "Bird Sounds in Nature Writing: Human Perspective on Animal Communication." *Sign Systems Studies* 37, no. 3/4. Special issue: Zoosemiotics. Guest editors: Dario Martinelli and Otto Lehto. Tartu: Tartu University Press, 2009.

Uexküll, Jakob von. *A Foray into the Worlds of Animals and Humans: with A Theory of Meaning.* Translated by Joseph D. O'Neil. Minneapolis: University of Minnesota Press, 2010 [1934].

Vadén, Tere. *Kaksijalkainen ympäristövallankumous.* Tampere: Rohkean reunaan, 2010.

van Dooren, Thom, Eben Kirksey, and Ursula Münster. "Multispecies Studies: Cultivating Arts of Attentiveness." *Environmental Humanities* 8, no. 1 (2016): 1–23.

Wolfe, Cary. "In the Shadow of Wittgenstein's Lion: Language, Ethics, and the Question of the Animal." In *Zoontologies: The Question of the Animal*, edited by Cary Wolfe, 1–57. Minneapolis: University of Minnesota Press, 2003.

Life as a Lynx: a Digital Animal Story[1]

Gunnar Theodór Eggertsson

Shelter 2 (2015) is an animal survival game created by Stock-holm-based studio Might and Delight. It allows players to embody a Mother Lynx who has given birth to a litter of four cubs. The game's objective is to keep the cubs alive, watch them grow and, eventually, see them leave the proverbial nest. In order to do so, players must keep them fed and safe from harmful predators. The game does not provide much direction, but rather presents players with abstract symbols and a non-linear gameplay that forces them to learn from experience and, more often than not, from failure. At the game's end, Mother Lynx returns alone to the empty den and players are free to begin a new game as one of the surviving cubs. Beneath this deceptively simple survival story a multiplicity of worlds lies hidden, a legion of lives lived and lost as the human player bodies forth into generations of lynxes.

This chapter will argue that *Shelter 2* differs in important respects from other types of animal representation in video games by examining how the game actively engages with an imagined animal viewpoint and creates an intermediary space between the human player and animal avatar. The game will be analyzed both in terms of its ludological elements, i.e. the interactive gameplay and "ludo-narrative" form, as well as its textual elements, i.e. the narrative techniques of animal representation in literature—more precisely, that of the genre of

[1] This chapter is based on two earlier papers given by the author: "Mother Lynx and Asshole Goose: Animal Stories in a Digital Landscape" at the inaugural symposium for the *Ratatoskr* Research Group for Literary Animal Studies at Södertörn University, Stockholm, December 5th 2019, and "Life as a Lynx: Engaging with Animal Viewpoints in Video Games" at the Fellow Travellers Conference at Wesleyan University, Middletown, September 29th 2016. Heartfelt thanks to all members of the *Ratatoskr* group as well as everyone involved with the Animals and Society Institute and Wesleyan Animal Studies programs.

"natural science fiction" and the style of "critical anthropomorphism." Finally, the game will be discussed in terms of animal ethics to speculate how representing the lives of animals through interactive gaming can help reshape and rethink human-animal relations.

Still from *Shelter 2*: A "family group": Mother Lynx with her litter of cubs.

Simulated life: engaging with animals in video games

The medium of video games is filled with animal characters, the majority of whom only have superficial connections to actual animals and are not integral to the gameplay. In his article "Cows, Clicks, Ciphers, and Satire," Tom Tyler refers to these sorts of interchangeable animals as "ciphers," being "empty, transposable placeholders who fulfil a vital function but have no significance in their own right," and further argues that the arbitrariness of these absent referents permits us to forget that these animals "are independent individuals, each with their own existence and experience."[1] As such, the animals serve their role as ludic elements (parts of the game mechanism) but the fact that they are animals and not, say, robots, is irrelevant, because

[1] Tom Tyler, "Cows, Clicks, Ciphers, and Satire." *NECSUS: European Journal of Media Studies* 4.1 (Spring 2015). Website.

their inherent animality has no fundamental bearing upon the game as a whole—put another species (or robot or alien) in their place and the game remains the same. Tyler discusses farming simulators *Farmville* (2009) and the satirical *Cow Clicker* (2010), but other examples include popular characters such as Sega's *Sonic the Hedgehog* (1991), Nintendo's *Donkey Kong* (1981), and the popular *Angry Birds* (2009) franchise, all of which reduce their animals to interchangeable ludic mechanisms. These "cipherous animals" serve as reminders that an animal protagonist does not necessarily make for an "animal game."

A more realistic type of animal representation can be found in the "immersive environment," where animals are portrayed as representations of real world creatures and exist within games as such, showing species-specific behavior, designed according to the look of actual animals and placed in an environment befitting their species. Open world fantasy games such as *The Witcher 3: Wild Hunt* (2015) or *The Elder Scrolls V: Skyrim* (2011) offer detailed and vast fantasy worlds, populated by naturalistic fauna, including bears, wolves, deer and hares, as well as horses, cows, chickens and the occasional pet, all of which are presented as specific animal species and not interchangeable as such. Regardless, these animals are rarely given any characterization and are mostly relegated to decorative purposes as part of an immersive backdrop. Players can let them be or hunt and harvest their bodies for resources (for cooking food, forging weapons, making potions or other craftable items). Although peripheral to most fantasy games, this element of exploitation becomes an integral part of the gameplay within the genre of "survival games," such as *The Long Dark* (2014) or *Conan Exiles* (2017), where animals exist first and foremost to be exploited as raw material in stories revolving around humans surviving at the cost of other animal life.[2] Even if these naturalistic animals retain their animality in-game, players do not actively engage with the animal viewpoint in any meaningful way.

---

[2] It is worth noting that *Conan Exiles* is decisively anti-speciesist by allowing the player to also skin and consume other humans, in addition to wildlife.

A rarer beast is the "trans human" animal game, to borrow a term from *The Deer God* (2015), a puzzle platformer in which a deer hunter is transported into a mythological realm of deers to make up for his violent behavior towards other animals. It is an animal game which allows players to control a member of a specific species within a fantasy environment and even if it has a human story at its center, the overall theme and the multiple viewpoints add an animalistic dimension. Similar "trans human" examples can be found in games like *Never Alone* (2014), where players shift controls between a young Iñupiaq girl and her fox familiar, and *Lost Ember* (2019), where players control a spirit which can jump between various species to solve puzzles. Both games allow players to engage with the viewpoints of other animals in an original and meaningful way by exploring the game environment from a non-human perspective, though the gameplay remains rooted in an anthropocentric storyline.

However, a much more prevalent role for animals in computer games reflects the most common use of animals in real life: namely, as objects of resource and exploitation, most notably as "meat."[3] From resource-building games such as Sid Meier's classic *Civilization* (1991) series, where animal lives are reduced to statistics in an economic system, to the gamification of animal exploitation in hunting simulators, such as the *Hunting Simulator* (2017) series, where naturalistic animals are objectified as trophies in the sport of killing. The same goes for any game that adapts animal exploitation as a core gaming mechanism, such as *Cooking Simulator* (2019), *Farming Simulator* (2008) and *Planet Zoo* (2019), which reduce their animal subjects to ingredients, resources and/or objects to be moved around and managed, and routinely disregard the animal viewpoint.

It is the genre of *wildlife* simulators that bears further reflection. These simulators harken back at least to the mid-90s,

---

[3] For further analysis of digital "meat," see Tom Tyler, "Meanings of Meat in Videogames," in *Literature and Meat Since 1900*, 231–247, edited by Seán McCorry and John Miller (London: Palgrave, 2019).

with games such as *Wolf* (1994) and *Lion* (1995), up to the more recent *WolfQuest* (2007/2015) and *Bee Simulator* (2019). Each of these games has, in one way or another, educational purposes, with much information for players to absorb. A clear sense of naturalism pervades these games: the environment is detailed, the animals are central to the overall design, and, most importantly, they are *integral to the gameplay*. As the term suggests, wildlife simulators actively engage with the animal viewpoint, allowing players to control their bodies and explore their environments. Changing the animal in these simulators would fundamentally alter the game itself, marking them out as true "animal games," but unlike trans-human games that use animal simulation to tell human stories, simulators are not emotionally engaging on a narrative level. They are precisely that—*simulations*—non-linear exploration games without a story structure. At first glance, *Shelter 2* seems to share much with the genre of wildlife simulation, but in order to understand what makes the game different from its more traditional counterparts, we need to examine the way in which *Shelter 2* forms, from its non-linear narrative elements, an engaging and emotionally driven "ludic animal story".

Still from *WolfQuest*: The photorealistic world of wolf simulation.[4]

[4] "About WolfQuest," *WolfQuest.Org*.

Animal play: how *Shelter 2* tells a story

When it comes to the narrative form, computer games are a complicated medium. As Espen Aarseth points out in his 2012 paper "A narrative theory of games," the metonymic term "games" is often mistakenly used to describe "software that in reality are integrated crossmedia packages,"[5] consisting of, for example, film-like scenes, text, music, board games or sports, often within a single program, and, therefore, equating a game with a novel or analyzing a game from a straightforwardly literary perspective runs the risk of oversimplifying or misconstruing the essence of what makes games a unique medium. In order to avoid the infamous "ludology vs. narratology debate" within game studies,[6] this analysis of *Shelter 2* will attempt to follow a "ludo-narrative" model, using the system devised by Aarseth, by acknowledging both the ludologic elements and the narratological aspects that together make up this particular breed of "ludic animal story."

A ludo-narrative analysis is a way to use and adapt certain tools or methods from traditional narratology in order to discuss how a story is formed in a given game. To better understand how *Shelter 2* weaves together its multilayered animal experience, it is helpful to examine what Aarseth defines as the four common denominators inherent to storytelling in both gaming and literature: *World, Objects, Agents*, and *Events*. Within the "ludo-narrative designspace" each of these elements can reside on a sliding scale between a purely narrative pole (more static, e.g. visual novels, where players are led through the narrative in a linear way) and a ludic one (more dynamic, e.g. open-world games where players move freely without being dependent on

[5] Espen Aarseth, "A Narrative Theory of Games." Paper given at the 2012 Foundation of Digital Games Conference (Raleigh, North Carolina: FDG 2012). Online version, 2.

[6] For more info, see Aarseth, 3, as well as Gonzalo Frasca, "Ludology Meets Narratology: Similitude and Differences Between (Video)games and Narrative," (Helsinki: www.ludology.org, 1999). Website [accessed 07–09–2020].

an aready establishednarrative). Most games shift between these two poles in various ways. *Shelter 2* is no exception.

The *world* of *Shelter 2* is mostly non-linear, which marks a fundamental shift from the game's predecessor, *Shelter* (2013), a thematically similar game but structured around a specific narrative route.[7] By adapting the sequel for an open world, the designers have alloted players more freedom and flexibility to explore the environment and personally contribute to the unfolding ludo-narrative. Objects within *Shelter 2* are static, in the sense that they can be interacted with by the player (e.g. rabbits can be hunted and eaten/fed to the cubs) while they are not craftable or modifiable. Less freedom in crafting gives players less control over the narrative, but this element is also of less importance in a game with animal protagonists, when players do not expect a lynx to craft items in a realistic manner.[8]

The *agents* of *Shelter 2* are particularly interesting, since the term has to be adapted to reflect an animal character that does not necessarily fulfill the basic criteria for human computer game characters. Aarseth divides agents along the narrative/ ludic pole and distinguishes between "deep, rich, round characters" and "shallow" or "flat" characters "with names and individual appearance, but little personality."[9] However, deep and rounded *human* characters benefit from having dialogue, making decisions that affect the story and changing as part of a character arc. The lynx does not speak or show inner thoughts and her narrative is rather simple: she shows love and affection for her cubs and tries to keep them alive, but it is really up to the player to fill in the blank space of how to play out her character. Therefore, the lynx rather belongs to the category of "shallow" or "flat" characters, not in the sense that the player necessarily

---

[7] This article was written before the publication of *Shelter 3* (2021) and therefore does not include any comparison with the third part of the game series, nor does it include references to the spin-off games *Paws* (2016) or *Meadow* (2016), both of which are fundamentally different in form to *Shelter 2*.

[8] Many animals can of course make tools and solve puzzles and it would certainly be possible to adapt such themes to a computer game, but in this particular example it is not an important or necessary part of the characterization.

[9] Aarseth, 5.

has a shallow experience of the lynx, but that the gameplay only offers a shallow agent onto whom players can project a certain degree of narrative, characterization and personality.

This finally brings us to *events* and the actual narrative of the ludic story. According to Aarseth's model, a sequence of events on the ludo-narrative pole can be plotted, selectable or open—from the most static or literary, to the most dynamic and ludic. Aarseth borrows from narratology and, using the terms kernel and satellites, suggests that while the former term applies to events that define the story and make it identifiable as a whole, the latter term refers to whatever constitutes "supplementary events that fill out the discourse."[10] The sequence of events in *Shelter 2* is a mixture of both open and plotted events; the narrative kernels are plotted while the satellites remain open and randomized. A playthrough of the game's storyline can there-fore be compared to a sort of framed improvisation—there is a predetermined opening and closure, with a specific temporal progression within the game (the cycle of life) and a certain overall tone (the looming threat of death), but in between these story points, players are free to do whatever they choose within the narrative limits of the game map.

There are five main kernels to the game: (i) giving birth to the cubs (the opening sequence); (ii) feeding the cubs (helping them out of the den); (iii) the passing of the seasons (the game takes place over the span of a single year); (iv) the cubs leaving (as spring returns) and finally (v) the lynx returning to the den, which marks the end of the game. Even if it is possible to work around them a little bit, these five kernels remain fixed parts of the ludo-narrative. So, for example, it is possible to refuse the call of the den in the game's prologue and not trigger the main story. It is also possible to leave the cubs to starve in the den and prematurely enter the final phase of the game. But the most obvious point of kernel control comes from the possibility for players not to return to the den at the game's end, thereby delaying the closure. This gives players a new sense of control

[10] Aarseth, 4.

over the environment, allowing them to spend time exploring, earning achievements, or even admiring the landscape.

In between these five kernels are the supplementary events that flesh out the "ludic animal story" of each individual playthrough. These include player decisions in terms of where to explore or how far to venture away from the relatively safe space surrounding the den. A constant satellite is the cubs' hunger, which must be dealt with otherwise players face the consequences of starvation (a narrative choice in and of itself). There are also other randomized encounters with different predatory animals, which can have the greatest effect on how the discourse of each story pans out. Cubs can be threatened by an eagle, a fox, a pack of wolves or a roaming bear, in addition to environmental dangers such as forest fires and fog. These narrative satellites depend upon random spawns (though the chances of encountering them differ between areas of the map) and player decisions and reactions. Overall a single playthrough can result in an engaging and tragic narrative discourse on a par with some of the finest animal fiction.

However, if we are to compare the ludic story of *Shelter 2* with the tradition of literary animal stories, then it is important to account for the fundamental differences between the two genres. While the literary story remains static, has a clear authorial voice and fixed plot elements, the ludic one offers a non-linear experience that makes each playthrough different from the next. This gives the player control over the narrative as part of an improvisational mode of storytelling. Players of *Shelter 2* are in constant dialogue with the game developers, the latter of whom can be considered as the composers of a piece of improvised music, with players having autonomy over their instruments. It would thus be misleading to compare the literary and the ludic stories on the basis of pure narrative similarities. It is rather in the representation of the animal viewpoint where these two modes of storytelling intersect.

Still from *Shelter 2*: The expressive and mysterious environment.

The ludic and the literary:
an anthropomorphic mystery

In 1902, Canadian animal storyteller Charles G.D. Roberts published his seminal article on "The Animal Story," an overview of the genre of realist animal stories popular around the turn of the 20th century, as well as a manifesto of sorts. There Roberts provides the following definition of what makes good animal fiction: "The animal story at its highest peak of development is a psychological romance constructed on a framework of natural science."[11] In other words, animal stories are never pure fiction, nor pure fact, but always a strange blend of both, each element anchoring the other. Without the framework of natural science, the animal story might lose itself in fantasy and become excessively anthropomorphic. At the same time, without the psychological romance the story risks ignoring the inner life of the animal, reducing their existence to pure behaviorism. This specific genre of animal fiction can be referred to as "natural science fiction," a term which emphasizes the genre's roots in naturalism (natural science), as well as transmitting an unavoid-

[11] Charles G. D. Roberts, *The Kindred of the Wild* (Boston: L. C. Page & Company, 1953), 24.

able sense of the fantastical (science fiction). It is thus a type of naturalistic fiction that does not strive for total realism, but rather aims to combine scientific truths with a sort of poetic truth about human-animal relations.

Whether or not natural science fiction can be said to accurately represent animal cognition or emotion is a philosophical question that touches upon the theory of mind and consciousness, and one that goes beyond the scope of this chapter. However, this caveat is built into the genre, which retains an inherent sense of self-criticism towards its animal representations by adapting a sort of "limited realism," in that any tale told from the viewpoint of an animal will inevitably encounter a chasm bridgeable only with certain leaps of the imagination. Such storytelling can therefore be rooted in verisimilitude, but unlike the field of natural science, these stories do not pretend to tell a scientific "truth" about animal life. Conversely, understanding them as pure fantasy is also misleading, since they are written to reflect real animal lives to some degree. This is the defining quality of natural science fiction—not that animal stories tell us *what it is like* to be another animal, but rather that they allow readers to imagine *what it might be like* to be another animal.

In examining animal computer games through the lens of natural science fiction, then the wildlife simulator seems the obvious case study; both genres aspire to verisimilitude in expressing the lives of animals. But we are immediately faced with a problem: wildlife simulators tend to be too literal and not literary enough and have more in common with nature documentaries than the poetry of animal fiction. They are lacking when it comes to the element of psychological romance that is so vital to the limited realism we find within the genre of natural science fiction. In this respect, *Shelter 2* differs greatly from other wildlife simulators: it shows a distinct lack of educational material, emphasizes immersive gameplay, and openly embraces the unavoidable fantasy of animal simulation. This is not to say that the game does not provide a non-verbal educational aspect, since the general framework of the design-space is realistic enough to give players the feel that the world of the lynx is firmly rooted in natural science and credible animal behavior. Like the realistic animal stories, *Shelter 2* effectively combines the detached human perspective (fact/natural science) with the immersive non-human perspective (fiction/fantasy).

On that note, it is worth briefly discussing Tom Tyler's analysis of the 2003 game *Dog's Life*. While not a wildlife simulator as such—it is an adventure game aimed at a younger audience, with a clear narrative structure and a talking canine protagonist—the game shares important characteristics with the genre. It is definitely an "animal game" in the sense that the protagonist is a central element of the game design; furthermore, it shares the educational aspect of many simulators, even if the designers more readily anthropomorphize the dog. The game's standout feature is its "smellovision" aspect, which shifts the traditional third-person perspective of animal simulators into the first-person point of view, transforming the design-space into muted colours and visualized scents and allows players to imagine a non-human view of the world. This makes it possible for Taylor to speak of the game's "anti-environmental potential," building on MacLuhan's idea of the "environment" as "an encompassing mileau that we fail to notice, but which nonetheless actively structures our actions and awareness."[12] Taylor suggests that by presenting the canine point of view, the game shows players "that the default, seemingly impartial third person perspective is, in fact, a *human* perspective."[13] The "anti-environment" of the canine protagonist therefore poses a challenge to the anthroponormative outlook, one that works to undermine the normalization of the human perspective and reminds players that "a human point of view is but one immersed, subjective perspective amongst many."[14]

The "smellovision" or "instinct mode" effect has seemingly become a standard element in recent wildlife simulators, pos-

[12] Tom Tyler, "New Tricks," *Angelaki* 18.1 (March 2013), 72.
[13] Tyler, "New Tricks," 72.
[14] Tyler, "New Tricks," 77.

sibly influenced by similar features in popular action games, such as *Batman: Arkham Asylum* (2009) and *Tomb Raider* (2013), which include features that transform the environment in order to highlight certain aspects of the gameplay. *WolfQuest* offers a "scent view", so as to smell out particular scent trails of other animals, *Bee Simulator* includes a "bee vision" feature, to see different coloured flowers, and *Shelter 2* has "lynx vision" which singles out possible prey as red shapes. Like *Dog's Life*, both *WolfQuest* and *Bee Simulator* make the jump from a third-person to a first-person perspective when entering instinct modes. However, *Shelter 2* breaks with this tradition and makes no such jump. Like Batman and Lara Croft, Mother Lynx stays within the third-person perspective in both regular and enhanced modes of play. This is because *Shelter 2*'s "anti-environmental" effects do not stem from jumping between perspectives, but by *integrating both perspectives at once*. The detached perspective retains the inherently human point of view, whereas the world building as a whole represents the imagined environment of the lynx.

Indeed, it is the artistic and abstract visual style of *Shelter 2* which truly sets it apart from other wildlife simulators. Roberts' mixture of realism and romance, of fact and fantasy, is an integral part of the game design, as players explore the expressive and mysterious world of the Mother Lynx. Unlike other wildlife simulators, the graphics make no claim to photorealism, but present a landscape that is both familiar and strange, representing that sense of shared space between species viewpoints. Colors are different. Forms are different. Freed from the constraints of the verisimilitude and didacticism of other simulators, *Shelter 2* makes the animal world more open to interpretation. This is an important point, since it creates a worldview that is both familiar to us humans, yet retains the notion that to the animal, it must look and feel otherwise.

As such, the game's visual style is comparable to the popular animal studies understanding of critical anthropomorphism, i.e. writing about animals in a self-reflexive way in order to "make the world of other animals accessible to ourselves and to other human beings" and "more readily understand and explain the emotions or feelings of other animals," to quote Marc Bekoff.[15] Anthropomorphism allows us to address animal inner lives, as long as we uphold a certain critical distance as a reminder that we can never directly access those experiences.[16] Understood in these terms, the heightened visuals of *Shelter 2* become neither a reflection of the "real world" nor a "fantasy world," but rather an artistic expression of the liminal space that exists between species viewpoints. Within this space, the role of anthropomorphism takes on a mysterious quality. In *Why Look At Animals?* John Berger argues that anthropomorphism was integral to the relation between humans and other animals until relatively recently. In the last few centuries, he points out, animals have been reduced to a mechanical view, leaving modern humans alone in the world. "Today we live without them," he writes, "and in this new solitude, anthropomorphism makes us doubly uneasy."[17] That is because the translative language of anthropomorphism reconnects us with other animals through a strange kinship, which, in the context of modernity, can evoke uneasy feelings, since it means acknowledging the animal viewpoint in an age of the increasing objectification of animals.

As Daston and Mitman further point out in their introduction to *Thinking With Animals: New Perspectives on Anthropomorphism*, debates over animal rights have added a new moral dimension to the subject of anthropomorphism, with current discussions taking place in a "highly electrified field" where "the stakes are high and are being played for openly in science, art,

---

[15] Marc Bekoff, "Wild Justice and Fair Play: Cooperation, Forgiveness, and Morality in Animals," in *The Animals Reader,* edited by Linda Kalof and Amy Fitzgerald (Oxford: Berg, 2007), 73.

[16] Just as games can employ different narrative modes within a single program, they can also employ different modes of anthropomorphism, e.g. *Dog's Life* is heavily anthropomorphized in the third-person perspective (the dog talks, makes jokes, etc.) but less so within the "smellovision" setting, which arguably has more in common with the moderately anthropomorphic space of *Shelter 2.*

[17] John Berger, *Why Look At Animals?* (London: Penguin Books, 2009), 21.

politics, and global commerce."[18] Anthropomorphism in video games is no less a moral subject when contextualized within larger debates on animal exploitation, where imagining the world from another species' perspective has ideological consequences. Jumping into the skin of another species means admitting that as humans, our understanding of the lives of animals will forever be limited. This is not a constraining thought. Rather, it is a liberating one. Such an admission breeds mystery back into animal life—a mystery that the modern age has all but destroyed. To quote naturalist Henry Beston, we need "another and a wiser and perhaps a more mystical concept of animals [because] the animal shall not be measured by man."[19] Here, engaging both critically and emotionally with anthropomorphism can be a valuable effort, as a way to think about and explore the strange kinship we have with other species.

The design-space of *Shelter 2* is a beautifully rendered mystery of animal life. As players embody the Mother Lynx, they become a narrative device of their own, improvising their way through this doubled life of human player and animal agent. Whether or not the experience is an accurate depiction of the subjective reality of a lynx is irrelevant. What matters is that players engage with and imagine this life in an emotional and intimate way, as they participate in a willing suspension of anthropocentric reality. The game makes no didactic claim to know exactly what it is like to be a lynx, but players enter into the simulation regardless, recognizing that living as a lynx must somehow be meaningful in itself—if players do not believe this, they would not take the game seriously enough to engage on an emotional level.

Shelter 2 therefore poses questions of poetic truth that help us to think outside of human subjectivity. What does a Mother Lynx feel when she loses one of her cubs? Many players, this author included, have been devastated playing the game, and

---

[18] Lorraine Daston and Gregg Mitman, "Introduction," in *Thinking with Animals,* edited by Daston and Mitman (New York: Columbia University Press, 2005), 4–5.
[19] Henry Beston, *The Outermost House* (New York: St. Martin's Griffin, [2003]), 24–25.

explaining such empathic identification away as mere anthropomorphism is too simple a solution. A Mother Lynx must feel something, even if it is not the same thing as we feel when playing—be it sadness, grief, longing, remembrance, guilt, regret—and through a mode of mysterious anthropomorphism, players partake in an analogous experience to better understand and imagine this animal viewpoint. And the game does touch players, as is evident in some of the top rated YouTube comments beneath the game's soundtrack:[20] "makes me feel violent with emotions"; "just so touching"; "this whole game made me cry" and, perhaps most notably, "this game put me in a world I could never fully understand in a lifetime."[21] It is an experience that stays long in the memory of players; through a mixture of storytelling and gameplay, players have imagined living and dying in that liminal space where species meet.

Photo: Jonas Bengtsson. Mother Lynx with cubs at Skansen zoo, Stockholm (Creative Commons (CC BY 2.0)).

[20] The game's soundtrack and music also plays an important part in the emotional narrative of the game, since it changes during certain scenes (e.g. predator attacks) and areas, as well as playing a soulful theme when the cubs grow up and leave the player.
[21] Quotes from users Fatrick Stare (2015), Rebekkah Katner (2016), _obscurity_ (2017) and J F (2017), respectively. "Shelter 2—Full Soundtrack," uploaded by "cat," on YouTube, June 13th 2015. Website.

Bestial memory: life after lynxes

So what does it mean for a real-life human player to be "put in a lynx's world"? It can mean acknowledging the emotional bonds between a Mother Lynx and her cubs, or challenging an anthroponormative ideology by elevating the animal viewpoint. However, from the game's standpoint, living as a lynx is relatively easy, since the protagonist herself is never in real danger, only her offspring. The lynx cannot be killed, which points to the problem with an otherwise near-perfect game as *Shelter 2*: apart from the player at the controls, there are no humans to be seen. According to one of the game designers, leaving humans out of the storyworld was a calculated choice and a way to keep the game apolitical.[22] But when it comes to the representation of animals in society, there is no staying out of politics, and excluding humans will always be a political choice. As such, this choice reaffirms the myth of a pristine nature and disregards human impact on lynx populations. Most obviously, in a game preoccupied with roles of predator and prey, the choice ignores the presence of human hunters.

Granted, for a wild animal, the Eurasian Lynx is relatively uncontroversial in society, since the species, resembling large housecats with tufted ears, generally shies away from humans, tending to keep away from livestock. In Sweden, the game studio's home country, the lynx has been protected since 1928 and the species' population is monitored annually in accordance with specific Scandinavian guidelines. According to the most recent estimate (2019/2020), 189.5 "family groups," i.e. "adult female lynx with dependent kittens" were registered in Sweden, corresponding to a population of about 1118 lynxes.[23] The reference point for favorable conservation status in Sweden is having at least 870 animals, which brings the Swedish popu-

---

[22] Q&A at the inaugural symposium for the Ratatoskr Research Group for Literary Animal Studies, Södertörn University, Stockholm, December 5th, 2019.

[23] Jenny Mattisson and Jens Frank, "Bestandsovervåking av gaupe i 2020," *Norsk Institutt for naturforskning.*

lation well over that mark.[24] But that also leads to systematic and monitored "culling" of the species with licensed hunts in selected counties. For 2020, the annual allocation of killings was set at 108 animals, spread over 11 counties.[25]

Here, animal life is reduced to simple statistics, but vivid illustrations to these numbers can be found on hunting websites such as the Swedish *Jaktjournalen* (*Hunting Journal*). News about lynx killings is accompanied by obligatory pictures of dead animal bodies, but perhaps none quite as relevant to the subject of this chapter as a trophy photograph published alongside a boastful 2016 news story about a group of hunters who managed to shoot three lynxes in one hunt—a feat so rare that when the group called the government office to report the third dead lynx, the respondent thought they were misreporting the second dead lynx twice.[26] The photograph shows three smiling men, each one kneeling above a dead lynx. All three were killed in the same area and within a limited timeframe. It was a "family group"; a Mother Lynx with two cubs.

Sometimes when playing *Shelter 2*, I like to imagine that my free roaming comes to an abrupt end, when I find a large fence enclosing the pristine wilderness, run into a highway filled with roaring trucks, or that an invisible bullet will bring down one of my cubs from afar, because leaving out humans is only ever part of the whole of any animal story. Immersive and engaging as the game might be, *Shelter 2* does not seem willing to directly engage with animal cruelty or exploitation, leaving one to wonder how such a game would play out—a naturalistic wildlife simulator that encompasses all the complexities of living "wild" in a world controlled by humans. Bringing the thought-exercise even further, one might imagine shifting the *wild* to the *farmed*, even bringing the animal viewpoint into that of contemporary animal exploitation, although a "factory farm animal simulator" is unlikely to see the light of day.

[24] Mirja Lindberget, "Fakta om lodjur," *Naturvårdsverket.*
[25] "Så blir lodjursjakten 2020," *Svensk Jakt* (January 3rd 2020).
[26] Per Jonson, "Makalös lodjursjakt resulterade i trippel," *JaktJournalen* (March 3rd 2016).

Shelter 2 is truly an "animal game" telling a dynamic "ludic animal story" through a complicated, yet deceptively simple, ludo-narrative. As such, it shows the same transformative power as animal fiction when it comes to issues of anthropomorphism and animal ethics, for imaginative storytelling can affect the way humans think about and engage with real-life animals. Even if a game like *Shelter 2* refrains from explicitly dealing with contemporary human-animal problems, it reaffirms the importance of considering the animal viewpoint as an integral part of our anthropocentric environment. This chapter has argued that animal games are part of a greater lineage of animal storytelling as well as a valuable addition to the growing field of both game studies and human-animal studies. Engaging with an animal protagonist—fictional, digital, textual or visual—and taking their lives seriously should have certain consequences in real life, since players have become tainted with a bestial memory which should not be easily ignored. The next time one encounters a lynx behind bars, chances upon strange tracks in the woods, or sees a photograph of proud hunters posing by carcasses, the mind might wander back to some time well spent exploring a digital landscape through the avatar of another animal.[27]

References

Aarseth, Espen. "A Narrative Theory of Games." Paper given at the 2012 Foundation of Digital Games Conference (FDG '12), Raleigh, North Carolina, 2012. Web version [accessed 07–09–2020].

"About WolfQuest." *WolfQuest.Org*, Eduweb. Website [accessed 07–09–2020].

Bekoff, Marc. "Wild Justice and Fair Play: Cooperation, Forgiveness, and Morality in Animals." In *The Animals Reader,* 72–90. Edited by Linda Kalof and Amy Fitzgerald. Oxford: Berg, 2007.

---

[27] The forthcoming game *Natural Instincts* from DreamStorm Studios (out in early access 2021) will allow players to command animals and help them survive in an environment that includes human intrusion, such as the threat of poachers and roads. Although it remains to be seen how the game engages with the animal viewpoint, it shows how the genre of animal games continues to evolve and therefore should remain of interest to gamers and academics alike.

Bengtsson, Jonas. *Lynxes from Skansen*. Photograph. Creative Commons (CC BY 2.0). Website [accessed 14–08–2020].

Berger, John. *Why Look At Animals?* London: Penguin Books, 2009.

Beston, Henry. *The Outermost House*. 75th Anniversary Edition. New York: St. Martin's Griffin [2003].

Daston, Lorraine and Gregg Mitman. "Introduction." In *Thinking with Animals. New Perspectives on Anthropomorphism*, 1–14. Edited by Daston and Mitman. New York: Columbia University Press, 2005.

Jonson, Per. "Makalös lodjursjakt resulterade i trippel." *JaktJournalen* (March 3rd 2016). Website [accessed 14–08–2020].

Lindberget, Mirja. "Fakta om lodjur," *Naturvårdsverket*. Website [accessed 14–08–2020].

Mattisson, Jenny and Jens Frank. "Bestandsovervåking av gaupe i 2020." *Norsk Institutt for naturforskning*. Website [accessed 07–09–2020].

Roberts, Charles G. D. *The Kindred of the Wild*. Boston: L.C. Page & Company, 1953.

"Shelter 2—Full Soundtrack." Uploaded by "cat." YouTube, June 13th 2015. Website [accessed 07–09–2020].

"Så blir lodjursjakten 2020." *Svensk Jakt* (January 3rd 2020). Website [accessed 14–08–2020].

Tyler, Tom. "Cows, Clicks, Ciphers, and Satire." *NECSUS: European Journal of Media Studies* 4.1 (Spring 2015).

Tyler, Tom. "New Tricks." *Angelaki* 18.1 (March 2013): 65–82. Web version [accessed 07–09–2020].

Humans, Cows, and Bacteria:
Three Modes of Reading the Film *Bullhead*

Amelie Björck

As Donna Haraway has been arguing throughout her work, knowledge production is a "story telling practice."[1] Humans use stories to organize knowledge in order to understand the world and to become familiar about what at first seems foreign. But stories tend to stick to old dramaturgies and scales. They typically put humans at the center, challenging us first and foremost to understand *ourselves*. As Francois Lyotard pointed out already thirty years ago, the backside of this focus on the human is that it prevents us from taking the diversity of agencies on this planet seriously.[2] While science offers us plenty of *information* about non-human life and events on planetary and microscopic levels, we still grapple with how to handle this material, culturally and aesthetically, without humanizing it beyond recognition. In short: How can we grasp what is going on with our planet on micro and global levels, and with other forms of life, if the human figure is our constant filter?

In the anthology *Telemorphosis*, environmental humanities professor Timothy Clark formulates the question slightly differently. He writes: "How then can a literary or cultural critic engage with the sudden sense that most given thought about literature and culture has been taking place on the wrong scale?"[3]

---

[1] Donna Haraway, *Primate Visions. Gender, Race and Nature in the World of Modern Science* (London/New York: Routledge, 1989), 4. Haraway's focus on story telling practices has pervaded most of her writings since the 1980s.

[2] Jean-François Lyotard, *Inhuman. Reflections on Time*, trans. Geoffrey Bennington and Rachel Bowlby (Cambridge/Oxford: Polity Press, 1993), 1–7.

[3] Timothy Clark, "Scale. Derangements of Scale," in *Telemophosis. Theory in the era of Climate Change*, ed. Tom Cohen (Ann Arbor: University of Michigan Library, 2012), 152. Clark develops his work further in Timothy Clark, *Ecocriticism on the Edge. The Anthropocene as a Threshold Concept* (London: Bloomsbury Academic, 2015).

For me as a literary scholar this is an important rephrasing, since it puts the spotlight on the reader and critic rather than the writer or creator. How can I, as a reader, navigate to help ablate human narcissism?[4]

Clark makes his contribution by proposing a reading of a short story by Raymond Carver that moves its scope from scale to scale. First, he reads the story, *Elephant*, on the familiar scale of the characters, then he looks at it on a national scale and in its close historical setting, and finally he reads it on a planetary scale, widening the timespan to a randomly chosen macro frame of 600 years. In that widened, earthly perspective, the story's entire ethic shows itself differently. The main issue is no longer the question of personal responsibility toward family and friends, when the main character gets tired of lending money to each and everyone. Neither is it the state of poverty and consumerism in the US—at least not restricted as a nation state problem. Rather, the story's whole infrastructure of people, cars, separate households and property owning comes across as a bizarre machine of destruction, taken for a stable and familiar reality. As Clark puts it:

> Plots, characters, setting and trivia that seemed normal and harmless on the personal or national scale reappear as destructive doubles of themselves on the third scale, part of a disturbing and encroaching parallel universe, whose malign reality it is becoming impossible to deny.[5]

In this wide perspective, having or losing a car is not a private thing, since CO_2 emissions is a global disorder, and the tragedy of poverty is hardly a tragedy at all in relation to an exploited earth. With its impersonal and ahuman outlook, Clark's third scale reading might seem counterintuitive and harsh, but nonetheless it does reveal a crucial drama. An earthly drama which is there, in the text, but easy to miss.

---

[4] It is implicit that I here use the term "reading" in the broad sense of engaging in and digesting a cultural expression in any medium or genre.
[5] Clark, 161.

Reading on different scales like this, and juxtaposing them to display the dilemma of conflicting interests, is obviously an experiment. It is not an experiment that claims to go beyond human logics; what is offered is not the kind of bewildering deconstruction that might in the end be needed to properly rethink hermeneutics in the Anthropocene. Still, I find the attempt important, since it has the ambition to widen our conventional mindset as critics. It trains us to see other stories besides the privileged one, thereby putting our accustomed knowledge production into perspective.

In this chapter I want to demonstrate in a slightly different way how different modes of reading might activate different kinds of awarenessess. In accordance with Clark, I will suggest modes that move increasingly further away from the human figure—but instead of a scaling up in time and place, I will focus on different kinds of agencies and interests, with the aim to unsettle the preconception of whose and what drama we are beholding. However, scale remains an important factor, and it will become apparent that the impersonal micro scale (which is closely conjoined with the earthly macro scale) remains the trickiest for the reader to fully do justice.

I tentatively call the three modes of reading:

- Traditional humanist reading
- Animal studies reading
- Microecological reading

By choosing these modes, I wish to acknowledge the fact that the research fields of animal-studies and ecocriticism have during the past decades challenged the humanities to read in the spirit of Clark: to look for other stories, with acute relevance in the anthropocene era, within and beyond the human framed story. Still, most readers, also within these fields, refrain from utilizing conflicting modes of reading for understanding the same story. Furthermore, there is an abiding reluctance to move too far beyond the (presumed) intention of the story's author. This kind of tactful hesitation to interpret absences or make overinterpretations must, with this reading experiment, be abandoned.

The focus of my study is the Oscar nominated Belgian film *Bullhead* (Rundskop) from 2011, created by Michaël Roskam. This film serves as pedagogical material since it touches thematically upon the boundaries between the human, animal and microbiological realms. As soon as I start recapitulating the story, one of the three modes of reading will be activated. For the sake of homeliness, I will start in the traditional humanist mode.

The traditional humanist reading

From this interpretive perspective the film is about a farmer, Jacky, who is head of a large cattle production plant in northeastern Belgium. Jacky is the silent, hardworking type, stuck in the mud but respected by his mates for his strong and bull-like physics, his highly productive animals and his connections to the black market. In a couple of bathroom-scenes we learn about Jacky's abuse of hormones, which is mirrored by his practice of injecting hormone and anti-biotic cocktails into his already supersized cows. 35 minutes into the film, in a terrifying flashback, we realize that Jacky suffered a bodily trauma as a boy. He was badly beaten by a mentally disabled and hyper-sexual juvenile, who decided to crush the younger boy's genitals. After his injury Jacky's parents and a doctor started treating him with hormones—along with a thick silence—in order to keep up an illusion of "normality." For Jacky the trauma seems to have resulted in a combination of overcompensating for the feared loss of masculinity and an inability to articulate emotions other than in brutal physical ways. Typically, his rage is evoked by gay men who do not honor the kind of reproductive heterosexuality from which he is himself precluded.

Jacky's complex biography makes him shy and awkward when he meets and tries to court his childhood love again. At this point he has also become more deeply involved with the hormone mafia, trading drugs and meat and violently avoiding to be exposed by a unit of detectives. It all ends with death. Jacky is hunted down by the police after his loved one has turned him in, and in a furious fight in the elevator he is shot by the officers.

The animal studies reading

So—if this is the traditional humanist reading, distinguishing the psychological and social pattern of a man's (mis)fortune—what, then, could an animal studies mode of reading pick up that the anthropocentric interpretation misses? It is a fact that non-human animals, and more specifically cattle, are very much present in the film. Cattle are seen cribbed at Jacky's and his neighbours' farms. They are exposed as receivers of drugs and when being handled during calving, their flesh is projected as merchandise and demonstratively subject to close-ups when grilled and consumed.

The visual mirroring between the man and the animals now calls for further analysis. I mentioned the correspondence between Jacky's bull-like body and his super-sized animals—an aspect which is highlighted in the visual marketing of the film. But the depiction acutely emphasizes the *fragility* of all these big bodies, more than their strength. These animals are exploited and confined cows rather than groomed fighting bulls. The setting is dark realism, exposing industrial commodification and bodily vulnerability.

It is not uncommon in fiction that the exposure of the harsh biopolitics of animal production is used to amplify the emotional content within the human sphere, suggesting a related hardship. Such tendencies abound in proletarian classics such as the report novel *The Jungle* by Upton Sinclair (1906) and the theatre play *Die heilige Johanna der Schlachthöfe* by Bertolt Brecht (1931). Both of these stories are set in the horrifying Chicago Stockyards, and picture animal as well as human suffering—but leaving no question that the human class struggle is the issue (rather than the salvation of the animals).

In *Bullhead* the mirroring intitially goes both ways. It is also worth noting that the mirroring does not limit itself to affirming a common victimization of cattle and human workers in the animal industry in a general way, rather it focuses on specific points of exposure in the animals' lives (and in Jacky's life). The practices of "body building" and "reproductive sexuality," emphasized by the mirroring, are certainly at the core of the animal trauma at any breeding plant. The animal studies reader would investigate this aspect, remaining close to the animal interest.

The Belgian blue is a breed in which a certain mutation has been promoted. As a result, the animals usually have a genetical inactivation of a special growth inhibiting hormone. This means that the calves are huge and generally have to be delivered by caesarian section. This total dependence on a human scalpel at the most fragile moment of giving birth adds another component to the already prevailing human command over the reproduction of these animals, who will never be allowed to breed without the assistance of humans, nor to keep their offspring for very long.

The animal studies reader would recognize the importance of this in the story. The film *does* seem unusually engaged in and knowledgeable about the reality of the animals. The cattle and the man are both presented as hostages of the hierarchical value system that Jacques Derrida has labelled "carnophallogo-centrism",[6] in which the intelligent, meat-eating macho man is at the top while the animal lies at the bottom of the order. In the film, this matrix of domination is reinforced by economic power structures—further entangling humans and animals. The hormone trafficking plot of the film involves both Jacky and, by force, the animals, in a criminal socio-economic network. Furthermore, the mafia network has a documentary background, which encourages the viewer to reflect critically on real

---

[6] Jacques Derrida, "'Eating well', or the Calculation of the Subject. Interview by Jean-Luc Nancy" [1988], in *Jacques Derrida: Points ... Interviews 1974–1994*, trans. Peter Connor and Avital Ronell (Stanford: Stanford University Press, 1994), 280–284. The term "carnophallogocentrism" is an expansion of Luce Irigaray's earlier term "phallogocentrism," acknowledging that the human power over other animals—ultimately manifested in traditions of sacrifice and eating—is a fundamental aspect of the "matrix of domination" that keeps human civilization in place.

life affairs. The use of hormones in meat production, to increase growth and thereby profit, has been outlawed in the European Union since 1989 because of the hazards for the animals, when their bodies become too heavy for their organs and skeletons. Since hormones are rather easily manufactured this has resulted in an active black market.

The film demonstrates the terror of the matrix of domination in its many different angles. It is when Jacky starts sliding from his dominant position—when his masculinity softens, when he tests perfumes in his loved one's shop, speaks soft French to her instead of rough Limburgish, abandons his mafia brothers and loses his cold rationality—that is, it is when he is no longer in place at the top of the order, that he becomes every bit as "killable" as his animals had been all the time.

The problem, from the animal studies point of view, is the increasing asymmetrical nature of this mirroring. The film eventually relapses into an anthropocentric perspective. It laments the debasement of the man but not that of the animals. The animals are abandoned by the narrative and the camera at crucial points. Take for instance the scene in which Jacky is seen assisting the gloved veterinary during the delivery of a new calf by caesarian section. As soon as the cut is made, the men coil an iron chain around the calf's leg, hoisting it from the safe haven in its mother's womb into the air. The camera then zooms in on the calf, placed in a cold and empty barrow, sniffing in vain for its mother's warm body.

Draped in solemn violin tunes the scene addresses the commodification of life, the brutal deprivation of closeness and the heartbreaking adjustment to loneliness—acute realities for the calf and experiences shared to some extent by Jacky. But instead of staying a little longer with, or coming back to, the calf to confirm reciprocity, the camera turns to Jacky, reducing the animal tragedy to an amplifier of his human misfortune. This is done by showing Jacky standing alone in the following scene and then contrasting his loneliness with a shot of his brother's big family. The futurelessness of the calf becomes Jacky's future-lessness and his misery is depicted as dependent on his sad relation to heterosexual reproduction: he will never have children of his own like his brother.

Along these same lines it is Jacky, the human, that the camera follows to his tragic end. The final scenes are all about Jacky's downfall and death. The destiny and assumed killing of the cattle he left behind takes place out of view.

The microecological reading

I will now move on to the microecological mode of reading, which would criticize both the anthropocentric and the animal studies interpretations for limiting themselves to the mammal scale and interest.

Just as the film in part appears to care for the animals, it also thematically evokes the microecological perspective, by pointing out the relation between micro-agents like hormones and antibiotics and big mammal bodies. The film makes clear that bodies are not self-sufficient entities, rather, with a phrasing from biogeographer Bruno Brown, they are "embedded in a chaotic and unpredictable molecular world."[7] The film seems to criticize the microbiological modification of both humans and animals as biopolitical interventions powered by destructive value norms and profit seeking.

A microecological reading of the film would "follow the micro-agents"[8] and point out how substances move around and permeate life beyond human optics and control. Via the meat eaten in the film, the human bodies receive doses of the hormones injected in the cows. When Jacky, in his desperation towards the end of the film, empties his stash of drugs in the

[7] Bruce Brown, "Biopolitics and the Molecularization of Life," *Cultural Geographies*, no. 14 (2007): 17.

[8] This is a consenting rephrasing of Ann-Sofie Lönngren's "following the animal" as a human-animal studies reading method, suggesting that the researcher should follow the track of the animal (rather than the human) throughout the text and beyond it, but with an active awareness that to follow must not mean to hunt and name; instead it might mean to be seen first or just being close and curious. Ann-Sofie Lönngren, *Following the Animal. Power, Agency, and Human-animal Transformations in Modern, Northern-European Literature* (Newcastle upon Tyne: Cambridge Scholars Publishing, 2015), 27–30.

sewer, it is a kind of peripeteia from a micro-perspective: this means that the substances will travel widely via the groundwater into new and other bodies and material assemblages.

Moreover, inside the cows' bodies, the injected substances—including antibiotics to prevent disease and promote extra growth—will eventually create more cases of bacterial resistance. Resistant bacteria will travel between cows and humans via touch, food, water and ground and might spread unstoppable diseases. Furthermore, the emission of methane gas from animal industries like Jacky's could be added to the micro scenario, as one of the main factors behind global warming.[9] The micro and the macro activities thus tend to be closely entangled. The microecological drama in *Bullhead* turns out to be a drama of global relevance. Within much less than Clark's timescale of 600 years, this drama has the power to change and rearrange the forms of life with which we are familiar.

From an anthropocentric humanist perspective, resistant bacteria are the enemy, since they threaten human life. But from a microecological perspective, the eventual rearrangement of life forms might be valued differently. After all, microbes were here long before our species and have developed extremely smart and resilient forms of existence. As Myra Hird concludes after a deep dive into recent research:

> Taken together, this research suggests that bacteria 'develop collective memory, use and generate common knowledge, develop group identity, recognize the identity of other colonies, learn from experience to improve themselves, and engage in group decision-making, an additional surprising social conduct that amounts to what should most appropriately be dubbed as social intelligence'.[10]

[9] P. K. Thornton, "Livestock Production: Recent Trends, Future Prospects," *Philosophical Transactions of the Royal Society B*, no. 365 (2010), 2853–2867.

[10] Myra Hird, *The Origins of Sociable Life. Evolution After Science Studies* (New York: Palgrave Macmillan, 2009), 52. The quote within the quote refers to Eshel

Why, then, should bacteria not take over after us? Anti-humanists like Patricia MacCormack and Claire Colebrook accept the idea of a flourishing and diverse future earth without our species.[11] Many others still hope for improved co-existence. Wherever our sympathy lies, in the light of the micro and macro dramas, Jacky's singular tragedy in the film seems like a tiny cog in a huge machinery.

In addition: from this microecological perspective, we become aware of the fixation on sexual difference and sexual reproduction in human culture and art. So many fictions attract their audiences by means of a theme of love and mating. The film *Bullhead* revolves around this theme, at the same time both consolidating and interrogating the idea of "natural" sexual reproduction as the given focus of mammal scaled life. Both for Jacky and for his animals, sexuality and reproduction are central, though in disharmony, depicted as mechanisms driven by frustrated desire, greed and longing, and upheld by technology.

As Clare Colebrook has shown, the human focus on "sexual difference" is paradoxical.[12] In a way, our culturally cheered interest in sex and reproduction is what keeps our species alive, but it has also lured us to think of other issues as less interesting—as if we were autonomous as a species and able, unhindered, to continue to reproduce no matter what happens outside our mesmerizing story of love and genetic exchange. This, Colebrook reminds us, is false since the system of sexual reproduction is extremely fragile to environmental changes. Much more so than other forms of reproduction, for instance

Ben-Jacob, Israela Becker, Yoash Shapira and Herbert Levine, "Bacterial Linguistic Communication and Social Intelligence," *Trends in Microbiology* 12, no. 8 (2004), 367.

[11] Claire Colebrook, *Death of the PostHuman. Essays on Extinction*, vol. 1, (Ann Arbor: Michigan Publishing and Open Humanities Press, 2014); Patricia Mac-Cormack, *The Ahuman Manifesto* (London: Bloomsbury Academic, 2020).

[12] Claire Colebrook, "Sexual Indifference," in *Telemophosis. Theory in the Era of Climate Change*, ed. Tom Cohen (Ann Arbor: University of Michigan Library, 2012), 170.

cloning—and as Myra Hird observes: "[…] bacteria invented cloning some 3.8 billion years ago."[13] While we have been preoccupied with our human stories about courting and sex, the human generated climate crisis has been growing in our peripheral vision—and now we are facing the prediction that the Y-cromosome might not endure for long.[14] Seen in a longer timespan, then, a changed environment might in fact slowly erase male virility—more effectively than any swarm of distressed juveniles with stones. Again: For good or bad? In a private perspective we see a myriad of personal tragedies lining up, but from the perspective of an overpopulated earth, on which a human steamroller is destroying diversity inch by inch, the drama is another.

Ransacking the readings and their relevance

Would it be possible to integrate the human subject's private perspective and the earthly perspective in one ethics—to see the individual as part of a kind of human super-subject, with a collective super-agency and super-responsibility in the era of the Antropocene? For instance, to see childlessness as a good deed from the part of the super-subject, and not only a private tragedy? This does not come easy.

So far, our storytelling practices in the West and North have schooled us to value "life" and "creation" in terms of anthropocentric criteria such as the survival of mankind, individual self-realization, and "personal liberal freedoms" such as the right to become a parent. With few exceptions, storytelling fiction has nurtured our sense of supersubjectivity (acting as a species/as Man) only when it comes to conquering different kinds of outer threats (like great storms, viruses or aliens), and less to cultivate an awareness of entanglements, responsibilities or a willingness to step back. Donna Haraway has labelled the fundamental heroic story, encountered in old myths, as well as in contemporary narratives including sci/fi and cli/fi, the "prick tale":

---

[13] Hird, 25.
[14] Colebrook, "Sexual Indifference," 167.

In a tragic story with only one real actor, one real world-maker, the hero, this is the Man-making tale of the hunter on a quest to kill and bring back the terrible bounty. This is the cutting, sharp, combative tale of action that defers the suffering of glutinous, earth-rotted passivity beyond bearing. All others in the prick tale are props, plot space, or prey.[15]

Looking at *Bullhead*, it is evident that its (porous) backbone is a kind of privatized "prick tale," with Jacky as the hero who tries but fails to break free and fulfill himself. The further our reading withdraws from the human figure, i.e. Jacky and his fate, the less support we get from the film's concrete narrative and visual articulations. As we have seen, the film touches on the boundaries to other agencies and scales, but asymmetry prevails. The animals are there, in sight, but the mirroring between the cows and the man weigh over until Jacky fills up the whole screen. In terms of the microecological aspect, it is not at all as elaborated as the mammal scaled dramas. In fact, its only visualization is in the form of bottles with substances for injections, in view in a few scenes. This means that the microecological reading edges the farfetched; it relies to a large extent on the reader's own imagination and previous knowledge.

To counterbalance the "prick tale" tradition Haraway proposes acts of "re-storying," that turn the attention away from heroic actions and toward the supposedly passive but in fact bustling "background." Her proposal is inspired by author and theorist Ursula Le Guin, who in 1986 formulated a "Carrier bag theory of fiction."[16] Le Guin's theory looks at storytelling in relation to the ancient (female) activity of gathering rather than hunting: a story should be a "holder" of a myriad of small things

---

[15] Donna Haraway, *Staying with the Trouble. Making Kin in the Chthulucene* (Durham: Duke University Press, 2016), 39.

[16] Ursula Le Guin, "A Carrier Bag Theory of Fiction," in *Dancing at the Edge of the World. Thoughts on Words, Women and Places* (New York: Grove Press, 2018), 165–170. Editors' note: Concerning Ursula Le Guin, see also Sune Borkfelt's and Michael Lundblad's chapters in this volume.

in subtle relations, rather than a journey toward a specific (heroic) goal. Le Guins novels, turning theory into practice, serve us with thick and messy story nets without a clear-cut progression from A to B. Indeed, it seems to take an experiment, in the sense of leaving narrative conventions behind, to do justice to the reality of the "mesh"[17] of earthly life. In fact, other genres or art forms than the novel or the motion picture might have a better starting position, when it comes to wiring humans to micro and macro perspectives—artforms like poetry, dance, sound art or visual art. These art forms are less hooked on elements such as a main character, causal storyline and a perfect closure. They are art forms that have a historical experience of exploring materialities and abstraction, beyond the contours of the human figure, and they currently show great interest in the more-than-human sphere.

Still, as I have tried to outline with my three readings of *Bullhead*, re-storying is not only a task for creators of literature and art, but also for critics and readers when encountering any particular story. As initially stated, one of the major points of making reading experiments, combining different modes of reading, is that they bring to attention what we take for granted and what we are willing to block out—not only when reading fiction, but when reading the stories of our own everyday lives. As Timothy Clark concludes:

> In sum, reading at several scales at once cannot be just the abolition of one scale in the greater claim of another but a way of enriching, singularizing and yet also creatively deranging the text through embedding it in multiple and even contradictory frames at the same time [...].[18]

With this kind of "deranging" readings we may come closer to a kind of truth: an acknowledgment of the frictions and ethical

---

[17] Timothy Morton, *The Ecological Thought* (Boston: Harvard University Press, 2010), 29. Morton coined the word "mesh" to account for the interconnectedness of all living and non-living things on earth.
[18] Clark, 163.

dilemmas that characterize being part of the entangled mesh of planetary existence.

References

Brown, Bruce. "Biopolitics and the Molecularization of Life," *Cultural Geographies*, no. 14 (2007): 6–28.

Clark, Timothy. "Scale. Derangements of Scale." In *Telemophosis. Theory in the era of Climate Change*, 148–166. Edited by Tom Cohen. Ann Arbor: University of Michigan Library, 2012.

Clark, Timothy. *Ecocriticism on the Edge. The Anthropocene as a Threshold Concept.* London: Bloomsbury Academic, 2015.

Colebrook, Claire. "Sexual Indifference." In *Telemophosis. Theory in the Era of Climate Change*, 167–182. Edited by Tom Cohen. Ann Arbor: University of Michigan Library, 2012.

Colebrook, Claire. *Death of the PostHuman. Essays on Extinction*, vol. 1. Ann Arbor: Michigan Publishing and Open Humanities Press, 2014.

Derrida, Jacques. "'Eating well', or the Calculation of the Subject. Interview by Jean-Luc Nancy." In *Jacques Derrida: Points ... Interviews 1974–1994*, 255–87. Translated by Peter Connor and Avital Ronell. Stanford: Stanford University Press, 1994.

Haraway, Donna. *Primate Visions. Gender, Race and Nature in the World of Modern Science.* London/New York: Routledge, 1989.

Haraway, Donna. *Staying with the Trouble. Making Kin in the Chthulucene.* Durham: Duke University Press, 2016.

Hird, Myra. *The Origins of Sociable Life. Evolution After Science Studies.* New York: Palgrave Macmillan, 2009.

Le Guin, Ursula. "A Carrier Bag Theory of Fiction." In *Dancing at the Edge of the World. Thoughts on Words, Women and Places*, 165–170. New York: Grove Press, 2018.

Lönngren, Ann-Sofie. *Following the Animal. Power, Agency, and Human-animal Transformations in Modern, Northern-European Literature.* Newcastle upon Tyne: Cambridge Scholars Publishing, 2015.

Lyotard, Jean-François. *Inhuman. Reflections on Time.* Translated by Geoffrey Bennington and Rachel Bowlby. Cambridge/Oxford: Polity Press, 1993.

Morton, Timothy. *The Ecological Thought.* Boston: Harvard University Press, 2010.

Thornton, P. K. "Livestock Production: Recent Trends, Future Prospects," *Philosophical Transactions of the Royal Society B*, no. 365 (2010): 2853–2867.

Artistic Intervention III

Jacob Broms Engblom: Still from *What does shrimp dreams mean?*, video, 2019.

Text excerpt from video:

> Dreaming of shrimp is an indication you feel inadequate in your reality. You may just want to hide away from the world for a while. Seeing a live translucent shrimp, where its skeletal parts are visible, means you make decisions using great wisdom. But, maybe you take too long making decisions that sometimes you miss opportunities.

> Catching shrimp with your hands can indicate possible health issues. Eating shrimp indicates you will have an erotic meeting. This may be with an unusual stranger in an exciting, passionate encounter. It can also mean you notice that things are coming easily to you at this time.

This boosts your confidence. Be careful though. Do not get overconfident. But, this is a powerful time for you. Eating shrimp also reflects you are in danger of behaving arrogantly. You may try to exploit whatever is too easy for you and make yourself look stupid through your arrogance...."

Note from the artist:

What does shrimp dreams mean? is a video collage of aggregated found YouTube-content of dream interpretations in a realm that can be called Keyword Culture, content shaped by the search ranking algorithms that present it. Text is here vacuumed from the internet, processed by text-to-speech algorithms and haphazardly assembled together with related imagery providing a mechanical stream of interpretations of our own dreams. This in turn can act as a sort of mapping between the subconscious inside ourselves and the networked one distributed online.

Reflection

Just like Marta Badenska Hammarberg, Jacob Broms Engblom was a student in my writing-class at the Royal Art Institute in Stockholm in 2019. Before the conference, I had seen Jacob's work several times through study visits, trying to keep up with his tireless work on artificially generated visual culture and his ability to scroll through the strangest feeds. I found that he turns inside out the digital spheres we digest more and more in our lives. He provides us with a re/assembly of these strange and twisted stories that get generated with and through these digestions. *What does shrimp dreams mean?* provides and molds a humorous and uncanny experience of technology as seeping out of our pores, as addictive to us as air. The still and the text aims at giving the reader an idea of the entire work of art as it was generously presented at the *Ratatoskr* inaugural symposium.

Emma Kihl

AFTERWORD

Humans and Seagulls, Paused:
Pipsa Lonka's *Sky Every day* (2020)
and Theater During the Pandemic

Elsi Hyttinen

In Pipsa Lonka's play *Sky Every Day* (*Neljän päivän läheisyys*, 2020), the last scene belongs to seagulls, and not just momentarily: of the play's 82 pages, the seagulls' multilogue takes up the final nine pages. These are not Hitchcock's scary birds attacking us, or white birds soaring in the sky to symbolize our longing for *elsewhere*. The birds are not here to carry any man-made meanings or to represent anything we would want them to stand for. One might begin reading the scene searching for such meanings, but the sheer length of the multilogue works against such intentions. The spectacle here is the existence of the birds, in all their bird-specific birdness. The play invites us to sit and let the birds' existence sink in. Animals exist, and not just for us: they exist for themselves.

kyow-kyow-kyow-kyow-kyow kyow-kyow-kyow-kyow kyow kyow-kyow-kyow-kyow

KLEE-UW! KLEE-UW!
kreeaah! krreenyah krreenyah krreenyah

KLEE-UW!
kreeaah! krreenyah krreenyah krreenyah huoh

kreeaah! krreenyah krreenyah krreenyah

krreeaah! kreeaah! krreenyah krreenyah krreenyah kek ke-kek kek ke-kek keow keow

kek ke-kek kek ke-kek kek ke-kek kek ke-kek kek ke-kek kek ke-kek

glie kreeaah! krreenyah krreenyah krreenyah kreeaah! krreenyah krreenyah krreenyah

kreeaah! krreenyah krreenyah krreenyah

kreeaah! krreenyah krreenyah krreenyah ### KLEE-UW! KLEE-UW!

glie kyow-kyow-kyow-kyow-kyow

kek ke-kek kek ke-kek kek ke-kek kreeaah! krreenyah krreenyah krreenyah

kyow-kyow-kyow-kyow-kyow KLEE-UW! KLEE-UW! glie glie glie glie

keow keow kreeaah! krreenyah krreenyah krreenyah keow keow keow keow keow

ke ke KLAIYYA-KLAIYYA! ke ke ke KLAIYYA-KLAIYYA! kei-a kei-a kei-a ke ke!

keow keow keow keow keow ke ke KLAIYYA-KLAIYYA! ke ke KLAIYYA-KLAIYYA! kei-a kei-a kei-a ke ke!

kreeaah! krreenyah krreenyah krreenyah KLEE-UW! glie kreeaah! kreeaah!

kreeaah! krreenyah krreenyah krreenyah KLEE-UUW KLEE-UUW kyow-kyow-kyow-kyow-kyow-kyow

keow keow keow keow KLEE-UW! KLEE-UW! kreeaah! krreenyah krreenyah krreenyah

KLEE-UUW!
kek krek ke-kek kek krek ke-kek kek krek ke-kek glie glie

kreeaah! krreenyah krreenyah krreenyah

kreeaah! krreenyah krreenyah krreenyah

kreeaah! krreenyah krreenyah krrenyah

When I made the first notes for this essay, in May 2020, it was week seven of Finland's first Covid lockdown.[1] Already then, I wrote about my strong, almost physical longing for live theater. Now as I'm typing these lines a year later, Finland has recently entered its second lockdown,[2] and I haven't set foot in a theater for a year. This is the longest period in my adult life that I've gone without attending any live performances. During the past

[1] A state of emergency was declared by the Finnish Government on 16 March 2020, and as part of the efforts to contain the virus, all national and municipal museums, theatres, the National Opera, cultural venues, libraries, services for customers at the National Archives, hobby and leisure centers, swimming pools and other sports facilities, youth centers, clubs, organisations' meeting rooms, day care services for the elderly, rehabilitative work facilities and workshops were closed. As of 23 March, the capital city area was isolated from the rest of the country for three weeks, with roadblocks, the police monitoring all crossings. Emergency Powers Act was lifted on 16 June 2020 and some theaters begun operating with a limited intake of audiences and other precautionary measures in place. As the epidemic situation worsened in the late autumn 2020, theaters largely closed again. See Government Communications Department, "Government, in cooperation with the President of the Republic, declares a state of emergency in Finland over coronavirus outbreak" (March 2020); Government Communications Department, "Use of powers under the Emergency Powers Act to end—state of emergency to be lifted on Tuesday 16 June" (June 2020).

[2] Government Communications Department, "Finland declares a state of emergency" (March 2021).

year, worldwide lockdowns have slowed down human activity in an unprecedented manner, leading some researchers to coin the term *anthropause*.[3] Originally, the term suggested that as human activity is reduced simultaneously all over the planet, the pandemic offers a rare opportunity for natural scientists to study how human activity affects wildlife. However, it has since been suggested that the anthropause might also be a chance to reconfigure the human–animal relationship, and that it could even be not just a pause but a portal to a new understanding of that relationship.[4]

In this article, I discuss Lonka's *Sky Every Day*, tracing the ways it participates in redefining the human–animal relationship in the anthropause. Pipsa Lonka (b. 1977) is a prominent contemporary playwright who has twice been awarded the Lea Award for Best Finnish Play of the Year. Her previous works also focus on the human–animal relationship in the Anthropocene.[5] Thematically, there is a clear vertical continuity between her earlier plays and *Sky Every Day*. However, as the play premiered during the anthropause, it also connects horizontally with the changes currently taking place in the world at large. *Sky Every Day* also offers me the opportunity to think about why the lockdown is making me long for live theater more than any other activities that the anthropause has put on hold.

Birds and humans, in close proximity

The English translation of Lonka's play is titled *Sky Every Day*: the name is a poem by Aram Saroyan and the sources and notes page at the end of the manuscript states Sarayan must always be

---

[3] C. Rutz, M. C. Loretto, A.E. Bates et al., "COVID-19 lockdown allows researchers to quantify the effects of human activity on wildlife," *Nature Ecology & Evolution*, no. 4 (2020): 1156–1159.
[4] A. Searle, J. Turnbull, J. Lorimer, "After the Anthropause: Lockdown Lessons for More-Than-Human Geographies," *The Geographical Journal* 187, no. 1 (2021): 69–77.
[5] Elsi Hyttinen, "Katso kyljystä. Toinen luonto ja poliittinen posthumanismi [Behold the cutlet. The play Second nature and political posthumanism]," in *Sotkuiset maailmat* [Messy worlds] (Jyväskylä: Nykykulttuuri, 2020), 337–354.

credited for the name. However, the original Finnish title of the play, *Neljän päivän läheisyys* would literally translate into *Four days of Closeness*, and indeed, the play conveys a strong message about the coexistence and equal value of humans and seagulls. The human–animal relationship is articulated primarily through how textual space is distributed between the species, and through the gaze directed at those beings in the fictional world. The play almost entirely discards the devices of plotlines, characters, and verbalized ideas. Even as a textual object, the play seems to anticipate the organicity of live theater. Theater scholar Carl Laverly has argued that theater's real purchase for rearticulating our relationship to non-human nature lies not in what a text says but in what a theater does: "[I]ts dramaturgical distribution of organic and inorganic bodies in actual time and space creates sensations and experiences in the here and now."[6] *Sky Every Day* makes full use of theater's spatiality.

The play is set in a holiday resort somewhere in the south. Whether the resort is in Andalusia, the Canary Islands, or Morocco, does not really matter. What is important here is the artificialness of the location. An unnatural environment that a resort is, it is however a place built for the purposes of enjoying what is experienced as nature: the sea, the sun, the weather. This is the milieu in which humans and seagulls will experience the four days of closeness. *Sky Every Day* gives equal textual space to humans and seagulls, and this is what makes it radical in its message. The text does not prioritize humans as the focus of attention.

The play begins with a preamble of seven sentences, distributed over seven pages. Short, descriptive sentences, to be interpreted either as parentheses or the observations by someone not specified, establish the scene: "A beach requires three: land, sea and sky. / The sand is mostly like this: a tiny crystal is next to another crystal. / The sea is murky and goes on and on. /

---

[6] Carl Lavery, "Introduction: Performance and Ecology—What Can Theatre Do?" *Green Letters* 20, no. 3 (2016): 229–236.

The sky is light blue and cloudless. / The gulls are mostly white and noisy. / Fish are mostly silver-skinned and slippery. / The humans are mostly rather reddish."[7] This setting of landscape is followed by the actual four parts of the play. The first two center on humans with the seagulls as part of the surrounding environment. The last two bring seagulls to the fore, and especially in the third part, a human body serves as part of their landscape.

In the first part, we are offered some tableaux vivants of what it is like to have a holiday in a resort. The play does not operate with any universal concept of the human. On the contrary, the humans here are very clearly like me: residents of the Northern Hemisphere, to whom holidays in a resort represent the good life, but in a slightly commonplace way. Nothing to boast about: just something we deserve once in a while. Taking holidays in these kinds of resorts is one of those habits we have that are disastrous for the planet, but which only recently have been perceived that way. However, the play does not moralize about tourism as a phenomenon; it just uses the resort as a sort of petri dish for the human and the non-human animals to meet. The moment we enter the fictional world, the resort loses its paradisiacal character. Its seashore is lined with smelly dead fish to which nobody except one child reacts. The humans repeat their holiday-making gestures in a manner that seems almost dignified in all its stubbornness: the man-made environmental disaster is creeping up to their paradise, but they cling to the leisure-signifying gestures of playing cards, spreading on sunscreen, lying on the sand getting tanned.

In the play, the human–animal question is not laid out as wilderness versus artificiality or culture. Rather, the species are represented as coexisting in an environment where the human touch makes itself known everywhere. This is the landscape of the Anthropocene. The text glimpses at various human holiday-makers, but the fictional humans have no lines and no real scenes to appear in. We are invited to perceive the humans much as we would watch animals in a documentary. The play's non-

---

[7] *Sky Every Day*, 2–8.

identifiable speaker, or theatrical parenthesis, describes some of this activity: "Room 202. A child has dumped Legos on the floor. The child assembles them into something, its form impossible for outsiders to decipher. A woman plucks her eyebrows at the mirror."[8] Nothing rare or awkward here. Just human life in the hotel and at the beach. In one room, a man has died and not been discovered yet. Even this is shown with a similar detachment. There is nothing spectacular in an organic life ending at some point. A death is just another occurrence at the resort.

The second part takes place in an outdoor restaurant where the holidaymakers flock for a meal. This is the only part of the play where the human figures have lines. However, their speech does not constitute a controlled dialogue. From the blurred lines, one understands that the mealtime is interrupted by a seagull colliding with the restaurant wall, collapsing and languishing between the tables until it dies. This unexpected event causes various reactions among the humans, from shock to disgust. In the end, one man takes the bird in his arms and walks toward the beach.

---

[8] *Sky Every Day*, 22.

but fives the best number
ok
five
all right

i dont know maybe ill
good you should

fives the best number

watch out
oops

five

almost stepped on it

here have some

look

that freaked me out so bad
whats it doing there

look over
oh my

my hearts beating so
what do you think
maybe we should go a little
is it like hurt or
maybe its wing or
it like flew into something

whats wrong with it

i dont see any blood
me either   here
what should we
tzho gross

whats wrong with it

should we help or
dont you think we ought
lets just go sit

This scene mirrors in layout and length the multilogue of the seagulls with which I began this essay. The seagulls' communication stretches over nine pages, the humans here make their species-specific sounds for fifteen pages. And that is all the attention the drama allots them, for the text shifts focus in the next section.

The play's third part takes us to the room of the dead man. The balcony door has been left open, and the seagulls have found their way into the room. First one, then many birds. There is some food in the room, and maybe it's the quietness that appeals to them as well; a sort of anthropause within the resort buzz. The birds don't mind the body on the floor. They don't destroy the body, either; they just pluck a few of its hairs out. They simply dwell in the same space, in close proximity, without paying any particular attention to the body. Human death is not a tragedy to them. It's just an occurrence in their environment, much like the seagull's death was just an occurrence for the humans in the previous part, something slightly startling and mildly disturbing to be forgotten by the next day. The fourth and final part is dedicated purely to the birds, their (to us) incomprehensible communication quoted in the introduction of this essay.

(Human) animals on stage

Rosi Braidotti, who for a long time has been involved in post-humanism, sees the Covid pandemic as a potential turning point in our understanding of the human. She argues that as the pandemic forces us to face our mortality, we could be seeing the beginning of a new era of affirmative ethics: "[L]ife as an inhuman, non-anthropocentric force (which I call *zoe*)—exceeds [these] negative conditions, because zoe exists independently of humans."[9] However, such changes in cultural conceptions do not just happen: life needs to be presented and re-presented over and over again in new ways for new concepts to take hold. In my previous work on contemporary Finnish drama,[10] I used the Gramscian concept of *interregnum* to discuss how our old concepts for the natural world are no longer valid while new ones have yet to be established. In an interregnum, things are simultaneously at a standstill *and* evolving, but we cannot proceed in any direction before the old sovereign is declared deceased. I suggest that *Sky Every Day* anticipates the kind of new understanding of the radical equality of lifeforms Braidotti is sketching out—one that perceives human and non-human lives as being on the same plane without placing one species above all others.

---

[9] Rosi Braidotti, "'We' Are In *This* Together, But We Are Not One and the Same." *Bioethical Inquiry* 17 (2020): 468.

[10] Elsi Hyttinen, "Antroposeeni kanallisella näyttämöllä eli *Maaseudun tulevaisuus* ja interregnum, jota elämme [Anthropocene at the national stage, or, the play *Maaseudun tulevaisuus* and the interregnum we are living through]," *Avain* 2 (2017).

Adam Searle, Jonathon Turnbull and Jamie Lorimer discuss what they, quoting Sarah Whatmore and Steve Hincliffe,[11] call "vernacular ecologies" in the anthropause: the ways humans interact with nature at an everyday level when our old ways have been put on hold. They note that the absence of noise has not solely altered the behavior of non-human animals, that the first researchers to discuss the anthropause were interested in. They argue, coming from a very different angle from Braidotti, that during the anthropause, humans are changing, too: "[V]ernacular ecologies signal changes in the sensibilities of urbanites towards their non-human companions."[12] We are getting better at seeing beyond the human horizon. What is more, Searle et al. claim that in the anthropause, "reconfigured mobilities reveal that urban spaces are already spaces for animals and that humans can—and should—learn to incorporate the needs of animals, commensal and otherwise, into more liveable cities in the Anthropocene."[13] An artwork made during the anthropause, Lonka's play also invites us to realize that we are already sharing space with other species. The play actually goes further than Searle et al. in that it does not prioritize human agents. The play is just as much about seagulls coexisting with us as it is about us coexisting with the seagulls.

Our heightened awareness of other animals inhabiting the spaces we are accustomed to thinking of as ours might open up ways for recalibrating the human, helping us in the ever more urgent task of becoming slightly smaller. In the early days of the global pandemic, in April 2020, the Indian writer Arundhati Roy wrote an essay with the suggestive title "The pandemic is a portal." Referring to Roy's essay, Searle et al. suggest that the anthropause might turn out to be not just a temporal halting of the world as it was, but a portal to a new phase in human–animal relations. Roy's essay zeroes in on

---

[11] Whatmore, Sarah & Steve Hinchcliffe, "Ecological Landscapes," in *Oxford Handbook of Material Culture Studies* (Oxford: Oxford University Press, 2010), 439–454.

[12] Searle, Turnbull & Lorimer, 72.

[13] Searle, Turnbull & Lorimer, 74.

India where the pandemic and the lockdowns mean very different things to people depending on their class, ethnicity, and wealth. Even though Roy's focus is primarily on Indian society, toward the end of the essay she expresses a desire for change, on which Searle et al. draw: "Nothing could be worse than a return to normality. Historically, pandemics have forced humans to break with the past and imagine their world anew. This one is no different. It is a portal, a gateway between one world and the next. We can choose to walk through it, dragging the carcasses of our prejudice and hatred, our avarice, our data banks and dead ideas, our dead rivers and smoky skies behind us. Or we can walk through lightly, with little luggage, ready to imagine another world. And ready to fight for it."[14] Searle et al. envision a future where we emerge from the anthropause with an altered understanding of planetary cohabitation of different species and lifeforms.

When describing vernacular ecologies, Searle et al. cover petkeeping, birdwatching and watching online video streams of animals in their natural environments. Through these, humans perceive their surroundings with a heightened interest in our non-human fellow beings. Pipsa Lonka's play accords with such activities in her bringing seagulls and humans into close proximity for us to really contemplate. But the play goes even further by portraying the human characters in such a way that we perceive them as we would animals. They are not individuals but rather representatives of their species, with all their species-specific idiosyncrasies. This view is further highlighted by an intertextual reference running through the play, but on a separate narrative level. Not belonging to the depicted world, it is located rather on the border between the play's world and our own.

---

[14] Arundhati Roy, "The Pandemic is a Portal," *Financial Times* April 3 2020. Roy's essay was originally published in *Financial Times*. However, when referring to the essay, Searle and al. refer to the Haymarket books website April 23 2020, not *FT*, even though the latter only provides a blog post about Roy's essay and a link to a youtube teach-in with the author, not the essay as a whole.

Throughout the play, a human cleans a seagull's skeleton with a toothbrush. In remarks at the end of the manuscript, Lonka explains that the figure is a reference to Marina Abramovic's performance *Cleaning the mirror* (1995), and that the process should continue throughout the play and remain external to the fictive world of the resort. In *Cleaning the mirror*, a five-part videotaped performance, Abramovic cleans a human skeleton with soapy water. The Guggenheim website explains: "this three-hour action recalls, among other things, Tibetan death rites that prepare disciples to become one with their own mortality."[15] Citing the performance highlights the understanding of *zoe* that underpins *Sky Every Day*, as Lonka's play departs in a significant way from the humanist legacy of *Cleaning the mirror* by replacing the original human skeleton with that of a seagull. All organic life ends in death. This is an inescapable reality, one that surpasses all distinctions between lifeforms. A bird is our mirror, and we are a bird's mirror.

Longing for live in the anthropause

Sky Every Day premiered as *Fyra Dagar av Närhet* in Helsinki at the Swedish-language theater Viirus in front of a restricted live audience in February 2021. In March, the month I am writing this essay, the play is live-streamed from Viirus three times, again echoing the times we are living through. During the pandemic, streamed theater has gained popularity in an unprecedented way. This is hardly any wonder; relying on electronic devices is about the only way for us to keep this cultural form alive during the lockdowns. Streaming makes it possible for theaters to maintain relationships with their audiences and for actors to practice their profession. This is not entirely without irony. Rosi Braidotti notes: "The COVID-19 pandemic is a man-made disaster, caused by undue interference in the ecological balance and the lives of multiple species. Paradoxically, the contagion has resulted in increased use of technology and digital

---

[15] Nancy Spector, "Marina Abramović: Cleaning the Mirror #1".

mediation [...]."[16] I shall end this essay by reflecting on my pandemic-long longing for live theater, and how watching the streamed version of Lonka's play intensified that longing and has affected my response to the play.

Media scholar Eleni Timplalexi has studied how the pandemic is changing what we mean by the term "theater." She states that previously, a streaming was generally understood as inferior to the real thing of a live event. Now, she notes that many shows produced during the pandemic become materialized within digital mediums. There is no indexical relationship between a taped play and the live one.[17] She even argues that the upsurge in streamed theater during the pandemic is invalidating the terms of the famous 1990s debate on liveness, known as the Phelan–Auslander debate. In 1993, Peggy Phelan explained what she perceived as the defining feature of live performance— that it only exists in the present: "Performance's only life is in the present. Performance cannot be saved, recorded, documented, or otherwise participate in the circulation of representations of representations: once it does so, it becomes something other than performance."[18] At the other end of the debate, Philip Ausslander stated that no such aura of the present existed, focusing his argumentation, however, around authenticity: "It does not even make much sense to ask which of the many identical productions of Tamara or Disney's Beauty and the Beast is the 'authentic' one."[19] Timplalexi claims that we are currently experiencing "the actual eradication of this very distinctiveness between the live and the recorded, the streamed or the mediatized."[20]

[16] Braidotti, 465.

[17] Eleni Timplalexi, "Theatre and Performance Go Massively Online During the COVID-19 pandemic: Implications and Side Effects," *Homo Virtualis*, no. 2 (2020): 50.

[18] Peggy Phelan, *Unmarked: The Politics of Performance* (Milton Park: Taylor & Francis, 1993), 146.

[19] Philip Ausslander, *Liveness—performance in a mediatized culture*. 2nd, revised edition (London & New York: Routledge, 2008), 55.

[20] Timplalexi, 45.

Sky Every Day exists in at least four forms: the written manuscript (and this in at least three languages, as the play has been translated into Swedish by Sofia Aminoff and English by Kristian London), a taped reading,[21] a theater production, and a streamed online performance. I first read the play in the Finnish-language textual variant, and, later on, I watched the performance directed by Susanna Airaksinen as a Swedish-language online stream. Whilst I agree with Ausslander that it would be impossible and indeed pointless to argue that some form in which *Sky Every Day* exists is the authentic one, I don't see how this would lead to live performance losing its non-reproducibility. And indeed, in all her enthusiasm for mediatized forms of theater, Timplalexi admits that "online theater and performance may serve some of us today as indexes or signifiers standing in the position of absent, signified cultural meaning, reminders of what theater and performance was before it all started,"[22] even if she then goes on to suggest that such nostalgia proves that theater performance is becoming "a potentially passé medium."[23] I'm sure it is in the nature of theater to adapt to new media. We've already seen that radio, film, and television happened, and they were not the end of live theater. That new, mediatized forms of performative arts might be born out of the halt forced upon the world's live theaters by the pandemic is one thing. But what live theater means to audiences is quite another. I strongly recognize myself as one of those people for whom a streaming is a painful remainder of the absence, and indeed forced halting, of live theaters globally during the pandemic.

In their research into pre-pandemic online theater, theater scholars Daniela Mueser and Peter Vlachos state that based on audience surveys, an aspect of liminality is important for theatergoers. Going to a theater is a structured ritual, and therefore attending a streaming may produce experiences that are

---

[21] "Fyra dagar av närhet – en posthumanistisk föreställning om måsar och människor".

[22] Timplalexi, 44.

[23] Timplalexi, 49.

similar to attending a performance live. This sense of *eventness* comes from seeing the streamed production in a movie theatre —a space that mimics the traditional venue for theater—and doing so in the presence of others, as part of an audience.[24] Mueser and Vlachos concentrate on people watching streamed theater in public spaces. However, another theater scholar, Erin Sullivan, has studied the experience of watching theater online at home. She finds that even online audiences prefer watching performances in real-time, because of the sense of togetherness it brings. Online theater has the potential to be regarded as experientially rich as long as it in some way "cultivates a sense of eventful togetherness."[25] Watching the stream, I experienced no such togetherness. Knowing my only peers were equally detached someones isolated at their screens somewhere was a melancholic feeling. Rather than creating a sense of meaningful eventness the situation highlighted the lack thereof.

Watching the streamed performance of *Sky Every Day*, I felt my longing for live theater only increase. This had very little to do with the qualities of the stream, more to do with the fact I watched the stream at home. As posthumanist scholar Stacy Alaimo argues, the home, in the western context, "has been erected as the spatial definition of the human."[26] The home's function of protecting the human inside from everything non-human outside has only intensified during the pandemic. Watching the theater stream at home, I felt trapped inside a nightmarish version of the Human. This feeling of disconnection amplified my reaction to the play's posthumanist aesthetics. My affective response to the lockdown intertwined

[24] Daniela Mueser & Peter Vlachos, "Almost Like Being There? A conceptualization of Live-Streaming Theatre," *International Journal of Event and Festival management* 9, no. 2 (2018): 185, 193.

[25] Erin Sullivan, "Live to Your Living Room; Streamed Theatre, Audience Experience, and the Globe's A Midsummer Nights Dream," *Participations* 17, no. 1 (2020): 114–115.

[26] Stacy Alaimo, *Exposed. Environmental Politics and Pleasures in Posthuman Times* (Minnesota: University of Minnesota Press, 2016), 20.

with the play's message, as if the streamed play had anticipated my longing for the live event.

I cannot attend a live event because of the man-made disaster the pandemic is. I am trapped inside the Human, unable to connect, watching a play that delivers a message of radical equality of all organic life, set in a profoundly Anthropocenic world where the distinction of culture and nature has very nearly collapsed. The play communicates an understanding of the profound kinship of all organic life. My viewing situation isolates me from as much organic life as possible, both human and non-human, in order to keep me safe from the virus. In a way, the very same damage I see on the streamed stage—in the form of dead fish surrounding the artificial paradise of a holiday resort—keeps me from attending the live performance. It is lonely being this much Human.

References

Alaimo, Stacy. *Exposed. Environmental Politics and Pleasures in Post-human Times*. Minneapolis: University of Minnesota Press, 2016.

Ausslander, Philip. *Liveness—Performance in a Mediatized Culture*. 2nd, revised edition. London & New York: Routledge, 2008.

Braidotti, Rosi. "'We' Are in this Together, But We Are Not One and the Same." *Bioethical Inquiry* 17 (2020): 465–469.

Government Communications Department. "Government, in cooperation with the President of the Republic, declares a state of emergency in Finland over coronavirus outbreak" (March 2020).

Government Communications Department. "Use of powers under the Emergency Powers Act to end – state of emergency to be lifted on Tuesday 16 June" (June 2020).

Government Communications Department. "Finland declares a state of emergency" (March 2021).

Hyttinen, Elsi. "Katso kyljystä. *Toinen luonto* ja poliittinen post-humanismi [Behold the cutlet. The play *Second Nature* and political posthumanism]." In *Sotkuiset maailmat* [Messy worlds], 337–354. Edited by Elsi Hyttinen and Karoliina Lummaa. Jyväskylä: Nyky-kulttuuri, 2020.

Hyttinen, Elsi. "Antroposeeni kanallisella näyttämöllä eli Maaseudun tulevaisuus ja interregnum, jota elämme [Anthropocene at the national stage, or, the play *Maaseudun tulevaisuus* and the inter-regnum we are living through]." In *Avain*, no. 2 (2017): 45–63.

Lavery, Carl. "Introduction: Performance and Ecology—What can Theatre Do?" *Green Letters: Studies in Ecocriticism* 20, no. 3 (2016): 229–236.

Lonka, Pipsa. *Sky Every Day.* Translated by Kristian London, un-published manuscript 2020.

Lonka, Pipsa. *Neljän päivän läheisyys.* Helsinki: ntamo 2021.

Mueser, Daniela & Peter Vlachos. "Almost Like Being There? A Conceptualization of Live-Streaming Theatre." *International Journal of Event and Festival management* 9, no. 3 (2018): 183–203.

Phelan, Peggy. *Unmarked: The Politics of Performance.* Milton Park: Taylor & Francis, 1993.

Roy, Arundhati. "The Pandemic is a Portal," *Financial Times* April 3 2020.

Roy, Arundhati. "The Pandemic is a Portal," *Haymarket books* April 23 2020.

Rutz, Christian, Matthias-Claudio Loretto, Amanda E. Bates, Sarah C. Davidson, Carlos M. Duarte, Walter Jetz, Mark Johnson, Akiko Kato, Roland Kays, Thomas Mueller, Richard B. Primack, Yan Ropert-Coudert, Marlee A. Tucker, Martin Wikelski & Francesca Cagnacci. "COVID-19 lockdown allows researchers to quantify the effects of human activity on wildlife." *Nature Ecology & Evolution*, no. 4 (2020): 1156–1159.

Searle, Adam, Jonathan Turnbull & Jamie Lorimer. "After the Anthropause: Lockdown Lessons for More-Than-Human Geographies." *The Geographical Journal* 187, no. 1 (2021): 69–77.

Spector, Nancy. "Marina Abramović: Cleaning the Mirror #1," *The Guggenheim Collection online.* https://www.guggenheim.org/artwork/4374 [accessed 30–03–2020].

Sullivan, Erin. "Live to Your Living Room; Streamed Theatre, Audience Experience, and the Globe's *A Midsummer Nights Dream.*" *Participations* 17, no. 1 (2020): 92–119.

Timplalexi, Eleni. "Theatre and Performance Go Massively Online During the COVID-19 Pandemic: Implications and Side Effects." *Homo Virtualis* 3, no. 2 (2020).

Whatmore, Sarah & Steve Hinchcliffe. "Ecological Landscapes." In *Oxford handbook of material culture studies,* 439–454. Edited by Dan Hicks & Mary C. Beaudry. Oxford: Oxford University Press, 2010.

Emma Kihl: *Hurray*, ink on paper, 2021.

Reflection

Emma Kihl's *Hurray*, putting an open end to this anthology, takes its visual cue from the tradition of activist posters with sharp-cut shapes and a handmade touch. The motif evokes the language question: do we understand each other over species borders, and if so—how and what do we understand? The closed eye of the bird reminds us that we might not be the intended addressees of this bird's communication. It might not care about humans at all. Yet, bird song means a lot to others than birds. Intention and comprehension is not everything. There is also the joy of expression and the celebration of being sensuous.

Amelie Björck

List of contributors

Amelie Björck is associate professor and senior lecturer in comparative literature and drama at Södertörn University in Stockholm, Sweden. Her scholarly work mainly encompasses human-animal studies in late modern and contemporary literature and culture. In several articles she has taken an interest in the relation between modes of narrating, reading, and animal ethics. Björck's most recent project focused on how narrative temporality in different forms of literature and art conditions the space and agency of farmed animals. The project resulted in the book *Zooësis. Om kulturella gestaltningar av lantbruksdjurens tid och liv* (Glänta Produktion, 2019).

Sune Borkfelt has a PhD in English literature from Aarhus University, Denmark, where he has lectured since 2007. He is author of *Reading Slaughter: Abattoir Fictions, Space, and Empathy in Late Modernity* (Palgrave, 2022). His work on topics such as non-human otherness, the naming of non-human animals, postcolonial animals, and the ethics of animal product marketing, has appeared in *English Studies, Animals, and Journal of Agricultural and Environmental Ethics* as well as in a number of edited collections. He is also editor of a 2016 special issue of the journal *Otherness: Essays and Studies* focused on animal alterity.

Jacob Broms Engblom is an artist and engineer based in Stockholm. He graduated from the Royal Institute of Technology in 2012 and from the Royal Institute of Art in 2020. His practice circulates above and within undocumented phenomenon, media processes and anxieties in our digital culture.

Karin Dirke is associate professor and senior lecturer in the history of science and ideas at Stockholm University in Sweden. Her scholarly work centers on human-animal studies and mainly concerns the relationships between humans and other species in history. Dirke has published numerous articles and book chapters investigating human encounters with, and narratives about, wolves, dogs, cats and rats. She is particularly interested in animal agency and how it can be understood through the use of historical sources.

Gunnar Eggertsson is an author, Ph.D., and an independent researcher in comparative literature at the University of Iceland in Reykjavik. His academic work coheres around animal stories as a radical form of literature, one that actively engages with and critiques dominant anthropocentric hierarchies. Eggertsson has written articles about Icelandic farm animal stories and is working on a critical anthology of Nordic animal fiction (in Icelandic). Concurrent to literary theory, his research interests branch out to storytelling in other media.

Marta Badenska Hammarberg is an artist based in Stockholm Sweden. She graduated from the Royal Institute of Art in 2020. In her practice she uses photography video artists' books and installation to portray human-to-human phenomena.

Elsi Hyttinen is adjunct professor and senior researcher at the University of Turku, Finland. Her research interests include early 20th century Finnish literature, contemporary drama, animal studies, queer theory, posthumanities and working-class literature. Hyttinen has recently co-edited (with Karoliina Lummaa) a research anthology on posthuman literary studies *Sotkuiset maailmat* ('Messy worlds', 2020) and a special issue of the Finnish literary studies journal *Avain* (2021), focusing on forests.

Emma Kihl is Ph.D.-student in comparative literature at Södertörn University in Stockholm, Sweden. In her thesis she explores the poetry worlds by Agneta Enckell with Isabelle Stengers philosophy. Emma also holds a MFA in Fine Arts from the Royal Institute of Art in Stockholm, where she is currently an adjunct lecturer in writing.

Claudia Lindén is professor in comparative literature at Södertörn University in Stockholm, Sweden. Her research interests include 19th-century Scandinavian literature, Gothic literature, animal studies, gender studies, queer theory, theory of history. Lindén is currently working on the animal studies-project "Bear traces: A study of the bear in national romantic literature around the Baltic Sea."

Karoliina Lummaa is adjunct professor and senior lecturer in Finnish literature at the University of Turku, Finland. She is currently affiliated with Turku Institute for Advanced Studies (TIAS) and BIOS Research Unit. Lummaa's publications include two monographs on Finnish nature poetry and post-humanist theory, five co-edited anthologies on Finnish literature, multidisciplinary environmental research and posthumanism, and research articles on environmental humanities, with topics ranging from waste studies and human-animal studies to multidisciplinary Anthropocene research.

Michael Lundblad is professor of English-language literature at the University of Oslo, Norway. He is the author of *The Birth of a Jungle: Animality in Progressive-Era U.S. Literature and Culture* (Oxford UP, 2013), the co-editor, with Marianne DeKoven, of *Species Matters: Humane Advocacy and Cultural Theory* (Columbia UP, 2012), the editor of *Animalities: Literary and Cultural Studies Beyond the Human* (Edinburgh UP, 2017), and, most recently, the editor of a special issue of *New Literary History* on "Animality/ Posthumanism/Disability."

Ann-Sofie Lönngren is professor in comparative literature at Södertörn University in Stockholm, Sweden. Her research interests include Northern-European literature after 1880, animal studies, interdisciplinarity, queer theory, transgender studies, ethics, education, indigenous studies and intersectionality. Lönngren's most recent book is *Following the Animal. Power, Agency, and Human-animal Transformations in Modern, Northern-European Literature* (Cambridge Scholars Publishing, 2015).

Małgorzata Poks is Ph.D. and assistant professor at the Institute of Literary Studies at the University of Silesia in Katowice, Poland. Her main research interests cohere around contemporary North American literature, indigenous studies, US-Mexican border writing, critical animal studies, Christian anarchism and Thomas Merton's late poetry. Poks has published widely in Poland and abroad. Her monograph *Thomas Merton and Latin America: a Consonance of Voices* (2006) received the International Thomas Merton Award. She is also a recipient of several international research fellowships.

Oscar von Seth is an author and Ph.D.-student in comparative literature at Södertörn University in Stockholm, Sweden. His main academic interest area is at the intersection of literature and queer theory, and his research interests include masculinity, animality studies, intersectionality and postcolonial theory. von Seth's debut novel is entitled *Snö som föll i fjol* (Calidris, 2017) and the focus of his forthcoming dissertation (due for publication in the spring of 2022) is queer friendships in the writings of Hermann Hesse.

Lightning Source UK Ltd.
Milton Keynes UK
UKHW020726040122
396586UK00005B/54